A Practical Spiritual Primer

A Practical Spiritual Primer

Ralph A. Steadman

Stellium Flame

Published in 2017 by Stellium Flame,
Plymouth, Devon UK
Tel: +44 (0)1752 367 300   Fax: +44 (0)1752 350 453

British Library Cataloguing in Publication Data:
A catalogue record for this book is available
from The British Library

Design and typesetting by Zambezi Publishing Ltd, Plymouth UK
Printed in the UK by Lightning Source
Stellium Flame is an imprint of Stellium Ltd

About the Author

After getting a law degree in 1954, Ralph Steadman spent nine years in the Army, mostly in Army Education. Returning to civilian life in 1963, he worked for IBM for a time, before using his computer knowledge to work in companies pioneering computerised insurance, and then computerised management of large construction projects.

In 1967, Ralph became a Training Officer in the newly formed Road Transport Industry Training Board, from which – many years later – he was 'head-hunted' to be Education and Training Manager of a large, multi-branch organisation in the retail Motor Trade. He ended his working life doing what he most loved, teaching – before retiring in 1999.

Ralph now lives in Torquay with his second wife, Sybil – a gifted clairvoyant healer – and is actively involved in local Spiritualism. He has written several books and still lectures at Spiritualist conferences. Ralph lists among his other interests, music, computers and learning languages (of which he has studied eleven, at one time or another!)

Ralph says of himself, 'For the last fifty years I have been interested in psychic phenomena in general and spiritual philosophy in particular. Over the last few years, this has expanded into the study of Metaphysics – what lies beyond Science and also Religion – which I believe is the area that contains the answers to all possible questions about the ultimate reality of life!'

Dedication

I dedicate this book to my two perfect wives:

To Eleanor, who loved and supported me unstintingly through almost forty years of marriage, and who taught me the real meaning of Love!

To Sybil, who healed me after Eleanor had made her transition, and with whom I have worked tirelessly for Spirit over the last twenty years,

And to Clare, a wife from a previous life and a dear friend in this, who introduced me to Sybil!

Acknowledgements

Many people contributed to the publication of this book, and sometimes it is difficult to appreciate their exact role, but I will mention some of the more important. There are four who were most directly involved in the recent past.

First and foremost, of course, must be my beloved wife Sybil, whose unfailing support has carried me through many bleak moments in the writing process of many of my books over many years. But, not far behind, was Laurene, a very dear friend to both of us. Laurene is an exceptionally gifted medium, and gave me the impetus to start a previous book when she 'brought through' one of the beings who wished to channel through me. In addition, she often provided a 'spiritual poker' to prod me when my innate laziness was holding up progress on the present book!

Then there was Clare, another very dear friend. My publisher suggested that the manuscript needed detailed proofreading, and Clare (who by coincidence had worked in that field) took on the arduous task, and found many errors that I had totally overlooked.

I must also thank Sasha Fenton of Stellium Ltd for her advice and encouragement; her expertise guided me through all the intricacies of the publishing process until the final product.

But further back in time, there were many people who had a very great influence on the development of my own spiritual philosophy, and probably the most important of these was Louise L. Hay, whose seminal book 'You Can Heal Your Life' inspired me so greatly, and which has formed the basis of my own philosophy ever since. I still use her book, teach her methods and recommend her book to all whom I meet.

N.B. With the exception of members of my own family and 'Little Sue', the names of all the people whom I quote have been changed to protect their anonymity, so any similarities to existing or deceased persons of the same name are entirely coincidental!

Contents

Preface

Everything happens at the right time. I attend a weekly demonstration of clairvoyance in Torquay (Infinity Clairvoyance) and last year I was asked to give a series of 10-minute talks on spiritual philosophy from scratch, assuming that the listener had no knowledge whatsoever about the subject. I gave 40 of these talks during the year before they were discontinued, because by then we were getting into some fairly advanced stuff.

Last year I was impressed to collate the talks into a book, and started to gather the material together. However, whilst doing so, 'by coincidence' I came across the script of another book which I had started writing two years ago, and which had been put on hold after a while, so I was impressed to see if I could collate the talks into it.

However, when I tried to do so, I soon found out that it wasn't possible. First of all, the two styles of writing were very different: the first was a narrative, (meant to be easy reading,) whereas the second one was a more formal teaching course. The second problem was that there were stories of events and people that I quoted in both scripts, and some of them overlapped. However, not all were treated in the same way - each was tailored so that it showed an example of a precise point that I was covering at that moment, and so was integral to that context only. When mentioned again in a different context, it might be treated in a far lengthier way. So therefore, choosing to mention the stories exclusively in one book would risk overkill on one occasion, and oversight on another.

So I compromised, and kept the 2013 book untouched as the main text, and the book of talks as the Appendix.

This is the result. I start with the preface of the 2013 book.

***

A Practical Spiritual Primer

It is almost ten years since I wrote my autobiography 'All is well', which was published privately and given to my children and close friends as a memento of my own spiritual journey through life, and a summary of what I had learnt. In that time much has changed in the world - many would say 'Not for the better'. But one thing that has changed dramatically and very much for the better, is that many people are starting to want answers to some of the principal questions about life that have been with us down the ages, and this has led to two diametrically opposed reactions.

On the one hand, people are flocking in large numbers to join modernist religious organisations - the Evangelical churches report large increases in membership - while orthodox churches show a continued decline. On the other hand, secularists, humanists and atheists are becoming more extreme and militant in their denunciation of religion, and one leading scientist and writer has vowed to destroy Christianity.

Somewhere in the middle, there are increasing numbers of people who are looking for answers, but don't want to be formally connected to any organisation, and now demonstrations of spiritualist mediumship are becoming popular, helped by more favourable TV coverage of the subject.

It is in this context that I have decided to re-write my book, and provide simple answers to questions that people are asking. I have decided to cut out most of the autobiographical material, apart from that which is essential for the understanding of the spiritual context of my own journey. In the revision of the material, I have updated some parts, where my own understanding has grown over the last ten years, so that now I believe that it provides a simple - and hopefully enjoyable - introduction to what may today be loosely called 'New Age philosophy'.

Those readers who want a more profound and scientific exposition of Metaphysics are referred to my new book 'A New Understanding of Life', which can be accessed via my website, www.wolfeagle.co.uk

The principles that I outlined in the original introduction remain the same, so I have left that untouched.

Ralph A. Steadman
July 2013.

~ PART ONE ~

Introduction

There comes a time in the life of all of us when we are faced with the fact of our own mortality. In most cases it is on the death of someone in our own family or of someone whom we know: sometimes it is on the death of a world figure, such as Princess Diana; sometimes it is triggered by the sights of the carnage of war, natural disasters or horrific accidents; but whatever is the cause, that day of realisation will inevitably come.

In my own case it was at the approach of my seventieth birthday - the date of the biblical 'three-score-and-ten years'. I had been thinking about my love of France, and my fluency in French, both of which I have at one time or other in my life tried to instil into secondary and adult students, with varying degrees of success. Then suddenly I realized that when I eventually die all of that knowledge will disappear. This led me to accept that whatever the skill or knowledge of *any* human being, unless passed on to others before death it is eventually extinguished. In the case of creative artists like sculptors, painters, musicians, actors or poets, their works may be studied long after their death, but for the rest of us, after the death of our physical body, the only way of passing on any knowledge or skill that we have had is by writing about it beforehand.

This led me to consider whether or not anything at all of that which I have learnt during the course of my life is worth writing about, and made me realise that perhaps what I now consider as 'obvious' answers to questions regarding spiritual philosophy are either unknown to others or scorned by them. Some religions or -isms have answers to the age-old questions of 'What is Life all about?', 'Where were we before we were born?', 'What happens when we die?', 'Why are some people born to a life of hardship, while others cannot seem to go wrong?', 'What is Love?', and 'Why do children have to suffer?' but most either shy away from them

Introduction

completely or produce a standard answer along the lines of 'This is one of the mysteries of Life which cannot be solved by human beings'.

That sort of answer never appealed to me, as I always thought that it was a cop-out, a complete cover-up, a way of hiding the fact that the individual who gave it just hadn't the basic knowledge to say anything meaningful on the subject. But I went along with it until I was almost thirty, when something happened which made me start to *deliberately* ask questions and try to find answers. I then found out that the more answers I got, the more questions needed to be asked - so I carried on. It has been a very slow process, but an immensely rewarding one - and it has certainly proved to me the truth of the saying 'When the pupil is ready the master will appear'. At each stage of my quest, when my progress seemed to have become totally stalled (sometimes for many years), either someone came into my life to help me or something happened which opened up new avenues to me and set me off on my spiritual travels once more.

Looking back now, I see that there is much in what I have learnt which others might find of value in their own spiritual journey. Not that I believe that what I *know* is right for me will be definitely right for everyone else: in fact, I know that it *won't*. For those who are devout followers of one or other of the World Religions, it is unlikely to prove very enlightening, nor will it be any more palatable to those who are humanists or atheists. In fact, no one from either group is likely to even read the book. But in between those two extremes there are a large number of people who want some sort of reassurance, some answers when they are experiencing moments of crisis in their lives, even some form of mental challenge to face up to the questions outlined above - and all of these people may find some value in reading this book.

Then comes another problem: between a third and a half of the content of the original book was spiritual philosophy - and I am well aware that most people find that fairly dry reading (unless, of course, they are already embarked on a spiritual pathway). Also I realized that if I just write about the philosophy, there might be a danger of others feeling that I see myself as some sort of 'guru', handing down wisdom from on high. But I am no guru - just an ordinary man. My life, although interesting and eventful, has not been so much different from that of millions of others with working-class backgrounds who were born in the 1930s, brought up during World War II and its aftermath, and then saw the world changing out of all recognition during the next fifty years or more. So therefore, to put everything in context, I needed to talk about my background and insert into that background the spiritual mileposts that I passed along my journey; it is that background which took up the majority of the first book. In general terms, the earlier chapters were 100% autobiography, the latter were 100% philosophy - and those in between were a graduating mixture of both.

Finally, I mentioned a large number of people whom I have met during my life, and of whom I have (usually) happy memories. Some of those mentioned figured in verifiable incidents, others didn't. Where I told a particular story, everything that I say happened was factual: the story was always seen from *my* viewpoint, although others may well have interpreted those facts in a different way. In none of these cases did I try to disguise names in any way. However, where I referred to people whom I have known who have had particular problems of any sort, I always disguised their identity in such a way - by giving them false names - that they cannot be identified by anyone who was not *aware* of the situation when it was happening at the time.

Each of us is on our own unique pathway through this life, and no one can live anyone else's life for them, nor ought they to try to tell other people how *they* should live their life. We all need to find our own individual way as we go on our *own* journey. I hope that readers may find the story of my journey towards spiritual understanding of interest, and ideally of enough value to help them in *their own* personal journey.

Chapter 1: Initiation

Although I was brought up in a Christian family - my mother was very devout and I was forced to attend church three times every Sunday; Morning and Evening services and Sunday School in the afternoon - the theology of Christianity never really touched me. The moral code was continuously hammered into me, of course, but conscious personal spirituality was far off in the future

I did, however, have my first psychic experience in early childhood.

It was early in the War: I must have been about six or seven, and I had some minor illness - possibly a touch of 'flu. I remember that I was given some vile medicine and sent to bed to sweat it off. Then suddenly I felt that I was floating round, up by the ceiling, looking down at myself lying in bed. I couldn't understand this, but for a while amused myself by flying round and darting backwards and forwards, twisting and turning. Suddenly I heard my mother's footsteps on the stairs. I was terrified that she would look up and see me, and say, 'What are you doing up there?' so I hid in the corner of the ceiling and kept very still. But I needn't have worried, as she bent over the bed, tucked me in and then went out again. Quick as a flash I zoomed down and got in bed again - and woke up. I now realise that I was having an 'out-of-body experience', where the consciousness is separated from the physical body, but I didn't know that at the time. I have tried to re-create the experience on many occasions in adult life, but unfortunately have never been able to.

After education at a local Grammar school, I went to Birmingham University to study Law (which I hated), and finished by scraping a Pass degree (the lowest level). The only thing of spiritual note that I remember from that time was when I first came into personal contact with Death. Uncle George, (or 'Skip' as he was known to most people, being the Skipper of the local Scout Troop,) died of cancer of the liver at the early age of 54. He was a lovely man, liked and respected by all, and the only really positive male-role figure whom I had ever known. I saw him for one last time a few minutes after he had died, and was struck by the look of complete peace on his face - and by the air of total stillness in the room. I remembered seeing him the evening before, gasping out his final hours of life, and the difference between seeing a person alive and seeing a corpse impressed me greatly.

Possibly that was when I realised that the difference lay in the absence of the personality, or to put it into religious terms, the soul. Since that time I have never deliberately gone to see anyone after his/ her death - there is no point in seeing an empty shell. I was with both of my parents and with my first wife Eleanor at the time when each of them passed, but I refused to go to see any of them again before the funeral.

The start of my journey into Spiritualism was in 1956, when I was a regular soldier: a Sergeant-Instructor in the Royal Army Educational Corps. I was fresh out of training and had joined my first Army Unit, a camp in Sudbury, Staffordshire. Little did I think, during those first few weeks there, that I was on the brink of something that would make an impression on me for the rest of my life - and it was all to do with Aunty Margaret, my first spiritual guru. In fact, she was effectively my spiritual mother, who started me on my own personal journey towards spirituality. She was Eleanor's aunt, and a very powerful medium, who had once served on the prestigious Marylebone circuit of Spiritualist churches in London. I was now about to have my first example of her powers, about ten months after Eleanor and I had married.

For my first six weeks in Sudbury, I commuted back to Bilston, Eleanor's family home, every weekend. Outside the camp, I caught the country bus that rambled round the countryside at a leisurely pace to Burton-on-Trent, from where I caught a train to Birmingham, another one to Wolverhampton, then a bus to Bilston. The journey was no more than about fifty miles as the crow flies, but usually took about two hours. I always arrived home at more or less the same time every week.

One particular Saturday, while I was waiting at the camp bus stop, a colleague stopped his car and offered me a lift as far as Tutbury, through which the bus had to pass, after having travelled in a wide loop for three miles. He dropped me off there, but now I had about half an hour to wait until the bus arrived, so I went into the local pub for a drink. Talking to the landlord, I asked if he knew of any accommodation to let in the area,

1: Initiation

and he told me that there were rooms in the large house opposite. I went over, saw the owners, and said that I was looking for somewhere to live with my wife. They showed me what they had, which was four rooms of the house. I agreed in principle to take them, subject to Eleanor seeing them, and then had to dash over to the bus stop to catch my normal bus, now chugging up the hill. I caught the same trains and bus that I always caught and arrived home at the normal time.

When I got back home, I walked into the tiny kitchen and found it crammed with people, all standing round the table, where Aunty Margaret was 'reading the cards'. Everyone turned round as I walked in, said 'Ssssh' and turned back to carry on listening. I stood by the door with a scornful look on my face, listening to these gullible people being told what I thought was a load of rubbish. But when she had finished with everyone else, they said to me, 'Come and have a go'. At first I refused, but was pressed. Eleanor said, 'Sit down!' So I finally gave in and sat down, certain that I would get nothing of any value.

The first words that Aunty Margaret said to me were, 'You are going to live in that house you have just been to see. They are nice people, and have a little boy'. I was amazed, and everyone else wondered what on earth she was talking about, as I had not had a chance to speak even one word since going in. She said, 'Eleanor is going to teach at that school. There will be three people who will interview her, and she will make a very good impression and will get the job. You are going to be very happy there, but you will live there for only one year exactly'.

Of course, everyone had been listening and wanted to know what it was all about. I explained what had happened, and Eleanor was most impressed. After ten months of marriage, still living with her parents and apart from me, she was eager to start up family life in her own home with me, so that we could concentrate on starting a family (which is a delicate way of putting it). She asked me to make an appointment for us to go to see the landlord, which I did as soon as I got back, and we arranged to go over on the following weekend to see the rooms.

She loved them on first sight. The house was a big square building, possibly a couple of hundred years old, and the rooms which we were offered were adequate for our needs, so without much ado we signed a tenancy agreement and moved in the following week, on Thursday March 15th, 1956. We loved it there: we were young, living together for the first time, and our time in Tutbury was very much in the line of an extended honeymoon. The old saying is 'A new home, a new baby' - and Eleanor was overjoyed when she found that she was at last pregnant.

She had always been a woman who needed to be doing something, as she found inactivity very irksome, so she went down to the local school to see if there was any possibility of teaching. She was told that 'by coincidence' one of the staff had that day been called back home to the other end of the country because of family commitments, and would not be coming back. Therefore, they had an immediate vacancy for a full-time member of staff for a few months until a permanent position could be advertised by the Local Education Authority. She filled in an application form there and then, and a formal interview was arranged for the following week. She was told that she would be interviewed by two people - the Headmaster and the Chairman of the Governors; but when she arrived for her interview, there was a third man there who was introduced as the local Primary School Inspector, who 'by coincidence' was visiting that day. So Eleanor got the job, and taught at the school until the new teacher arrived - a month or so before our first son was born. Synchronicity!

Skipping forward many months, I had gone away to do an Officer Training Course at Eaton Hall, near Chester, and Eleanor had been joined by her sister to keep her company and to help look after Michael, our first-born. Then on March 1st 1957, the landlord called on her to say that his wife's sister had just lost her husband, and would be coming to live with them in Tutbury, so the rooms that we occupied would no longer be available. He gave Eleanor a fortnight's notice, and she left on March 15th - exactly a year to the day after we had moved in.

One of the themes of this book is that everything happens at exactly the right time in our life, and that everything happens to further our own spiritual progress. Of course, it is only when we can look back, sometimes after many years have elapsed, that we can appreciate that fact - and the Eaton Hall episode in my life was a perfect example of this. At the time, I did not appreciate it - in fact, I lived through Hell for several months - but I can now look back and see it as part of a pattern. I failed the course, and was returned to my unit - the dreaded RTU - which was an incredible psychological blow. It was that weekend, in appalling emotional conditions - something that was to have immense repercussions later in his life - that my second son Robert was conceived.

1: Initiation

On one level, Eaton Hall was a total disaster for me. On another it ensured that I was in exactly the right place at the right time to prepare me for one of the happiest times in my life, and to ensure that Robert would have the perfect start for the difficult life that he had chosen for himself.

So started my spiritual journey, which has to date lasted for 60 years, and is still continuing as I learn more and more about the meaning of Life itself.

As my previous post in Sudbury had now been filled, I was sent back to the R.A.E.C. Headquarters, Wilton Park, in Buckinghamshire for a few months, until my next posting could be arranged, and that stay at Wilton Park was a great healer. I found that I had a totally new status now: previously I had been a mere trainee, but now I was a fully-fledged Sergeant-Instructor who was waiting in the Pool between postings, and as such, I had virtually no duties whatsoever. The powers-that-be did try to find things to keep all of us in the Pool occupied, but none of our duties were very onerous, and life was very pleasant for the short time I was there.

But never in all my wildest dreams could I have imagined where I would be posted next. One day I was called in to see the Postings Officer, and was asked how good my French was. I was surprised but, as I had got a double Distinction in written and oral French in School Certificate eight years before, I answered without hesitation that it was excellent, and fortunately, he did not press me further. He then told me that there was a posting for a French-speaking R.A.E.C. sergeant coming up in the British Army Camp Support Unit with the NATO forces in Fontainebleau, France and asked 'How would you like to go there?' How would I like to go there? I was speechless, as this was one of the most sought-after postings in the world. I assured him that I would certainly be able to cope with the French language - which the duties involved - and it was settled there and then. So that was how the pattern of my future life was irrevocably changed.

I had a wonderful time in France for three years, and two more sons were born there, Robert and David. I can't say that much happened there to forward my spiritual life, although there was one incident which has now, almost sixty years later, shown me how 'what goes around comes around'. There was an establishment of one R.A.E.C. Warrant Officer and two sergeants at the Unit, and when I got there the Warrant Officer was Harry, who was about to be replaced by Frank.

A Practical Spiritual Primer

There was a period of time when both Frank and Harry were in the Unit together, as a few weeks had been allowed for a hand-over/take-over of duties. They got on very well together, although they were totally different in character. The one thing that they had in common, however, was that they were both rather hard of hearing - and this led to some amazing scenes. The sort of thing that would happen was as follows:

One would come into the office first thing in the morning, and find the other already there, and this sort of conversation would be heard:

A: It is a nice day today.
B. Pay - we don't get paid till Thursday.
A. Thirsty - it's a bit early, but I wouldn't mind a drink.
B. Think - what do I think? I can't understand.
A. Band - I can't hear any band............

And so it would carry on, with both of them getting increasingly muddled up, and anyone who happened to be listening (usually the other sergeant, John, or me - or both) reduced to paroxysms of helpless laughter.

Re-telling this story has made me realise that *I* am now like that: in my latter years I have become increasingly hard of hearing, and without my hearing aids a lot of conversation is reduced to unintelligible gibberish - so I am now 'getting my come-uppance' for having laughed at the same infirmity all those years ago in France.

After three years in France I was posted to Malta for two years, and it was at that time, when I saw how the Maltese Catholic Church treated the local population, that I came as close as I have ever been to becoming an atheist - or at least, an agnostic. Looking back now, with the wisdom of more than fifty years of hindsight, I can see that in spiritual terms my experiences were a sort of paradox.

A paradox is when something happens which leads to the opposite result to that which was either intended or expected. My experience of orthodox religion in Malta brought me to a state where I became very anti-religion - but at the same time, it provided a catalyst for me to start thinking about spirituality, and what it really means.

Perhaps what I was experiencing was what is sometimes called 'The dark night of the soul'. This is a term that is used to describe the state of utter despair, which results in a total loss of faith in all that which one has

1: Initiation

previously thought to be true and valid. The most dramatic example of it was what the disciples of Jesus felt after the Crucifixion, but all of us experience it in one way or another at some time in our lives. Everyone reacts to it in a different way: some feel hopeless and helpless; others sink into deep depression, or even react with violence and anger.

The state may last only a few weeks, but on occasions, it can last for months - or even years. The only thing which is certain is that one day it will end - as every situation has to end sooner or later. When I think of 'the dark night of the soul', I rationalise it astrologically by thinking of the planet Uranus. He is the destroyer of fixed conditions, and has the job of preparing us for new things to come into our life. He gives us the jolt we need to get us out of any rut that we might have got into, which is stopping our further development. If we are faced with a situation that proves to us that our previous ideas are no longer valid, then that forces us to start thinking about what *is* valid. I am no gardener, but I understand that after a very hard winter, during which the soil has been frozen for long periods of time, it is particularly easy to work once the Spring comes again. Perhaps in my case the 'freezing-out' of my old beliefs meant that my mental soil was being prepared for new seeds to be sown.

Chapter 2: Getting in Deeper

After almost nine years in the Army, I was made redundant, when the R.A.E.C. became an all-officer Corps, and I took redundancy, rather than become an officer. (Memories of Eaton Hall!) This decision proved to be a major turning point in my personal life, but it was also important from a spiritual point of view, and once again, it was all because of Aunty Margaret. She had given me my first psychic reading many years before, and had shaken my supercilious belief that all talk about Spiritualism and mediums was total hocus-pocus - but that effect had by now largely worn off, and it was time for me to have another experience.

At that time, she was running a Spiritualist church in a local Community Centre in Wolverhampton, and every time that she came round to see Nanny - her sister, Eleanor's mother - we met. I tried to tell her that Spiritualism was all a load of rubbish, but she invited me to come to a Service one night and see for myself what happened. I went along, more to humour her than with any idea of learning anything, and had my second great shock. I deliberately sat at the back of the room, where I could watch what was going on while not being directly involved, and I listened as the presiding Minister, Albert Taylor of Birmingham, led the hymns and prayers and gave an address. So far, there was little difference between the service and a normal C. of E. service. But then came the clairvoyance, and I listened in amazement as he spoke to various members of the congregation and told them of people who were there and who wanted to give them messages. They all appeared to understand what was happening, but though I looked all around every time he was describing someone, I couldn't see anyone remotely resembling that person. So I concluded that he was hallucinating, although he looked like a fairly normal, kindly old man.

2: Getting in Deeper

But then, to my absolute horror, he spoke to me. 'I want to come to that young man at the back', he said. I crouched down in my seat and pretended not to be there. 'Speak up', he said, 'and let me hear your voice'. Still I said nothing, but a large woman in front of me turned round and said, 'He's speaking to you. Say 'Yes!' So I said 'Yes' and his first words to me were, 'You have a great work to do for Spirit'. Then he began to describe someone to me, whom I didn't know. I racked my brains, went through all my friends and relatives and couldn't recognise anyone. So he started on another, with the same result. Finally, Aunty Margaret told him that I was new, so he gave up and just said to me, 'Always remember what I have told you tonight - you have a great work to do for Spirit' - and my ordeal was at an end.

Afterwards, I asked Aunty Margaret what all that rubbish was about, as I didn't recognise the description of either of the people he had mentioned. When she told me that they were the spirits of people who had now 'passed over' - and when I realised that that phrase meant 'died' - I was horrified, especially as one of the descriptions matched that of a very dear relative who had died many years previously. Then she told me that certain people, known as mediums or clairvoyants, have the gift of being able to see and/or hear those who have died - and that Mr Taylor was one of them. I told her that it wasn't possible, and I vowed that I would prove that it was all a load of rubbish. So I started to study Spiritualism and attend Spiritualist services regularly, and became more and more interested in the subject; eventually, after five years, I ended up by proving to my own satisfaction exactly the opposite - that it was totally valid - and that is how I took the first step towards my own spiritual enlightenment

*****

I had three jobs over the next five years, and all of them involved working away in London. One interesting thing happened during that time: I had seen an advert inviting applications to join MENSA, the organisation of highly intelligent members, which had the idea that, with a combination of intelligent people, the world could be changed for the better. I am not sure that that concept is really valid, but as I had always prized Intelligence very highly, I applied to join. I was told to go to London University on one particular evening, where there were about 150 candidates in a large hall, and we were all given an Intelligence Test.

A Practical Spiritual Primer

This consisted of having to work our way through a very thick booklet of questions, which had to be completed in one hour. I finished in about fifty minutes, checked my answers and then sat looking round rather smugly at all the other candidates who were still sweating away working. Then 'Time' was called, and we were all told to hand in our booklets, *face down*. It was only when I turned my booklet over that I found, to my horror, that there was a whole page of questions on the back of the booklet which I had not even seen, far less attempted. I was eventually told that I had scored 152, which was high enough for me to be admitted as a member - but it just underlined the difference between intelligence and commonsense. I have a lot of the former, but am woefully - almost completely - lacking in the latter.

But while all this was happening to me in the working environment, things were also happening at home. Eleanor was finding it more and more difficult to control the children, particularly Robert, who was now nine years old and was getting into trouble at school. (One of his troubles was the fact that he was dyslexic, which had not been diagnosed)! Michael had passed the Entrance Exam for the local Grammar School - my old school - and needed running round to various school functions, and the other children were starting to make demands on her time as well. I had been living in London for most of the last four years, commuting back to Wolverhampton only at weekends, and I was really needed at home. So we decided that I would look for a job in the Midlands, where I could live at home and be part of the family once more.

Chapter 3: Spiritual Progression

Some people believe that a person's spiritual progression can be plotted like a straight-line graph. Possibly you remember that sort of graph from schooldays: it started at the bottom left-hand corner and carried on uniformly to the top right. Well, the truth is that spiritual progression doesn't work that way at all. The graph starts somewhere on the left, but need not start at the bottom - after all, we do not all have the same degree of spiritual knowledge from birth. Then it rises erratically, sometimes steeply, sometimes more gently - but for most of the time it does not rise at all, just remaining on the same level, on a plateau. A simple way to visualise the graph is as a series of sloping rises, at the top of each of which is a horizontal line, followed by another sloping rise, etc.

The reason for this is quite simple: each of us is capable of taking in only so much new knowledge at a time, and then we need time to digest it. In fact, if we think of our own digestive system, it provides a very good example. We cannot continuously eat food: we need time to digest what we have eaten; and the bigger the meal we have had the longer we will need to digest it.

So it is with spiritual growth: the occult saying is, 'When the pupil is ready, the master will appear'. So, when we are ready for another meal of spiritual food, someone or something will come into our life to provide it. Then, for a period of time, we will grow rapidly in understanding, before slowing down and remaining on a plateau until the next time when we are ready. In my own case, I have had such experiences on four different occasions.

The first one was with Aunty Margaret, my first guru and Spiritual Mother. The second was when I had been on a spiritual plateau for several years. By 1967, I was employed by John Laing Construction Company, working away in London during the week and commuting home only at weekends, but I had been seconded to a construction site in Bristol for several months. One evening, being at a loose end with nothing in particular to do, I decided to go to a service in Bedminster Spiritualist Church.

At the end of the service, I was speaking to the President of the church, and asked her about a particular aspect of Spiritualism that was puzzling me. She said, 'Oh, you should have been here last week. Mr ... was taking the service, and he is an expert on that'. I asked for his telephone number, rang him up and asked to see him. He didn't seem to be at all surprised at a stranger contacting him in that way - in fact, if anything he seemed to be expecting it - and so I went to see him in his home. We talked for about an hour and a half, during which time he not only answered all my queries but also gave me much more to think about, and set me off on a new path, which carried me on for the next few years. I never met him again, and by now have even forgotten his name, but he did me a great service as my second guru in providing another step on my own spiritual ladder.

However, there was another thing that happened, which was a direct result of my working in Bristol: I got into Astrology, which has proved to be a great influence in my life and philosophy. It all happened like this:

I was commuting home every weekend from Bristol back to Wolverhampton, and going back down to work the following Monday morning. Now that particular journey took a long time: although it was only about 80 miles, the train seemed to stop at every possible station en route - and the monotony could only be relieved by reading something. At the time, I did a lot of reading, and I found that I had read most of the books on sale in the tiny bookstall on Wolverhampton Station. The only one that I hadn't read, and which might be of any interest to me whatsoever, was an Oxford University Press book, 'Teach Yourself Astrology', so I bought it and read it from cover to cover. Despite a certain amount of scepticism, I found myself becoming interested in the subject, and so I decided to try it out. In order to set up a chart the book said that it was necessary to get an Ephemeris for the year of the birth concerned. (An Ephemeris is a booklet that contains a set of figures showing the positions of the Sun, Moon and all the planets on each day of the year concerned). The book also gave sample interpretations of the meaning of the placements of the planets in the different signs and of the angles between planets (the aspects). So that week I went into a bookshop and

3: Spiritual Progression

bought an Ephemeris for 1958 - the birth year of one of my sons, Robert - and started to set up his chart.

Robert had been conceived in extremely unfavourable astrological circumstances, and had had a very difficult childhood. He has now become a mature adult, and an expert craftsman, and I am very proud of him. However, at this time in his early life he was having problems, so I wanted to see if his birth chart could give us any clues about how to help him overcome them.

I did everything which the book said was necessary, working in a totally mechanical way and not understanding a thing about what I was doing, and managed to create an astrological chart for the first time. Then came the task of interpreting it. For this, I could only read out the sample interpretations that the book had given, as I had no knowledge of the real meaning of planets, signs or relative positions whatsoever. As I read out the meaning of each of them in the chart that I had created, a shiver ran down my spine: I was reading Robert's character. Then, when I went back home that weekend, I read out the sample interpretations to Eleanor, and asked whom I was describing. She immediately said, 'Robert, of course!' - and was just as shocked as I was to find out how I had arrived at those interpretations. From then on, I started to take Astrology seriously, and bought a Reference Manual with which I taught myself the subject.

I know that many religious people will be horrified at the thought of using Astrology in any sort of spiritual context, but I believe that it is just a tool to help us to know ourselves, and face the basic traits of our own character. After all, somewhere there is a spiritual maxim 'Man, know thyself!' In my recent book, written seven years after 'All is Well', I explore the subject in much more detail, and show how Astrology is, in fact, an integral part of the whole process of Life itself and plays an important role in the formation of the new soul coming into incarnation. Much later in life, when I started to do voluntary spiritual counselling, I developed a technique of drawing up a horoscope for the client and showing him/ her how the chart - which could have been drawn up ten minutes after the birth - had set the framework for his/ her whole life. I found out that this was very effective in helping to reduce initial nervousness.

So my stay in Bristol had achieved the two objectives for which Fate had brought it about, and soon after that, I saw positions advertised for Training Officers in the newly formed Road Transport Industry Training

A Practical Spiritual Primer

Board. The only problem was that I would have to take a huge drop in salary, from £2,200 p.a. down to £1,600 p.a. I discussed it with Eleanor and we decided that the overall benefits would justify the lower salary, so I applied for a position in the Birmingham Regional Office of the Board, and was accepted. Best of all, I was given a company car and a patch to look after which consisted of Wolverhampton and some of the surrounding countryside - so at last I could come home and live a normal family life, for the first time since I had left the Army. I started my new job at the beginning of December 1967.

Our five children viewed my impending homecoming with mixed feelings: in some ways, they were glad, as I would be there to take them out to places during the week, but in others, they were very wary. I had become an 'Avenging Angel' figure, dispensing justice and punishments at the weekends for misdeeds done during the week, and they were not sure how things would work out when I was there all the time. But the most amusing reaction was that of Nicola, who was only three years of age at the time. Each of the children was allowed to sleep with Eleanor on one night of the week, and looked forward to 'having their turn'. So Nicola stated that I could only come back home if I took my turn sleeping with their Mother like they had to.

At the same time that life was evolving in career and the home, I was starting to get more deeply into Spiritualist matters as well, and I eventually became the vice-president of a little Spiritualist church in Bilston. By this time I had gone far beyond the stage of needing to be convinced about whether the survival of the personality was a fact or not, and I wanted to know what life was all about.

In the church I was initiated into 'sitting in circle', where a group of people sat and meditated together with a view to seeing if contact could be made with those who had passed on from this world. I found that I had no apparent gifts as a clairvoyant medium, but I did receive information from various souls who wished to talk about spiritual philosophy, which was something in which I was - and still am - greatly interested. When I say I 'received information', that is the only way I can describe it: I did not *hear* anything, but words just seemed to come into my mind. Not only did I receive the information, but I told the others in the group what I was receiving - what is normally described as 'channelling'.

3: Spiritual Progression

I had been prepared for this by the evening that I had had with my second guru in Bristol: up to that time I had no idea that it was possible to be contacted and used as a channel by those who were in the Spirit world. I knew that they could come to us via a medium, and I knew what sort of work mediums did - but channelling was a totally new concept for me. I had also learnt that spirit beings often refer to the persons through whom they channel as their 'instruments', because those people allow themselves to be used for the purpose of Spirit, without trying to interfere and impose their own thoughts or will upon those who are giving the information.

I learnt other things in that little church in Bilston, and possibly the most important one was about the power of Healing. We had a healing circle one evening every week, and during that circle members of the public used to come in and ask for healing to be given for their various illnesses or complaints. I saw some wonderful happenings, but one of the most dramatic was the healing of a woman who came in with a large lump on the neck. I believe that it was a goitre, or something similar. One of the most powerful healers and teaching mediums in the church was Pat, who went to the woman, prayed for a time, and then put her hands on her neck. She stayed like that for about ten minutes, and when she removed her hands, the lump had gone. How or why, we never found out. Physically, it was impossible, and yet the woman walked out of the room without the lump.

Another case that comes to mind was that of a woman who was carried into the room by her relatives. She appeared to be dreadfully deformed, and was crouching and curled up as though trying to defend herself against an unseen enemy. We were told that she had been a witness to an experiment with a Ouija board, which had unleashed some harmful force that had attached itself to her and could not then be cleared. The woman had been in and out of psychiatric hospitals for the last three years, had endured all sorts of treatments - electrical, drug and others - and was still as bad as ever. So in desperation her relatives had brought her to us as a last resort.

We sat her in a chair and formed a circle round her. 'By coincidence' there were seven healers there that night, and seven is the number of spiritual power. We all tried to get rid of what was possessing her, and seemed to have some success, but the woman was saying, 'It is still there'

- meaning that whatever 'it' was, was waiting until we had gone before it would re-possess her. So the President of the church, who was leader of the circle, put his own crucifix, which was on a golden chain, round her neck. There was an immediate reaction. I had never understood what the words 'The scream of a banshee' meant - until that night. The woman let out an unearthly cry, her body went rigid and she slid along the floor as stiff as a board. Then, after about a quarter of a minute, during which time we were all standing transfixed by the hideous wail, she got up and asked for a cup of tea: she was healed.

Let me say something about Ouija boards and planchettes: these are both devices round which one can sit in a circle in order to communicate with Spirit in a very simple way, and many people have used them to experiment with making contact. When they are used correctly, and with sincerity, they can work well: at one time, Eleanor and I used to use them when sitting with friends, but we always made sure that we were well protected, and of course, we had implicit trust in each other, and knew that everyone involved was a genuine seeker of Truth. The problem is when you are with people whom you do *not* know: if any one of them is evil - or even just downright mischievous - then things can go badly wrong, as they did for the poor woman whom I have described in the last paragraph.

The problem is that a spiritual circle, like a chain, is only as strong as its weakest link, and if the weakest link is evil or mischievous, then that is the sort of influence which will be attracted. After all, like attracts like, or - as the old adage says - 'Birds of a feather flock together'. Then once an entity has been attracted, it may take far more skill or knowledge than any of those in the circle have to get rid of it again. On balance, I always advise people who ask me about Ouija boards or planchettes to avoid them. As I explain, you wouldn't deliberately leave your front door open at night, for fear of who might come in: if you did, you might not be able to get rid of your unwanted guests. Using either of these devices is the psychic equivalent of doing just that: you leave the door open at your peril.

Chapter 4: Reincarnation

One of the things that Astrology had taught me was that the pattern of a person's life is basically set at the moment of birth, and that a birth chart drawn up ten minutes later could be used to predict what would happen to the person in childhood, adolescence or even adulthood. I reasoned that if this was so, then the whole of everyone's life was subject to an arbitrary rule, based on the moment of their birth - and this seemed totally unfair to me. Why were some people 'born with a silver spoon in their mouth', while others never had a chance from the moment of their birth? So I was facing the basic dilemma of all people who try to make sense of an apparently senseless existence.

However, some of the times when I was channelling I received tantalising hints that it was possible to have lived at several different periods of time in the past, and this opened up the whole concept of Reincarnation to me - and something interesting happened. I have said previously that 'when the pupil is ready the master will appear' - and this proved true yet again. This time it wasn't a person who came into my life, but a book. I happened to be in a second-hand bookshop one day, when a particular book 'jumped out of the bookshelf' at me. (In fact, it didn't move at all, but my attention suddenly became riveted on it, so that I had to pick it up). It was called 'There is a River', and was all about an incredible man called Edgar Cayce (pronounced Casey).

Edgar Cayce was an American who lived from 1877 until 1946, and found that he had an amazing gift of being able to go into trance and then to not only diagnose the physical or mental illnesses from which people were suffering, but also to prescribe medicines or treatments to cure them, although he had no medical training whatsoever. He did this on more than thirty thousand occasions, and all the transcripts of what he said were recorded and have been published by a company called the Association

A Practical Spiritual Primer

for Research and Enlightenment, (A.R.E). But even more amazing were the times when he said that the cause of the illness had its roots in a problem in a previous life, and gave details of that life. I found that there are many books about Edgar Cayce that are still published, and I read many of them. (For those readers who wish follow my example and delve further into his remarkable life, I suggest they should look for the official website about him on the internet: just put 'Edgar Cayce' into Google, or whichever search engine you are using).

But before I start to talk about Reincarnation, let me say something about the words 'Spirit', 'Soul' and 'Personality' - or rather about the way in which I see them To me 'Spirit' is the creative force of the Universe, what people may call 'God', 'Allah', 'Jehovah', 'the I AM' - or whatever their particular concept of this force is. 'Soul' is a particle split off from this Force, which is able to live through many dimensions of existence in many worlds, and as far as we are concerned on this planet is able to have many individual lives. 'Personality' is the sort of character that we have chosen to be during any one lifetime. As soon as we choose a different life, that former 'personality' is replaced by the new one - although it still exists as part of the 'record of existence' of the journey through successive lives of that particular 'soul'. Usually, of course, the word 'soul' is used indiscriminately to describe not only the permanent particle but also the personality during an individual life - and in general, that is how I use it in this book.

Once I had started to study reincarnation, I found that it answered many of the questions that I had been asking. If we have only this one life, then the inequalities of it are blatantly obvious; if, however, this life is only one in a long succession of lives, then what happens this time can be seen as part of a much broader picture, so that in the longer term there are no inequalities at all.

Since that time in the early 1970s, I have continued to study the subject, both in books and in meditation, and I have come to certain conclusions. The first is that what most people think that reincarnation is - 'Karma', or the Law of Retribution and Reward - is only a crude outline of what it really is. It is in fact far more complex and all-embracing than that. There are three main strands of reincarnation, which can be called 'the Three Cs' - Continuation, Compensation and Consequence.

4: Reincarnation

The first strand of reincarnation is the case of a soul who has decided to continue some course of study or refine some talent in several previous consecutive lives, and so he/she is able to excel in the field chosen in this current life. Such cases are what make child prodigies - like, for instance, Mozart, who composed his first symphony at the age of eight. Other examples are the cases of children who are apparently born as mathematical geniuses, who take GCSE at the age of eight or nine and who are at University before they are teenagers.

The second is when a soul, through a series of incarnations, has become unbalanced in one area or another, and needs to seek the opposite trait in order to regain its equilibrium. If a person has become too male-orientated, for instance, a lifetime as a woman might be needed to redress the balance - or, of course, vice-versa. Someone who was totally orientated towards mental pursuits might need a lifetime in which only physical stamina or power was respected, or vice-versa. Someone who had little time for anything of an artistic nature might incarnate with the gifts of a dancer, painter, or musician. Whatever the imbalance that has been created over a series of incarnations is, the thread of Compensation can be chosen in order to re-balance the soul for its onward journey. (I have said that *a* lifetime may be chosen: in fact, if the balance has become seriously disturbed, *several* lifetimes may be needed).

Interestingly enough, this is borne out by something in Astrology. In a birth chart, there are two points that are called the Nodes of the Moon. The South Node, or the 'Dragon's Tail', shows the sum total of what we have achieved in all our incarnations to date, and therefore shows where we have got to so far; on the other hand the North Node, or the 'Dragon's Head', shows why we came into this incarnation in the first place, and indicates where we are aiming to be by the end of our life. As the two Nodes are always diametrically opposed to each other, it shows that the object of a series of incarnations is always to try to achieve perfect balance.

The third strand is the classic case of 'Retribution and Reward', or as it is usually known the Law of Karma. However, the former part, Retribution, is not so much a question of punishment as a different aspect of Balance, an opportunity to see the other side of the story; this helps us to realise that we are all part of the same life force - and so the ideal life is to do one's best for all others, regardless of the circumstances. The

A Practical Spiritual Primer

latter, the Reward aspect, is what happened to Edgar Cayce, as in a previous life he apparently honed his skills of concentration so much that he was able to use those same skills in this last life. (Of course, it can also be taken to be another example of Continuation).

But these three strands are only the *main* avenues of Reincarnation. There are countless others, as each individual soul that comes into incarnation has its own agenda, and in order to fulfil that agenda will choose different gifts, talents - and disabilities.

Many years ago a famous name in the field of football caused uproar when he suggested that people with a physical disability are being punished for misdemeanours in a past life. It is a very dangerous thing to make public pronouncements about a subject which is outside one's own field of competence, and which one has not studied very thoroughly - and I believe that he said what he did out of a complete misunderstanding of the whole subject of Reincarnation: he knew of part of the Consequence strand - 'Karma' - but nothing of the others.

As we go through our many incarnations, we become more and more spiritually evolved, and the further we get on our journey, the faster we want to progress. This means that we are more likely to take on heavier burdens, and greater challenges than we would have done at an earlier stage. Anything and everything that affects us adversely in life can be seen in two ways - as a problem or as a challenge. If we see it as a problem, then we tend to do nothing about it, and we give up the ghost and get no further forward. If, however, we see it as a challenge, then we try to find ways to get round or overcome the difficulties, and it is in doing this that we make spiritual progress. The spiritual maxim that describes this is usually expressed as 'There are no problems in life, only opportunities'. (Interestingly enough, one of my grandchildren has a degree in Maths, and he has told me that the mathematician's equivalent is 'There are no problems in life, only solutions - even if the solution is that there is *no* solution').

I am reminded of the tragedy of Thalidomide in the 1960s. A lot of the babies who were born at that time were dreadfully deformed, and yet many of those, who are now in their fifties, have managed to overcome their problems and lead happy and productive lives. But it is not only the babies themselves who were faced with the challenges: their parents also were, and had the job of trying to get what was best for their children out

4: Reincarnation

of the appalling situation. I believe that just as those souls who incarnated at that time were very special children, they also chose very special parents, who were evolved and strong enough to take on the exceptional burden with which they were faced at that time.

Possibly the most evolved of all are the souls who take on not only a physical disability but also a mental one as well. These - and their parents - must be some of the most spiritual people on the planet at any one time: the children themselves are locked in a body without the opportunity of expressing what they really are or think, whereas their parents are in a situation that demands total and unconditional love at all times. It is no wonder that those who know such souls speak with wonder of their spirituality.

As far as the idea of the higher the level of the soul, the quicker it wishes to evolve is concerned, I have discussed this in more detail later on, in the chapter, entitled 'The Journey', so I will not expand on the subject here.

Much later in life, I was given a practical lesson in Reincarnation when I had my first 'flashback' - a spontaneous memory of a past existence. We were on holiday in South-West France, an area which we had never visited, and were visiting the mediaeval walled city of Carcassonne. I had driven up to the visitors' car park outside the walls (mediaeval cities are not very car-friendly) and when I had locked the car, I turned round and saw the walls in all their splendour for the first time. I was rooted to the spot: I couldn't move and I couldn't speak. I was re-living the last time when I saw those same walls, several hundred years before, when I was a soldier in an army that was besieging the city. I saw myself climbing up a long ladder which had been put against the wall at one place; then, when I was about halfway up, someone threw some scalding-hot liquid down on me, and I fell into the moat - and knew no more. I must have been standing there for at least two minutes without moving, and Eleanor was terrified, not knowing what was happening. When I did finally 'come back' I was badly shaken, and the experience has stayed with me to this day.

I have had several more flashbacks since that time, very often when I meet someone for the first time. In some of these flashbacks, I have seen myself in Atlantis, Ancient Egypt, Greece and Rome, in the Middle East during Biblical times and in France during the French Revolution. In fact,

A Practical Spiritual Primer

I know that I have had at least three lifetimes in France, which is probably why I always feel totally at home when I go there.

Sybil - my second wife - and I know that we have lived together before, in a very deep and loving spiritual relationship, some three thousand years ago in Ancient Egypt. We also know that many of our closest friends - all ladies - have figured in some of our previous incarnations. In two of those lives, Sybil was a mother to one close friend, and a daughter to another. For my part, I was a sister to another friend in one life. We were inseparable - almost like twins - until parted by the early death of one of us (I don't know which). Another close friend was a male friend to me in a past life, somewhere in Eastern Europe, probably now Poland. When I first met this lady in this life, I felt a compulsion to do everything that I possibly could to help her, and this I do even today. After a while, I realised that what I was doing for her must have had a Karmic origin, (came from a past life,) and when I meditated on it I saw a steeply wooded river valley - and realised that my friend had saved my life when he rescued me from drowning. No wonder I can't do enough for him/her today.

But the most dramatic, and detailed, recollection I have of a past life with someone was part of the amazing story of Ann, which I tell later in the book.

I have been told that any foreigner who has an obsessive love of France was probably living there in the time of the Cathars, a Christian sect in the 13th Century. The fact that I was a Cathar at one time was brought to me in a most unusual way. A few years ago, Sybil and I had a holiday in the Dordogne, in South-West France, and we spent a lot of time visiting some of the lovely old castles and small towns in the area. In one of them, which was built into a steep hillside, there was a shrine at the top that was accessed by a pilgrims' staircase of three to four hundred steps, which the faithful used to climb on their knees. We decided to climb in a more comfortable manner, but stopped every fifty steps or so to regain our breath. One of these stops was on a small landing, where there was a bookshop; all the books were in French - except one: this one was the history of the Cathars, their organisation and beliefs - and it was in English. Only the previous evening I had been thinking that I would like to know more about them - and there 'by coincidence' was the book that could tell me all that I wanted to know. I read it from cover to cover - and

4: Reincarnation

realised that I knew most of the information in the book already - I had just needed someone or something to remind me of it again - and finding the book had happened at exactly the right time.

This was just one in a series of strange happenings which have proved to me that there is no such thing as 'coincidence', and that what we think of as such is really 'synchronicity'. We put out thoughts into the ethereal planes, and depending on how strong those thoughts are, we set up a series of events that eventually bring to pass the things that we desire. Note the word 'desire': this is not the same as the word 'want' - it is a far deeper and stronger word, and is more appropriate for bringing things of a spiritual nature to us. I have developed these ideas more in the chapter about Synchronicity.

Chapter 5: The Journey

One day I asked my inspirers to explain how Reincarnation fitted into the picture of human life, and I was given the following little story:

Once upon a time, there was a land in very mountainous area. The people there lived a miserable existence, having to work hard to scratch a living out of the difficult, stony soil. The country was totally ringed by mountains, and the people were cut off from contact with any others anywhere - so they thought that their own land was all that existed in the whole world. No one knew how their ancestors had originally reached this desolate country, but there were ancient legends that told of a journey from a far distant 'land of milk and honey', which the ancestors had originally inhabited Some great catastrophe had taken place, which meant that the people had been forced to leave, and ever since that time their descendants had lived out their pitiable existence in this poor mountainous terrain.

Then one day there was great excitement in the country, when mysterious posters appeared all over the place inviting the people to take part in a journey back to the land of their original ancestors, which they were told was called 'Paradise'. They were warned that it would be a long, hard journey, but when they arrived, they would find themselves in a state of happiness such as they had never dreamed of before, in a place where life would be perfect in every respect. All that they needed to do was to enrol to go on this journey, and the rest would be explained to them in due course. Naturally, everyone wanted to go, so they all enrolled.

When they had enrolled, they were told of the conditions that would apply throughout their journey - and these seemed to be very strange. The first was that the journey would take a very long time, and they would be travelling for many months. At the start of each day, they would be shown a map of the overall area, and would be invited to choose the way that they

5: The Journey

thought would be the best one to take. They would have advisors to help them, and to tell them the general direction of the 'Promised Land' - but the advisors would not have the power to tell them which way was best - they would have to make that decision for themselves. However, the advisors were allowed to tell them what sort of equipment and clothing they would need, according to the different routes each one had chosen. They would then be issued with whatever clothing and equipment they needed, and food and drink for the day, and everything would be put in the rucksack with which they would also be supplied. Then they would be told to memorise the route that they had chosen well, as once they started the map would be taken away from them.

The second condition was that every night they would be picked up from wherever they had reached and taken to a hostel, where they would meet their advisors once more - but the next morning they would have to start from the same place that they had reached the previous night. When they met their advisers at night, they would be shown the map and would see what they had wanted to do - and what had in fact happened. They would then be able to discuss what progress they had made, where they had gone wrong and strayed from their planned route, which parts of the day's journey had gone really well and - most important of all - what they intended to do the next day. They would then have to choose their route again - remembering that they had to start from where they had left off - and would have to memorise the map once more, as it would be taken away before they started the next day's journey.

Everyone was still willing to make the journey, despite the strange conditions, so on the appointed morning they all set off. Some walked fast and with purpose, intending to make the best progress possible during their first day, while others dawdled and dallied, reasoning that if they had a journey of several months before them, they didn't need to go very far on each day. Most kept to the main road which led away from their starting point, but one or two took some of the minor side roads, which they had previously calculated would be short cuts and would save time. All went well for the main party until they came to the first major fork in the road: some remembered which way they had planned to go, but many had forgotten, and so the parties on the road split up, going their own separate ways. This process continued at every fork in each road, until there were travellers scattered over a wide area of country.

A Practical Spiritual Primer

At the end of that first day, the travellers were picked up, tired and weary, and taken to their hostel for the night, to be fed and watered and to have their planned meeting with their personal advisors. Some had kept to the main road all the day, and had achieved what they had hoped to achieve, whilst others had pushed themselves hard and were in fact far beyond their original planned destination for the day. But whatever had happened, all were faced with the necessity of planning for the next day.

When they met their advisors, they were shown the map again, and the place that they had reached was indicated - and many realised with horror how far that they had strayed from their planned route. The general road led upwards and round the mountains, but many had taken side roads which led them in a downwards direction, and so they now had to decide how to get back to where they would have been had they followed their original plan. They could, of course, just retrace their steps and go back to the start, but that would mean accepting that the first day's journey had been totally wasted - and none of them wanted to do that. So in most cases they chose a rougher path to get back to the original road - or even chose to abandon all paths and just scale up the hill through the tangled undergrowth in order to get back on course as quickly as possible.

They soon got into the daily routine of planning, travelling and then resting each night while surveying the progress that they had made. They always travelled in the company of others, but usually it was with people they didn't know. Sometimes, however, they met people with whom they had travelled before, and their reactions to them depended on what they remembered of the previous meeting. If they had had a pleasant journey together, or if the others had helped them in some way, they welcomed them with pleasure, but if the others had harmed them in any way, then their reaction was hostile from the beginning - although they could do nothing to stop those people from travelling on the same road as them. In fact, they usually found that when they met such people, *they* would be just as hostile in return. Occasionally they met a group of several people with whom they felt totally comfortable from the start - and only realised much later that they had all travelled together on a good day in the past.

More mystifying were the times they met someone and took an instant dislike to the person from the start - and couldn't find out why - until at the end of the day they asked their advisor, who explained that they had

had a bad experience with that person on one stage of the journey, but it was so long ago that they had completely forgotten it.

The travellers had realised from the very first day that there were little stalls from time to time along the road, and all these stalls proclaimed that they knew the best way to go to the destination. For a small fee, such stalls would even give out what they claimed were accurate maps of the area. However, having bought such maps on one or two occasions in the past, and having found out that the maps were only partly correct, giving a very limited view of a portion of the overall map, our travellers realised that the best way was to rely on their own memory and follow the route which they had chosen personally before the start of each day.

Then one day, when they were fairly advanced on their journey, they found out a remarkable fact. Before the start of each day, they had always been given all the tools and equipment they would be likely to need during that day's journey, and these had been put in the rucksack that each one carried on his/ her back. One day, when examining the rucksack more closely than he had done previously, one man found that it had, built in, a tiny two-way radio, which was tuned into the frequency of the hostel where they all met their advisors every night - and he told the others in the party. From that time onwards, things became considerably easier, as when they were lost, they could always 'ring up' and get advice from their own personal adviser.

Another thing that they had realised by now was that they could take short cuts from time to time, without running the risks of losing themselves, which they had experienced in the early stages. When the road snaked backwards and forwards in a very mountainous stretch, they realised that by doing a vertical climb to the road above on one day, they could save themselves many days' travelling, as the road would lead round to that very spot eventually. Granted, it would mean that they would have an incredibly difficult day's climb, but they would have all the equipment necessary to do it, and would be able to 'tune in' to the experience of their adviser - so many decided to do exactly that, and voluntarily accepted one difficult day's journey in order to save many other days of time. In fact, the nearer that they got to their eventual goal, and the more they started to feel the buzz of excitement which that knowledge brought, the more they were likely to go for the short cuts and do far more than they would normally have planned for one day.

A Practical Spiritual Primer

There was another strange thing that they realised after a long time on the journey: they started to occasionally meet people who appeared to have a great deal of knowledge about the whole journey, as if they themselves had already made it to the finish. Such people never told anyone what they *should* do, but were always available to listen to ideas and to stimulate the individuals to take responsibility for their own decisions.

The end of the story, of course, is that everyone eventually finished their own personal journeys - and found that all the legends were true, and that the land to which they came was the Paradise which they had expected: in fact it was far better than anything they could have ever wished for - and looking back over the months of travelling they realised that it had all been worthwhile.

***

I was given that little story as a parable of our own journey back to the Paradise from which we originally came. We travel through a series of lives, each of which represents one day's journey, and at the end of each life we are taken back to the 'hostel' where we are allowed to rest and take refreshments. We then review, with our own Higher Self*, (our personal spiritual advisor,) what we have achieved during that last life, the triumphs we have had and the difficulties we have encountered. We see how much of our original plan we have fulfilled, and we decide what we need to do in order to get back on track or to make even more rapid progress during the next life, as the case may be.

* N.B. I say more about our Higher Self in a later chapter.

When we first come into life, we have a master plan, which we have conceived during our rest period, but as we go through the life, we are often distracted from what would be our best way, and so we make detours or run into blind alleys, from which we have to extricate ourselves. However, nothing is ever wasted, as we learn from 'mistakes' we have made, and in learning we complete some of the lessons for which we came into life in the first place. Finally, we realise that there are never any real 'mistakes' in life - there are just 'learning curves'.

The people in our life with whom we feel an instant rapport are those with whom we have travelled in previous lives, and of whom we have

5: The Journey

pleasant memories, whereas those we meet and instantly dislike are those with whom we have had difficult relations in past lives. It is interesting that the reason they have been brought into this present life to meet us again is to see if we can resolve those past problems, so that we can wipe the slate clean and get rid of things which are holding up our own spiritual progress. (This, of course, works both ways, as *we* have been brought into *their* life with the same intention).

The stalls we see along the way are the different religions, philosophies and -isms which we encounter in life, all of which claim to provide the only true way to get to the 'Promised Land'. However, each of these mind-sets provides only a limited view of the Truth, the reality of which is far greater than any one of them could ever indicate. That Truth, in all its complexity, can be seen only when we reach the end of our life, and are shown the overall map again by our Higher Self.

Finding that all travellers carry a personal two-way radio, which came only at a late stage in the journey, is the realisation that each of us has a direct connection with our own Higher Self, and if or when we decide to start to use that connection we find that things become a lot easier in our own journey through life.

When the travellers neared the end of their journey, they started to feel the buzz of excitement that that brought, and realised that they could cut the journey by several days if they voluntarily took on a particularly difficult climb. So it is with us: when we become spiritually developed enough, we are likely to take on greater burdens during our life in order to make faster spiritual progress. We often see that many people who have enormous mental, physical or emotional problems in this life are in fact some of the loveliest and most advanced souls whom one could ever wish to meet. However, in the story all the travellers had always arranged to take all the tools and equipment needed for the next day's journey with them - and so it is in our earthly life: we always possess all the gifts and talents necessary to help us to get through our lessons - although many of us refuse to accept the fact on a conscious level. There is an old saying that 'No-one is ever given a load which is too heavy to bear' - and if we only accepted the truth of that and used the gifts we have, we would find the inner strength to face many of the challenges of life which at times might seem insurmountable.

A Practical Spiritual Primer

Finally, the strange travellers who appeared to have done the journey before are those enlightened souls (or 'Ascended Masters') who have in fact finished their cycle of earthly journeys and who have voluntarily either stayed behind or have come back in order to help humanity to progress onto the next stage of its spiritual journey. We are presently at the end of a cycle of evolution when the human race is on the verge of taking a massive leap forward in consciousness, and there are many highly evolved souls who have volunteered to come into incarnation at the moment with the express purpose of helping us to make that next quantum leap.

One of the heartening facts about the doctrine of reincarnation is that it means that we don't need to do everything in the one life. In many religions and mind-sets, you have one chance, and one chance only, and if you 'blow it', then you are condemned to eternal damnation. Once you realise that you have many lifetimes in which to reach the state of perfection, the pressure is off. However, the doctrine of 'Karma' still applies, and sooner or later, we must sort out all the problems we have caused in all our lives - although we don't need to do it all in one lifetime.

However, a belief in reincarnation has other, more immediate results. One of the precepts of many religions is that of doing to others what we would wish that they should do to us. If this idea just remains a platitude, to be trotted out and quoted when it suits us, or when we are trying to impress someone with our own spirituality, then it does not do much good. However, if we realise that it is a real fact of life, (in fact, that whatever we do to others *will* be done to us,) then we can start to behave towards others in a different way, and treat them as we ourselves want to be treated in our own future - and this starts to have dramatic results in a short time. The Law of Spiritual Interest* kicks in, and we quickly begin to reap the benefits of what we are doing - once again, biblically, 'We reap what we sow', or - to put it into the modern idiom - 'What goes around comes around'.

* *N.B. I talk more about the Law of Spiritual Interest in a later chapter.*
Another result of the doctrine of reincarnation is that fundamentalism in any religious mind-set is seen for what it really is - ridiculous. If one can be a Muslim in one life, a Christian in another, then a Jew, Hindu or Buddhist in the next, the absolutism of each religion is obviously totally inappropriate. However, each religion has much to contribute to our

5: The Journey

overall understanding of the essence of what 'God' (or whatever name we care to use) actually is - so seen from that perspective each religion has an important part to play in the spiritual evolution of the human race. Each one sees Reality from one viewpoint, and by looking from several viewpoints successively, we have a greater opportunity of seeing more of the whole picture.

I am reminded of the old story of how a wise ruler in India once called together six blind beggars and said that he would put them in front of an object and ask them to identify it. Whichever one then identified it correctly would be given riches untold. The first beggar touched the object and announced confidently that it was a spear. The second was equally confident that it was a rope. 'Not so', said the third, 'It is a large leaf'. Each of the other three had his own interpretation, one saying that it was a wall, another a tree trunk and the last one a snake.

Each one was wrong - and yet in a way, each of them was almost right, as the object that he touched was similar to what he had said. It was an elephant! Each beggar had touched a different part of its body - a tusk, its tail, an ear, a side, a leg and its trunk - and so had made his identification. The whole story could only be found by putting together all the different views - and no one had done that.

I think that it is symptomatic of our human condition that we are all searching and want to find *the* answer to the meaning of life. The problem is that there is not just one answer - there are as many answers as there are questions, and each of us has a different way of interpreting any one answer which is ever given. In fact, as there are over seven billion of us on the planet, there are those many views as to what the answers really mean.

I once heard a story about four men who wished to climb a great pyramid. They had been advised that the best way to climb it was by starting from one corner and going up the ridge of the pyramid, rather than by starting in the centre of one of its sides and going up its face. The only problem was - which corner to start from? They walked round to every corner in turn, and saw a crowd of people at each one, all extolling the value of starting from there and following their particular route. Eventually, they each decided on the corner they thought best - and by chance, each one chose a different corner.

A Practical Spiritual Primer

Once they had chosen their corner, each one was congratulated by the noisy crowd at that point, and was cheered as he started to climb. However, as he got higher and higher the noise of the crowd faded away, and he could now concentrate on what he was doing. He saw others climbing by the same route, but found that they were not very talkative - they were all too intent on where they were going. The higher he got the more difficult the climb seemed to become, but he persevered and finally reached his goal on the summit - to find that all his friends arrived there at about the same time. So the noise and fuss at the start had all been useless, as it didn't matter which way any one of them had taken, they all reached the same destination eventually.

Doesn't this little story contain a lesson for each one of us? The lesson is that eventually we all have to make our own decisions which way to take, and we can't choose the path for other people, any more than they can choose the path we should take. Whatever we do is right for us, but may well be totally wrong for another - and vice-versa. The only thing that we can do is follow our intuition and do whatever we feel is the right thing - and let others follow their own intuition, without judgement on whether what they are doing is right or wrong. In fact, there is a verse somewhere in the Bible that says, 'Judge not, so that you are not judged'. If only we could all follow that precept, what a different world it would be.

The other thing that one learns from this little story is that all the people who were making the most noise were those who were at the *foot* of the pyramid. Once the four men had started the ascent there was no one to tell them whether they were doing right or not. Isn't this indicative of much of human life? The ones who do the most shouting are usually not the most advanced on their own journey - if they were, they would be far too concerned with their own spiritual progression to worry about what others were doing about theirs. This ties in with what someone once told me about true gurus: the way in which you can always distinguish them from less spiritual teachers is that they will never *tell* you what you *should* be doing - they will always *ask* you what you think you *could* be doing.

Chapter 6: Forgiveness

At one time in our life together, Eleanor and I bought a small private hotel in Wolverhampton, which provided a lot more room for the growing family of children, of whom there were now six. There was a church about a hundred yards from the hotel, and the children who were still at home used to go there, and also go to the Youth Club which was held in the Church Hall. For a time also our youngest daughter, Penny, who had a good singing voice, was in the choir. I was persuaded, a bit against my better judgement, to go and join the Men's Bible Study Group, which that year was starting a journey through the Old Testament. I went along for several months; although it wasn't really my style of religious philosophy, nothing was said with which I violently disagreed. However, we then came to a part of the Israelites' journey through the desert when they besieged a certain town and slaughtered everyone in it, men, women and children - and the general consensus of opinion in the group was that all this was a good thing, as those particular people did not believe in 'the true God'.

That was too much for me to stomach, and that night, when everyone else had gone home, I stayed and talked for an hour or so to the vicar. I told him that in my opinion the slaughter of innocent people, just because they do not agree with one's own dogma, was nothing but the worst kind of religious bigotry - and could never have anything to do with the 'will of God' at all. Then I explained to him something of my own philosophy. He was kind enough to say at the end that it was the most comprehensive statement of Spiritualist beliefs that he had ever heard - but we decided, by mutual consent, that there wasn't much point in me continuing attendance in the Group.

Fifteen or more years afterwards, there was a curious echo of that event. I received a letter from the current vicar of the church, saying that he had heard that I had been badly treated at that time, and apologising for the unsympathetic way in which the matter was handled - and asking for my forgiveness. I was flabbergasted, as I had totally forgotten the incident. I think that the vicar had been talking to David, my 'Born Again Christian' son, who had remembered what had happened, and whose church was now into asking forgiveness for past wrongs committed. I wrote back and gave my complete forgiveness - although I pointed out that there wasn't really any need for it, as no harm had originally been done.

This brings me on to the question of forgiveness in general. There are two ways of looking at the subject: one is to say that if one carries a grudge for a past wrong through one's life, then one is carrying a needless amount of negativity, which does no good at all. The past is the past, and hanging on to anything that is not spiritually uplifting from that past can only harm us in the future. In fact, going on the hypothesis of Louise Hay, (about whose book more later,) the more rubbish that we carry about from the past, the more likely we are to suffer psychosomatic illness because of it.

The other way to look at it is to realise that what has happened in the past has made the present 'Us'. Whether past experiences have been 'good' or 'bad', they have created a situation that has moulded our present character, and made us what we are. In fact, each of us is at present 'perfect'! I hasten to add that I do not mean to imply that we are 'perfect' in the absolute sense of the word: if we were, there would be no point in us being in incarnation as human beings at all. But we are 'perfect' in the sense that we are now the exact person who we were *meant* to be, and facing all the challenges that we were *meant* to face, at this moment in time. When *we* decide that we are no longer what we want to be, then we can change ourselves - and once more we will become 'perfect' for that new phase in our life.

It is an old truism that we can look at problems in our life in two ways: if we are negative, we see them as obstacles; if we are positive, we see them as challenges. Now, since we can progress spiritually only through facing up to challenges and overcoming them, anything that has brought us to where we are now must have been of benefit to us - and we should not ever consider it as 'bad' at all. So as far as forgiving those who have hurt us in the past is concerned, we could go even further than *forgive* them - and *thank* them.

6: Forgiveness

I realise that this is a very difficult concept for most people to accept, and many will never be able to do so. If someone has hurt you so badly in the past that you cannot *forget* the hurt, even the act of forgiveness will seem totally alien to you, let alone anything far more advanced. (This applies even more so if a person has hurt someone whom you love). But it may be of value to you to think about past hurts in the following way:

- There was an incident in which someone hurt you.
- That incident is now past, and there is nothing that you can ever do to alter it.
- Remembering the incident still hurts you.
- So why do you carry on holding on to it if it only succeeds in prolonging the agony of the past?

One famous spiritual guru put it very simply by likening past hurts to stones that you are carrying in a rucksack. Why do you continue to carry them, when taking them out and throwing them away will make your future journey a lot easier?

Each of us is hurt many times as we go through life, some in simple ways, which are easy to forgive and forget, others in far more profound ways, which are difficult - if not impossible - to forget. However, if you are in the latter position hopefully something which has been said in this book will help you, in the fullness of time, to move on to a greater understanding and acceptance so that you can lay down the heavy load of bitterness and move forward on your own spiritual journey.

*****

Seven years before the end of my marriage to Eleanor, we had moved down to Devon, and were living in an ancient farmhouse, West Iddlecott. We had been married for thirty-one years, and during that time, there was not much to distinguish it from any other marriage. There were the good times and the bad, but as time went on, things deteriorated until eventually, we were doing little more than living together and just tolerating each other.

So we came to the day in October 1986 - probably the most fateful day in our whole marriage - when it all changed. We had been arguing about something or other - probably money, which was in perennially short supply. She argued her case very well, proved (once again) that I was in the wrong, and so I gave in rather ungraciously, and said, 'Right then, from this time on I shall do everything you ever suggest'. She replied, rather acidly, 'I'll believe *that* when I see it' and stormed off to do something or other. At Iddlecott, there were plenty of rooms to go to if you wanted to be alone for a while.

Nanny was living with us then - in fact, she had been with us for about nine years - and the day before, at the dinner table, she had been talking about some couple whom she knew, and about the way that the husband fussed over his wife and did every possible thing for her. She had finished by saying, 'He is *too* good to her. No, on second thoughts, no man can ever treat a woman *too* well!' I had been struck by that conversation, and had thought to myself at the time, 'I bet that I could'. So when I was thinking what I had said to Eleanor, I remembered that conversation, and I decided to make Nanny eat her words.

From that day on, I did what I had said that I would do: everything that Eleanor said she wanted, I did. I started to ask if she wanted things doing - errands, washing-up, cleaning, hoovering and the lot. I asked her advice about everything, and almost behaved like a newly married husband. I even started to use a new name for her when talking to the children: I called her 'She who must be obeyed'. (This title was one that I remembered from an H. Rider Haggard book I had once read about Ayesha, the Queen of a lost world). At first everything was done in an attitude of irony, as if to say, 'This is what you wanted - are you satisfied at last?' - but then something strange started to happen.

I still remember one of my favourite French poet/guitarists, a man called Georges Brassens. In one of his songs about a man who tries to find religious faith, he sings words that mean 'Just pretend that you believe, and very soon you *will* believe'. And this was exactly what happened to me. I played the part of a dutiful and adoring husband so well, that I started to enjoy it. And the more that I enjoyed it, the more I did it. A 'vicious spiral', is where things go from bad to worse: I don't know what the phrase to signify the opposite is - perhaps a 'beneficial spiral' - but whatever it is I now found that I was in it. Things went from good to better.

Although at first highly suspicious, Eleanor started to relax more when we were together, and then began to enjoy the new attention she was getting. In fact, things were even better now than when we first got married: she wasn't getting *more* attention, but she was getting *better*

6: Forgiveness

attention. In the early days, I used to look after her, but in a very controlling way. She had been brought up to the idea of a woman being controlled by her husband, so it was just natural for her to accept that sort of attention as the norm. But now, I was doing everything for *her*, not for *me*, and she was able to say what *she* would like to do, with the certainty that it would happen. In fact, she was able to start living for *herself* more, doing the things *she* wanted to do, in the full knowledge that I would support her - which was a totally new and refreshing experience for her. So as the months went on, the initial love which she had had for me began to re-surface, and she started to be able to demonstrate her love verbally, in ways in which she had been too inhibited to do all those years ago.

From my point of view, although I was initially going through the motions of being a dutiful husband, I was soon doing it for real, and as Eleanor started to respond to me, so I responded to her, and fell in love again - although I don't really like the phrase 'fell in love'. I have always maintained that 'to fall in love' is to be out of control of oneself, putting the other person on a pedestal and not being able to see any faults in him or her. Then, when the scales fall from one's eyes, one 'falls out of love', and the relationship is in trouble. What had happened to me was not 'falling in love' but, for the first time in my life, genuinely *loving*. After all, having lived with each other for more than thirty years, neither of us had any illusions about the other's character; but as far as I was concerned, I now wanted Eleanor as an equal partner, not as a mere household servant and bed-mate.

There is a saying that 'What goes around, comes around' - in other words, what you do to others you will have done to you. And this is exactly what happened to us. I dedicated my life to Eleanor's happiness, and she did the same for me, so that the next six years passed in a haze of requited love and fulfilment for both of us. Even when things became tough, in the last year of her life, the love never failed, and it is still there just as intensely as ever, more than twenty years after her passing. The great regret that I have had for all these years, of course, is that I found that wonderful love only in the last seven years of our marriage. For a long time I bitterly regretted having wasted the first thirty-one years. However, a few years ago, through a Spiritualist medium, I was given a message from Eleanor thanking me for the good times and the bad... 'but especially for the bad times, as that is when I learned and made most spiritual progress'. Although I was totally devastated at the memories those words brought back, it does reinforce the philosophy that 'Everything happens for a purpose' - and reinforces what I have said about *thanking* those who have hurt us!

Chapter 7: Eleanor's Departure

Our idyllic life was eventually shattered when Eleanor contracted three different types of cancer in succession. She fought - and overcame - the first two, but the third was incurable, and nine months after the initial diagnosis she breathed her last.

I was totally convinced that she would pull through, and even when I was called into the hospital on the final morning and told that she was not expected to last the day out, I refused to believe that it really was the end. I stayed there all that day, being joined by my second daughter, Nicola, in the afternoon, and was still optimistic. I was even talking about her recovery when we heard the death rattle in her throat - which I refused to recognise. And then, suddenly, at 3.19 in the morning of August 19th 1993, everything became still - and I went totally numb. I called the nurse, and she expressed her condolences and went back into the office. We sat for a few minutes in silence, and then I kissed Eleanor for the last time, refused the routine cup of sweet tea that was offered by the nurse, and drove home in silence with Nicola.

There are three main stages of mourning: the first is just shock, total numbness, where the person cannot take in what has happened. In this state, one can function as normal, carry out everyday chores and go through the usual routines - and to the casual observer, one can be absolutely fine. This is the state into which I went, and because I had been in denial about the reality - and finality - of Eleanor's illness, it was very deep numbness and lasted for over a year Another contributing factor was the absence of tears. There are ways of suppressing emotion, and I mistakenly used one of them, so that I couldn't cry. I said 'mistakenly', but I now realise that there are no 'mistakes': whatever we do is meant for a purpose, and in my case it was more appropriate that my tears should be deferred, as I will explain later on.

A Practical Spiritual Primer

One of the main reasons for the shock and numbness one feels when bereaved can be explained fairly simply, and once understood the conditions can be alleviated a little. When two people are in a relationship - any relationship, whether marital, partnership, parent and child, friendship, brother or sister or any other - there is always a two-way communication between them on a psychic level. The closer the relationship, the stronger the communication, and this bond has little to do with physical closeness. If you really love someone, they can be at the other side of the room or the other side of the world - and the bond will still exist. It is almost as though each person has a dedicated 'walkie-talkie' radio, which is permanently switched on and broadcasting to the radio of the other person.

Now when one of the pair passes, for a period of time their radio is put out of action, until they find their feet in their new existence and are able to start transmitting again. But if the one who is left, believing that the communication can no longer exist, switches off his/her own set, there is now total, 'deafening' radio silence - which produces the numbness which is felt. If the person had only left the radio switched on, so that the dear- departed could contact when it became possible, then the numbness would still exist, but would be considerably lessened. Of course, after a period of time when the loved one finds out how to come back, many people start to feel his/her presence once more - and that is the origin of the phrase 'Time is a great healer'.

In my case, I was well aware of the reality of survival after death - by then, I had been spiritually aware for almost thirty years - so I knew that Eleanor would come back as soon as she could. I didn't know how long it would take, as the length of time it takes depends on how *ill* the person is at the time of passing. This sounds a strange thing to say - but I discuss it in more detail in the chapter on Death.

After Eleanor's passing I decided to 'keep the radio switched on', and the channel to her open, so that when she was able to come back I would know immediately. I had a copy of one of her last photos enlarged and placed on a chest of drawers by the door in our bedroom, so that I would see it every time I went past, and I looked at it and spoke to her every time I went in or out. Sometimes I just said something like 'Hello, sweetheart' or 'I love you'; at others I would spend several minutes there, pouring out expressions of my love for her, in a way that I had never felt able to before. (Men very often have problems in expressing their deepest emotions, and as a detached Aquarian, I was no exception). It could not bring her back, but at least it allowed me to feel that I was still in contact with her.

Whenever I speak or write to someone who has been bereaved, I recommend him/her to do the same thing. After all, you don't stop loving a person just because they have died, so why should you stop telling them that you love them? Love is eternal, and can't be overcome even by Death, because Love is the material of the very building blocks of the whole universe. Keeping the connection open by talking to loved ones not only helps you, but it also helps them: first, it helps them to re-adjust to their new existence in as short a time as possible, then it helps them to come back when they are able to, as it provides a beacon for guidance. Pope John XXIII was very much loved by people all round the world, (and not only by Catholics,) and the love that was sent to him when he passed over enabled him to make his transition in the gentlest and least stressful way possible.

I went round on autopilot through the next few weeks, not really getting involved in what was happening. If that sounds strange, it was as though I was working on two different levels at the same time: I was going through the motions of doing all the administrative things which have to take place on bereavement, collecting belongings from the hospital, registering the death, putting notices in papers, arranging for the funeral, etc. - but it was almost as though it was happening to someone else, as emotionally I was completely detached from what was going on.

As a Spiritualist, I wanted to have a funeral service which reflected the spiritual philosophy that Death is only the gateway to another phase of life, but it wasn't to happen quite like that. The vicar of the local parish church censored the hymns that I had chosen: he was charitable enough to say of one of them (which starts with the words 'There is no Death') that he quite liked the sentiment, but as it wasn't specifically Christian, he couldn't allow it. He did, however, accept as borderline cases the other two, 'Morning has broken' and 'Lord of the Dance'. The latter was to prove to have a very important significance a few weeks later. We had chosen that particular song as Eleanor had loved dancing, and had herself danced in two of the dancing shows staged by my daughter Ellie.

A Practical Spiritual Primer

When I discussed the arrangements for the funeral with my daughters, we decided that we would have flowers from only the immediate family, and that the money that everyone else would have spent on flowers could be far better employed as a donation to the local hospital for use in connection with the welfare of cancer patients. I realise that many florists are upset by the trend towards donations in lieu of flowers, but I have always found it very sad to visit a crematorium and see so many beautiful bouquets from previous services lying on the ground wilting, until the time comes for them to be put in the rubbish bins. So there were only eight red roses on the coffin, one from each of the children and Nanny and one from me. That was also to prove very significant later on in life.

We then set up the Eleanor Steadman Memorial Fund to be a vehicle for donations, which poured in, as Eleanor was well-known and loved by many people all over the country, particularly in the Midlands, where she had worked for so long. The fund remained open for a year, and was closed when my daughter, who ran the local Dancing School, put on a Dancing Show. The profits from this night were added to the Fund, and we invited Eleanor's cancer specialist and his wife to attend the show. Afterwards, we had a little presentation ceremony and were able to give him the massive sum of £1,200 for patient amenities in the ward in which Eleanor was treated.

The funeral passed without undue incident. There were quite a lot of people there, many from other parts of the country. The organist, an elderly lady, played everything very slowly, at a *truly* funereal pace. It was depressing enough for any tune, but ridiculous for 'The Lord of the Dance', which is meant to be played at a very lively tempo. The main service was held in the parish church, and then all the mourners except the immediate family went to a reception in the Village Hall, while we went to the crematorium in Barnstaple, eighteen miles away. When we came back and joined the rest of the mourners the atmosphere became lighter, as many people there saw each other only infrequently, and I was told later by Mary, a local lady who had organised the refreshments, that she was amazed at how relaxed we all were.

It is only after the funeral that the reality of bereavement starts to sink in. Up to that time there are a lot of arrangements to be made, people are calling and offering condolences and quite a lot is happening; but then everything stops, and the task of starting a new life alone begins. For

7: Eleanor's Departure

me, there were letters to be sent to people who had not been able to attend the funeral, thanking them for their cards and donations, and enclosing a copy of Eleanor's last photo, and there were legal and insurance matters to be sorted out - but then I was faced with the routine of living in a large empty farmhouse. I say 'empty', as although Nanny was still there, the whole place now seemed to be a complete vacuum without Eleanor's physical presence.

To get away from it for a time, I invited Eleanor's nephew Mark and his fiancée to go away with me to our static mobile home in Normandy, and we stayed there for a week or two. Then came the first thing to lighten the gloom of the last few weeks: I was driving home at the end of the holiday, when I suddenly had the impression of 'The Lord of the Dance' being played and sung. The last time, it had been a dreary, draining experience, but now it was played at the normal speed, and with an intensity that defied all description. It filled me with glorious excitement, and I found myself singing with the tune (fortunately under my breath, or else Mark and Ruth would have thought that I had finally flipped). The tune ended, but then repeated itself after an hour or so, and continued repeating itself at intervals until the end of the long journey, by which time I was totally invigorated, and was certain that I had received the message that Eleanor was now all right.

This message was confirmed through a dream a few nights later, just twenty-six days after Eleanor's passing, when Aunty Margaret came to me and said that Eleanor was still recuperating, but would be with me as soon as she was able. Then, after a total of about six weeks, Eleanor herself came to my youngest daughter, via a medium, to confirm that she was now able to communicate. The first time she came to me was in a Spiritualist service: the medium came to me and said she had a lady with her who was offering me a single red rose - could I understand it? I realised that it represented the rose from me that had been on Eleanor's coffin, and when she described the lady, it was confirmed, as the description was that of Eleanor. She has been to me many times since then, and each time she comes, she brings the single red rose as a token. Sometimes she comes through a medium, but often she comes to me personally, and puts thoughts directly into my mind. In fact, I often have conversations with her, as I still love her just as much as when she was here on the earth plane.

A Practical Spiritual Primer

But then came another major landmark in my earthly journey, not only personal but also spiritual. Positive thinking is of major importance in everyone's life - and never more so than after a time of bereavement. After the initial numbness has passed, the second stage of grieving - the natural reaction of most people who are in a deep relationship - is to pity the loved one for all which they might have had if they had survived - long life, happy retirement, the pleasure of seeing children or grandchildren grow up, etc. But then comes the third and worst stage of the process, where the one who is left starts to feel sorry for him/herself. 'How will I cope, what will become of me, where will I go, what will I do without...?' Many sink down into a state of depression from which they are unable to emerge without professional help, although at the other end of the scale there are those who do the equivalent of mentally shrugging their shoulders and getting on with their life. I was lucky in that two or three months after Eleanor's passing, my attention was drawn to a book which changed my life.

Chapter 8: Positivity

The book was 'You can Heal your Life' by Louise L. Hay, published by Hay House Publishers (copyright 1984 & 1987). I am not sure how I came to read it: I might have had it recommended to me, seen a reference to it in some article or other in a magazine, or just simply picked it up when browsing in a bookshop. At any rate, I started to read it - and became totally enthralled. Without trying to paraphrase Louise Hay's life, her story is that of a woman who had many disadvantages in her journey through life, finally being told at a relatively early age that she had an incurable cancer. But instead of accepting that, and dying quietly, she decided that she was going to survive - and she did. The book proposes the theory that what we experience on a mental or emotional level during our childhood and early years can affect us on a psychic level - and that imbalances on *that* level can eventually seep down in later life and cause ailments in the physical body.

This in itself is nothing more than many doctors have maintained for a long time, but Louise Hay goes further, and attributes a psychic cause to a list of about 400 diseases and ailments. Further, she suggests that just as each of us has become mentally conditioned at some time in our life to think that certain things are true about ourselves, if that conditioning has led to such an imbalance that it has caused an illness in the physical body, it is possible to neutralise the original conditioning by what she calls 'affirmations'. An affirmation is simply a statement that says the opposite of what the original conditioning said - for instance, if the original conditioning was something along the lines of 'You are stupid', then a simple affirmation might be 'I am clever'.

Following this reasoning, if the original conditioning is neutralised, then there is no more reason for the disease to exist, and the change of conditions can eventually lead to the disease itself being neutralised. This is a very simple explanation of a long and interesting book, but I hope that it is sufficient to give an idea of what the book is all about. Louise Hay has now written many books on the subject of positive thinking: all of them are excellent reading and I can thoroughly recommend them.

When I had read the book, I went to the end and looked through the list of illnesses to find out what the psychic causes of Cancer were, and - chillingly - found out that one of them was 'Resentment'. I say 'chillingly', as once I read that word, I knew *exactly* what had killed Eleanor. All her life she had bitterly resented the fact that she was a woman in a man's world, and the focus of that resentment had been her mother, Nanny. She often told stories of various things which had happened in her life to make her feel that she was in some way inferior to her brothers, and one of the saddest was the following:

When she was about eight, there was a school concert, and Eleanor had a star turn as a soloist, just after the opening number. Her brother Jack, two years older, was also in the concert, and Nanny was getting the children ready to go out. However, she was very late starting to get them ready and, despite Eleanor's protestations, she got Jack ready first; that meant that by the time that Eleanor eventually got to school her turn had passed, and her big moment, for which she had been rehearsing for weeks, was not to be.

That incident must have etched itself deeply into her memory, because she recalled it only three weeks before her death, while reminiscing one day in the local hospital, some fifty-five years after the event. That shows how devastating early emotional shocks can be in our life.

The mechanics behind psychosomatic illness are very interesting. Each of us has a physical body, but this body is surrounded by a force field known as 'the aura'. Most people have never heard of the aura, let alone seen one, although it can be seen by psychics. However, with training it is possible to be able to recognise not only one's own aura but also that of other people. There are also products on the market known as Aura Goggles, through which some people are able to see auras directly.

Nevertheless, one does not need to be able to see something in order to realise that it is there. (For instance, no one can actually see electricity with the physical eyes - but you can certainly see the effects of it as it drives machinery or is used for lighting, heating or cooking). Many people often have the impression that someone is standing behind them, turn round - and see the person. What has happened is that the auras of the two people have come into contact with each other, and the effect is registered on the brain, telling the person in front that the other one is there. A similar effect occurs when we go into a room where there are people, and we suddenly feel either happy or sad, depending on the situation. What we are doing is picking up the collective emotions of those in the room, as expressed in their auras, which are interacting with our own aura. There are even people who are so sensitive that they can pick up the auras of others who have been in a room but have now left - their emotions having been imprinted on the room permanently. A particular example of this is where a psychic picks up the atmosphere of a long-forgotten tragedy, death or murder in a 'haunted' room.

We talk of an aura as if it were a single unit - but in fact, it is composed of many different layers, all of which makes up the complete aura. Each layer is a little bit more refined than the previous one, until the final layer is the spark of Spirit which is the eternal 'Us' - a part of that eternal power which has had a multitude of names in the history of Mankind - 'God', 'Spirit', 'Allah', 'The I AM', 'Jehovah', etc. In fact, every religion since the dawn of consciousness has given a different name to the ultimate creative power behind the Universe.

I asked my own guides many years ago how I could understand and explain to others the mechanics of how psychosomatic illnesses are created, and was given the following ingenious little parable:

A man got up in the morning, put on his underclothes, his shirt and trousers, his pullover, jacket, coat and then a light raincoat, and went out in a thunderstorm. At first, the raincoat got wet, then soaked through, until finally the rain passed through it without hindrance, and the coat started to get wet. It also became soaked through, and the jacket started to get wet. The same thing happened to the jacket, pullover, shirt, and vest, until the man was totally soaking, and the clothes could hold no more water - and then his skin started to get wet. It took a long time to get to that stage, but once it was reached, and the clothes were completely sodden, it was worse than if the rain had been just falling on his skin, as now he had the weight of the clothes to cope with as well as the rain.

And this is exactly what happens to us in life: whatever we experience, emotionally or mentally imprints itself on our aura, and very gradually seeps down through its layers until finally, it reaches the physical body, and we start to have the diseases or ailments that the experience has caused. This whole process starts, of course, in childhood, from the moment we become aware of our surroundings - or even before then. (When a child is first born, it is a pure spirit, and wide open to every kind of influence. If it is born into an atmosphere of love, it will be imprinted with that from the start; if into an atmosphere of hatred or rejection, then that will be what is picked up). It is said that in the Catholic Church, members of the Order of Jesus (the Jesuits) used to say, 'Give me a child for the first seven years of life, and he/she will be mine forever'. Whether or not that was actually said in those precise words, every psychologist knows that the character of a person is formed within the first five or six years of life, and is very difficult to mould after that time.

By the same token, the conditions round the mother at the time of the *conception* of her child are also important: I have already told of the conditions that surrounded Robert's conception, and the effect that they had on his life.

So for all her life Eleanor had fought against the unfairness of sexism and, as the eldest daughter of the family, against the need to look after all her brothers (even the eldest one), because her mother thought that that was her 'right'. (This was a strange misuse of language by Nanny, which I found difficult to understand when I first met her: she always mixed up the words 'right' and 'duty' - so that if she ever said that people had a 'right' to look after their aged parents, she was really talking about their 'duty').

But then again, Eleanor had chosen to come into those conditions before she first came into life: she had chosen to live in conditions of poverty and deprivation, and to endure the hardships of a sexist North-country upbringing. It made her tough - and I do mean tough! She had a lot of illness as a child, with spells in hospital, and so she missed her 11-plus examinations, which would have allowed her to have a Grammar-School education. However, by pure hard work, in the first two years of secondary school, she caught up on all that she had missed and then was able to get a transfer at the age of thirteen to a Grammar School - only to find that she was still behind the rest of her class. They had been learning for the last two years at an enhanced rate, compared with that of the Secondary School, so once more she had a hard slog to catch up with them.

8: Positivity

Not only did she catch up, she was now so used to working at this super-charged rate that she overtook all her classmates, ending up as the head-girl and top scholar of the whole school. Then she went to Teacher Training College, where she could take only the three-year general course, instead of the four-year special Home Economics course that she wanted, because her parents could not afford to keep her at college any longer - her wages were needed at home.

She came out of college to find herself faced with the harsh brutalities of a man's world, a world in which she was earning little more than a half of the salary of the new male teachers who were in the same school: in fact, she used to tell me that her first *month's* salary in 1952 came to the princely sum of £28. Much later on in life, still employed by the Education Committee, she went into the Youth Service, only to find that it was even more male-orientated than teaching. She fought her way up through the Service until she was an Area Youth Worker, supervising nine Youth Centres, had started up two Community Associations from scratch and was supervising a third, and was the Senior Tutor for the Authority's Senior Youth Leaders' training course.

On the recreational (?) side, she started up and ran three small one-woman businesses in Floristry, specialist Cake-making and Bridal Dresses (she had been taught by her mother in her early years and did a major project in Dressmaking and Design at College) - and all this while bringing up a family of six children. She packed more into 24 hours than any woman I have ever known, always driven by this burning desire to show that she was at least the equivalent of any man. In fact, if the subject of the 'Equality of Women' was ever mentioned, she always used to say, 'I have no wish ever to be *equal* to a man: I am *superior* to a man'. Looking back on her life, I wonder if she would have ever achieved even half as much as she did if that major early stimulus had been missing.

After she had passed over, she came back to me through a medium and said that when she was going through her last illness, she knew that it was her time to leave this life and she accepted that; the only thing about which she was worried was how I would cope by myself. She also knew that I had to remain because of all the work that I had to do in the future. I still haven't found out what that work is - perhaps it is teaching - but doubtless, I will find out at the appropriate time.

A Practical Spiritual Primer

To go back to Louise Hay's philosophy of positive thinking, it is most important to start children off on the best possible footing by continually telling them how good they are, praising them for every little success and encouraging them to do even more. There is nothing like a bit of praise in order to motivate a child - or for that matter an adult as well - and children who are continually told that they *are* clever, they *can* do things well and that they *are* loved, always feel good about themselves. Such children are far more likely to want to do more and to be adventurous in their learning process than those who are always being told that they are stupid, useless or - worst of all - unloved.

Author's note: I have studied and used Louise Hay's method and affirmations extensively over the last twenty years, both in my personal life and in voluntary spiritual counselling, and have seen how amazingly powerful affirmations can be. In the case histories I quote below, I used only Louise Hay's affirmations (unless specifically stated). I have written briefly about them with the intention of proving how powerful the method and the affirmations are, not with any intention of claiming any credit for me. For anyone who wishes to research the subject further, I strongly recommend the purchase of her seminal book, 'You can Heal your Life', which deals with the subject of 'positive thinking' very extensively! I give details of the book above. To get a full list of her works just put 'Louise L. Hay' in Google, or whatever search engine you are using!

I personally have had many experiences of the power of positive thinking, of which the following are only two examples:

One of my granddaughters, Eleanor, is now a beautiful young woman living in Australia. She was a very bright young girl, and at her Junior School was in the class above that of children of her own age, and coping very well. She was due to go to Senior School in a year's time. However, as her parents intended to have a house built in a different township, they made provisional arrangements for her to go to a very good selective private school in that area. Some of her classmates started to be very nasty to her, saying that she thought that she was better than they were, and so was going to go to a different school - and the situation deteriorated so badly that it started to affect Eleanor's health. So her parents moved her to another local school for her last year in the Juniors.

8: Positivity

However, Eleanor's confidence had been badly affected by the months of torment, and when one of her 'friends', who attended the new school, started to be nasty to her and cut her out of her own circle of cronies, Eleanor took it very badly indeed, and started to become quite introverted. When I heard of this, I suggested to her that if she would say 'I love and approve of myself' - what I call Louise Hay's 'Master Affirmation' - to one of her aunts twenty times a day, I would pay her 50 cents - 25p - and would continue to do that for each day she said it. Not surprisingly, she took me up on it, and then did it regularly, to get some extra pocket money. When I asked about her a few weeks later, during my weekly phone-call to her mother Ellie, I was told that she had made a lot of lovely friends in her new school, and was happier than she had been for a long time.

That is a very simple example of how one can quickly bring change into a child's life - before a situation has become so ingrained that it becomes very serious. However, I had a far more dramatic event than that which happened in my own life.

It was in the summer of 1995, and I was at the mobile home in Normandy by myself. I had scheduled a stay of 6 weeks, and realised that one good way of helping to pass the time - and promoting my own health - was to take regular exercise every day. So I decided to start a walking regime, and did one kilometre (half a mile) on the first day, two on the next, then three, etc. I walked at first along the towpath of the Orne Canal at Bénouville, and then gradually went further afield.

On Day 8, I had got about a couple of miles away down the towpath when I felt a crippling pain in my right big toe and knee and came to a sharp halt. The pain was agonising, but what was I to do? I was miles away from any road, and the nearest civilisation was the Camp on which the mobile home was. So I turned round and very slowly and painfully hobbled back along the towpath. When I got back, I went straight to the place where I had left Louise Hay's book and looked up 'Mobility and Joints'. The psychic cause of problems of mobility was given as the inability to change direction in life easily, and the remedy was to say the affirmation 'I easily flow with change. My life is divinely guided and I am always going in the best direction'. I memorised this affirmation, in case I might need it in the future.

A Practical Spiritual Primer

The next day I started out without any problem, but at approximately the same spot, the agonising pain in the toe and knee came again, so I turned round and started to hobble back along the towpath again, saying the affirmation all the time. By the time I reached halfway back, the pain was starting to ease, and it was reasonably bearable when I got back to the mobile home. I then sat down and started to try to understand what was happening.

I already knew that, astrologically, there was a major change coming into my life in a few months' time, as Uranus - the destroyer of fixed conditions - was hovering round waiting to enter Aquarius, my own sign, which he ruled. I knew that everything which I had considered as fixed and stable until then was about to change - and I realised that I was fighting against the change. Now the one thing that you cannot do is fight against Uranus - or, more correctly speaking, you cannot fight against him and *win*. He is the lightning, the thunderbolt, and *will* bring about change, whether you like it or not, in whatever part of your natal horoscope he is transiting. With me, it was the house of the home - but also the areas of self, career and relationships were affected. So that was a fairly good signal that there was going to be massive change in all of those areas - and I was fighting against it.

It is an interesting thing that if you fight against Uranus and *appear* to win, then you can get ready to have an accident. One of the things that are connected with Uranus is accidents, so if he can't bring change into your life through your normal mental processes, he is likely to do so through the physical body. My second wife, Sybil, had an example of this a year or so after we had met. She had been warned by Spirit to slow down and take a rest, but had ignored the warning. Yet Uranus was hovering round waiting to bring a change of routine into her life - and so she slipped on a loose step and hurt her back badly. This meant that she had an enforced rest of six weeks, which then led to her new change of routine, and a far more laid-back style of life. When she looked back, she had to ruefully admit that it would have been far less painful to heed the warning in the first place!

Most human beings are strange in that they shun changes of all kinds: Shakespeare said, 'We would rather bear those ills we have, than fly to others that we know not of' - and there is a bit of that sentiment in all of us. So I decided that if change was inevitable, I would go with it, and I said the affirmation a dozen or so times just to show that I really meant it.

The next day I got to about two and a half miles away before the pain started, but I turned round and resolutely set off back, silently chanting the affirmation all the time, to find that the pain had completely gone before I had got halfway back - and thereafter it never came back at all, as I was saying the affirmation continually on the way out as well as on the way back.

Whether it would have done any good for Eleanor to have said the appropriate affirmation for cancer or not, I don't know. Perhaps, as she had already decided on a soul level that it was time for her to leave this life, it wouldn't have made any difference. If I had had the right to decide, she would still have been here today, but then, none of us has any right whatsoever to decide what is going to happen in the life of another adult - and certainly not to decide when is the most appropriate time for them to leave it.

Note that I have just said 'decided on a *soul* level'. There are actually two levels of decision-making for each of us - the conscious level and the soul level. The Higher Self makes the *soul* level decisions - the most important ones - in our life; these are what the overall lessons of the life will be, when we will be born and when we will go back 'home'. The brain makes the *conscious* level decisions in our everyday life. Where there is a conflict between the two levels, the soul level always wins - so that if it has been decided that it is time for the person to end this life of experiences, it *will* happen, regardless of how strongly the conscious mind fights against it. In Louise Hay's personal life the Higher Self had decided that she would survive her terminal illness and had recruited the conscious mind to fight to ensure her survival - and the result that she was able to bring a new understanding of life to the world.

The more that I studied Louise Hay's books the more I was convinced of the validity of using 'positive thinking' as a basis for one's life and I started to use her book as my own personal 'bible'. In fact, all of her books are now some of the most valued, and used, books in my own extensive library. I also started to suggest that other people try the method as well. In my early days as a voluntary spiritual counsellor I used to give copies of 'You can Heal your Life' to my clients, but then as the price of the book gradually went up it became too expensive to do. However, I did use it and start to teach the philosophy to others.

I had many opportunities to do this, as I was a teacher by profession, and eventually became a Home Tutor. By that time all of my students were boys of secondary age who had been either expelled from school (these days 'excluded' is the term - it sounds better) or who had short-term medical problems and could not attend school at all. In all I taught a total of 53 pupils over a period of about three years. I say 'taught' but many of them simply refused to do anything at all, and most were half-hearted to say the least. But at least I did manage to get over to some of them the value of thinking a bit more highly of themselves. This was a new concept to most of them: the typical boy was the product of a broken marriage, had had difficulty in learning to read and/or write - and certainly to do any Maths, my subject - and had been totally switched off education long before his final year at school. Ninety percent of them had been expelled for behavioural problems during their last year.

Many of them were deeply into crime - one of my boys was reckoned by the local police force to be personally responsible for almost one-third of the town's crime figures - and almost all had had experience of drugs, with one or two having serious problems. So I was on a hiding to nothing before I started with the majority of them. However, as long as the Local Education Authority assigned a tutor for the boy, and provided the tutor turned up at the boy's home by appointment ready to teach, the requirement of the law had been carried out - even if the boy didn't let him in! I did, however, have some small successes: I remember one boy who had been expelled for persistent truancy (he always liked fishing more than school): he saw the error of his ways too late to do much about GCSEs, but I was able to get him up to the exam in Maths - and I believe he passed. The success there was probably because his mother was also interested in Maths. and sat in on our sessions; she possibly took the exam herself - I can't quite remember.

One very interesting case was Richard, who was thirteen when I first met him. Richard was born into a family where both his parents were teachers and his two elder brothers, who were highly intelligent, continually snubbed him and slapped him down verbally at every opportunity. He developed a very severe stammer, (psychically he had been stopped from expressing himself) and started to do badly at school,

8: Positivity

although he was a very intelligent boy. He had finally been put in a Care Home because of his increasingly erratic behaviour both at school and at home.

I taught one or two boys at that Home, and I managed to do some academic work with Richard, and realised that he was capable of far more than he was doing, but just couldn't get enough motivation. So I started to sow the seeds of positive thinking in his mind. Now Richard was considered a total oddball by almost everyone at the Care Home, staff and pupils alike, and so was derided by most of the pupils and tolerated wearily by staff. One day, I had talked to him about being positive in his attitude - and said that if he were really positive then he could actually change his life. I asked him what he would most like to do, and he replied, 'Get out of here'. So I suggested to him - rather rashly at the time - that he could do just that if only he believed in himself.

One of the main affirmations taught by Louise Hay - what I call the Master Affirmation - is 'I love and approve of myself' - and so I told Richard about this affirmation, and suggested that he might like to try it. I suggested that, when he was in the bathroom by himself, he should look into his own eyes in the mirror and say the affirmation a dozen times - but not aloud and not when there was likely to be anyone who could see him. Above all, I advised him not to tell anyone (meaning any of the other children) what he was doing or else they would mock him.

I was called in to see a very irate Home Manager the next week, asking what the devil I had been doing to Richard, as he had developed the habit of going to the bathroom and staring into the mirror, muttering some sort of gibberish to himself - and when asked what he was doing, telling everyone that he had been told to do this by me - and also told not to tell anyone at all about it. I explained what I had suggested, and was told in no uncertain terms that Richard was a very emotionally disturbed young man, and that I should leave the child psychology to the experts and just stick to my own academic work!

There is an interesting sequel to this story: the Management couldn't break Richard of his 'bathroom habit', so they just resigned themselves to it - and the other children kept even farther away from him. However, his behaviour did improve, and he lost his stammer. The next time the Educational Psychologist made his rounds and saw Richard he was so impressed by the change in him that he recommended that he should be transferred to a special residential school for non-violent pupils - and he was. So he got his wishes after all and started a new phase in his life away from the Home that he hated. I spoke to the Manager of Richard's new Home a couple of times during his first months there, and found that he was a model pupil and was making great progress in every way. I lost touch with him after about six months, but I would love to know what eventually became of him. I am sure that his case can be cited as an example of the success of positive thinking and of Louise Hay's methods.

In many cases, I went to teach a boy at his home, and found that his mother was probably as much in need of positive thinking as he was. One such boy was James. He had been a user of LSD, which had so distorted his 'psychic receptors'* that he found it physically painful to be in the presence of another human being for more than a few minutes. At one time, he would stay in his bedroom all day, listening to his Hi-Fi, and when his mother Ann had his meal ready, she would call him to come downstairs. He would come down to the kitchen, seize his plate of food, and rush back upstairs again, as he could not bear to be sitting at the same table as her for even five minutes.

* N.B. The body's 'psychic receptors' are usually known as 'the Chakras'. The technical explanation and discussion of their operation is beyond the scope of this book.

I was assigned to James for about six months in his last school year, and never managed to get him to do any academic work at all. However, what was quite an achievement, I did manage to get him to sit and talk to me for up to an hour at a time, about his hopes and fears, what he would like to do in life, how he would cope, etc. He became a little bit more positive in his general outlook, but was still deeply pessimistic about his ability to integrate with other people again. One example of his attitude was the following little story, which could be thought of as a joke, if it weren't so deeply tragic. I was talking to him one day about the possibility of him going to College to try to make up for his lost year at school, but he said that he wouldn't be able to manage to last the course. I urged him to be more positive in his attitude, and to say affirmations like 'I *can* go to College', 'I *can* cope with the work', etc. After talking a little more about this idea of positive thinking I asked him to make up a little affirmation

8: Positivity

which he could say about college, and he said, 'OK, then - I am *positive..*',
and I held my breath wondering whether I had made a breakthrough - only
to be disillusioned when he finished by saying, '............. that I *can't* get
through college'.

So, as far as anything academic was concerned, my time with James
was an absolute failure: but on another level, he was one of the most
important pupils I ever had in my life. In fact, when I look back on my
story from then over the next year or so, I am amazed at the synchronicity
of it all.

Chapter 9: Synchronicity

Some people will not have met the word 'synchronicity' before: however, they will easily understand the word 'coincidence'. The words really mean the same thing, but from two totally different mind-sets. If we talk about coincidence, we are saying that when two things that affect our life happen at the same time, there is no possible connection between them. If we talk about synchronicity, then we are aware that there *is* a connection. The connection will be on an ethereal level, so it might not always be obvious in the physical, rational world - but it is there.

It was the famous psychologist Carl Jung who first used the word 'synchronicity'. He had been stimulated by the work of an Austrian biologist, Paul Kammerer, who had put forward a theory that events, objects or occurrences of a like kind assemble in space and time, through an unknown process. He called this supposed phenomenon 'Seriality', and suggested that there might be some unknown Law of Nature that *tended to bring like and like together.* Jung took the idea further, coining the word 'synchronicity' for what he considered was a meaningful coincidence between one's *inner state* and the world outside. The important thing, as far as Jung was concerned, was that the coincidence should have some meaning in the life of the individual concerned.

Just to give an example: at one time, I had an accident in my car: a young man ran into the back of me, when we were in a slow-moving line of traffic. He had not been driving for very long, and had probably taken his mind off what was happening in front of him and lost control. My car received only a small dent in the back bumper, whereas his damage was a lot more severe.

When I look back, I can see various things that happened to bring about the situation in which I was at that precise spot, in front of him, at that point in time. There had been a series of unusual events that had

9: Synchronicity

brought me to that particular place; had there been the slightest variation in time in anything that we had done - even by as little as a minute - we would not have been at that precise place in the line of traffic.

As the damage to my car was minimal, I just got it checked over by my garage and did not claim against the young man's insurance. For his part, as a new young driver - he was an engineering apprentice - he was already paying a phenomenal amount in insurance premiums to get any insurance cover at all, and a claim against his insurance would almost certainly have meant that he would be unable to have afforded cover in future, as a hefty surcharge would have been put on his premiums. Paying for his own damage, rather than going through the insurance, would probably be far cheaper in the long run for him. Why did the accident happen? I don't know - I think it had something to do with his life rather than with mine - I just happened to be a convenient person available to give him the experience. Probably another person would have put in an insurance claim regardless of the amount of damage, and would have made his life considerably more difficult - and the fact that I didn't will make some impression on his personal philosophy in future.

This is obviously a very simple example, but when we look back on our life, we see major events that have been caused by a series of little coincidences - or even by just one. When the survivors of 9/11 were talking of their experiences, many weren't at their normal place of work at all because of a 'coincidence'. With one man, it was because it was his turn to get the doughnuts that day, with another because - exceptionally - he had to drop his daughter off at school. A third had just bought a pair of shoes, which had rubbed his heel and raised a blister - so he stopped off at the chemist's to buy a packet of Elastoplast. All fairly minor, unimportant, everyday events - and yet in each case it saved the person's life.

Sometimes, as in the above examples, the chain of events leads to a fortunate outcome, in others it leads to disaster or death. How many people on 9/11 died because they had changed their normal routine so that they were actually *in* one of the buildings at the fatal time? How many had changed the date of a holiday, looked in at the office on the way to a meeting in order to pick up files forgotten the night before, arranged a meeting in one of the buildings for that very day rather than another - we shall never know. When the horrific act of terrorism on the Spanish

A Practical Spiritual Primer

Railway took place some years ago, two little boys lost both of their parents on one of the trains. The parents normally drove from home to the centre of Madrid: on that particular day, 'by coincidence', their car had been booked in to a garage for routine servicing, so they took the train. A simple, everyday event - which had such a devastating effect.

One of the books that influenced me considerably when I first read it was 'The Celestine Prophecy' by James Redfield. In it, he talks a lot about this phenomenon of synchronicity and studying the subject, I personally have come to the conclusion that there are four stages of working with the concept:

- To accept that there is such a thing as synchronicity - i.e. that everything which happens has a meaning on some level or other.
- To look out for synchronicities in one's life, noticing what is happening and seeing what develops from it.
- To *expect* synchronicities to happen: this is a more advanced stage than the previous one, as it implies the possibility of controlling what will happen by thought. Putting yourself in a positive state of mind is more likely to bring positive synchronicity into your life.
- To *make* synchronicities happen. This is the final stage, and is really the process of manifestation.

To go back to James, little did I think, when I was first assigned as his tutor, that he would be so important in my life. In fact, he was one of the elements in the chain of events that led me to a greater spiritual awareness. The reason was that through being assigned to him, I met his mother, Ann. She was a woman who had had just about every trauma a woman can experience in her earlier years. She had been brought up in a poor family as the eldest of six children, had lost her mother before becoming a teenager and then had *had* to take on the role of mother to the rest of the family, cooking each night for seven people, while still attending school. After several years, the stress finally gave her a mental breakdown, and she was put into a mental hospital, where she was raped by two inmates. Having come out 'cured', she escaped the drudgery of her life by marrying, only to find that she had 'jumped from the frying pan into the fire', as her husband had as many psychological problems as she had, if not more. There were two boys born of the marriage, which finally broke up in an acrimonious divorce.

Both of the boys got into drugs, and the eldest - the apple of his mother's eye - started to experiment with the effects of different drugs. One day he took 1,000 magic mushrooms: it didn't kill him, but it totally scrambled his brain and he remained an incurable drug addict for many years, serving several prison sentences for having committed crimes to get drug money. At one time, he was sectioned under the Mental Health Act and spent some time in a Psychiatric Hospital. In fact, much later in life, after some years 'clean', he was persuaded to try drugs again - and an overdose killed him.

The younger son was James, of whose problems I have already spoken. Some time before I met her, Ann had decided that she needed to get some sort of qualification to earn herself a living, and had started a course of hairdressing, aromatherapy and massage at a local Technical College, and she was now halfway through her final year.

I was to spend quite a lot of time with Ann, as on the day I visited her son, she was not at College. After every session, she asked what had happened, and we talked about James' problems and - inevitably - we started to talk about her own. I began to stay on for an hour or so talking to her and letting her unload some of her problems, which seemed to help her. I mentioned the Louise Hay book and spoke in general terms about positive thinking - but her first reaction was that it was possibly valid for other people, but not for her. However, I persisted and gave her a copy of the book - and she started to think seriously about doing some work on herself.

When I first tried to tune in to her psychically, I had the impression of being in a car without lights or brakes, and with faulty steering, which was careering down a narrow road on a dark night at an ever-increasing pace - and at the time that just about summed up her life: things were getting worse rapidly: she was under a great deal of stress at College in the run-up to her final exams, her son was a constant source of irritation, and - worst of all - her financial position was little short of desperate.

When she first agreed to start to work on herself, I suggested that she try the Master affirmation proposed by Louise Hay: 'I love and approve of myself'. Not surprisingly, she couldn't. I say 'not surprisingly', as I have only ever met two or three people who had low self-esteem who could. I pointed out that the reason she couldn't say it was because it wasn't at that moment true - but if she succeeded in saying it, she would be starting to undo all the years of conditioning that had brought her to her present state of emotional and mental torture.

She agreed to try to work on the problem over the next week, and to talk to me again after James' next session with me. We did so, but she still had a blockage - she was literally unable to bring herself to say the words - even individually, let alone as a sentence. However, the next week she told me that she had made a breakthrough. I asked, 'Can you say the affirmation now, then?' - but she said, 'No, but what I can say is, 'I love myself a little bit more today than I did yesterday". I was amazed at her ingenuity, and congratulated her, and she almost cried. I don't think that she could remember having been congratulated many times in her life at all. She carried on saying that affirmation for another fortnight, until she announced triumphantly that she had cracked it - and could now at last say that she loved and approved of herself.

She had been attending a counselling group for many months when I met her, but she said that she always seemed to be depressed after one of the sessions there. I told her that the reason was that she was a very psychic lady, and that what was happening was that she was picking up negativity from other members of the group, and so was coming back home in a worse state than when she was going out. I suggested that she needed to protect herself every time that she went to the group, and told her how. She put up her protection before going to the next few group sessions, and felt much better, but after a while decided that she was making more progress outside the group than she had done inside it, so she stopped going.

If the need for protection seems a bit puzzling, let me explain it: I have said that there are different layers of the aura: two of them are the mental and the emotional levels. Now if someone is putting out negativity on either of those levels, and they come into your company, the interaction of their aura with yours will inevitably mean that your own aura will start to become contaminated with their negativity. You will not immediately feel anything physically, but as this starts to seep down to your physical level, you will start to feel a vague unease. If the length of time when you are with the person is fairly short, it won't affect you too much, but the longer that you stay with him/her the worse it will get, until you become conscious that you yourself are feeling depressed. Not only that, but the more psychic and sensitive you are, the quicker this is likely to happen.

Now if this can happen with only one negative person, just imagine what happens when you have a roomful of them together. If you yourself are ultra-sensitive in such a situation, it is virtually inevitable that you are going to pick up negativity, which could well counteract the positive work that is being done by the group leader. So how do you protect yourself in such a situation?

There are many ways to protect yourself, of which the following are only some examples:

- Imagine yourself in a big transparent balloon, and then fill that balloon with dazzling white light.
- Imagine that you are in a silver sphere, and that the outside of that sphere is coated with mirrors, so that any ray or wave directed against it is automatically reflected away.
- Surround yourself with an imaginary cloak, which is an electric-blue colour.
- Invoke a spiritual being to protect you.

This last method needs a bit of explanation: different religions have their own concepts of what the term 'God' means, and have different names for their own deity; and since the dawn of religion, people have called on their gods to help them in times of crisis in their life. I went to Australia in 2002, and flew by Royal Brunei Airlines. Brunei is a Muslim state, and before the start of each leg of the flight, while the aircraft was waiting at the end of the runway, the Muslim prayer invoking Allah for the safety of the flight was broadcast, and printed on the screen at the front in Arabic and English. The prayers must have been very effective, as we had a perfect flight in every case!

In the Christian religion, of course, many call on the help of Jesus Christ in times of trouble, and those of the Catholic faith have a wide range of saints whom they can invoke in different situations (the word 'invoke' means - literally - 'call in'). For instance, a woman might invoke the Virgin Mary to protect her during childbirth, a traveller could invoke St Christopher for protection, or someone who is having financial problems might invoke the help of St Martin of Tours.

A Practical Spiritual Primer

Others invoke their guardian angels, if they know their names, or one of the angels or archangels. I personally invoke the Lord Michael, better known as the Archangel Michael. (He is Lord of the Heavenly host, which is where he gets the title 'Lord Michael' from). Lord Michael's role is that of protection, so invoking him is totally appropriate.

To invoke spiritual beings, it is necessary only to call them by name three times, and they are compelled by spiritual law to be present. So if I am going into a situation where there are likely to be negative conditions, and I want to protect myself, I invoke Lord Michael with the following words:

'Lord Michael, Lord Michael, Lord Michael, I ask you to be with me now. I ask you to protect me and, with your blue sword, to cut through all conditions of negativity which may be around me when I am in .... and this I ask in the name of the One whom we all serve'.

One of the loveliest and most spiritual women whom I have ever met is Sue (as she is only 5ft and half-an-inch tall, she is always known as Little Sue - but the adjective 'little' is never used by people in a derogatory sense these days: they daren't). When I was counselling her and helping her to sort her life out many years ago I told her about invoking Lord Michael for protection, and now she does it automatically whenever the need arises. The most fascinating story about her is of when she was on holiday in Turkey several years ago, and there was an earthquake. She and her current partner both woke up, felt the building shaking, and said simultaneously 'Earthquake!' Her partner was terrified, but Sue just sent out a quick invocation to Lord Michael to protect them and all the people in the hotel from any danger - and promptly turned over and went to sleep again. Most of the people in the hotel spent the night outside, but she slept peacefully through it all - and the hotel was not damaged. That is what can properly be called 'Faith'.

To go back to Ann and to group counselling: I have no quarrel with Group Therapy, as it provides a very valuable safety valve for people who have no-one to talk to about their problems. (That is why the Reverend Chad Varah was so phenomenally successful when he started 'The Samaritans': people were able to talk to someone anonymously about their own problems, and in doing so, they very often solved those same problems themselves). However, at best a group can provide only a temporary crutch for people while they are in the process of working on

9: Synchronicity

healing themselves, and at worst it gives them the idea that it is a *substitute* for the process - which it definitely isn't. It can also be the vehicle to allow other members of the group, less qualified or skilled than the leader, to say, 'Ah, but you should have said/ done... .' in a 'holier-than-thou' sort of voice, which serves to boost their own self-esteem but does little to help the persons being criticised.

Ann made rapid progress once she really got into the swing of working on herself, and began to accept that some of the crises, which still happened to her (although by now slightly less regularly), were challenges rather than insurmountable problems. One such major crisis was at the end of her College course. A few days before the end of the term, when all the course work was being gathered together prior to being sent away for validation, she was asked where her project was. She asked, 'What project?' and was told that she was supposed to produce a project on how she would set up her own business when she left College. When she protested that no one had ever informed her of this project, she was told that everyone had been informed some months previously, and that without the project she could not pass her course. (It later transpired that she had been off ill when the class had been given all the information about the project - and no one had ever bothered to check up on it before the final few days of the course).

Rather than go to pieces completely, as she might have done a year earlier, she discussed with me what she could do in order to do the work (which normally would have taken a month) in the few days which were left before the final deadline for submission. She was quite capable of producing the information, but writing it all down by hand would probably give her a severe case of 'writer's cramp' - even if she could do it in time. However, we decided that I could help her, and that if she dictated the information, I could type it into my computer and then print it off - and that is what we did. We produced about twenty pages of A4 typing, which was certainly enough to satisfy the examiners, and it was handed in on the final day with about an hour to spare.

By this time, Ann's life had really started to change, and her attitude was becoming considerably less negative. One of the ways in which this was showing itself was in the improvements to her own health. She had always been totally paranoid about cleanliness, and was terrified of eating any sort of germs that would cause her stomach problems. She always seemed to be having infections of the lungs also, and having read Louise Hay I can understand why. The lungs are connected with taking in air, which symbolically means taking in life; therefore sadness, depression and the belief that you don't deserve to have any happiness all mean that you can't live life to the full, as it is meant to be lived.

Another important thing is the question of Fear. It is often said that the only thing which you ever need to fear is Fear itself - and that is certainly at least partially, if not totally, true. The way in which Fear normally shows itself in the life of most people is, of course, through Worry. We all tend to worry about everything - whether something will happen, whether something won't happen - the possible causes of worry are endless. I always tell people that 95% of all the things about which we worry in life never happen - which is true. However, a few years ago I heard a wonderful definition of 'Worry', which is well worth remembering: 'Worry is like paying interest on a debt which you may never even owe'.

Fear is a negative emotion, and surrounding yourself with negativity has a devastating effect. In the world of Physics, opposite poles attract, and negative and positive are brought together. In the world of human life and behaviour, the opposite is true: like attracts like, and we even have the old saying that 'Birds of a feather flock together'. The reason is not hard to understand: if we associate with people who are like ourselves in character, then we can be completely at ease with them; if we are with those who are not like us, whether we consider that they are superior or inferior, then we are more likely to be on our guard all the time while in their company - and since that is stressful, we tend to avoid doing it as much as possible.

This leads to some unexpected - and some would say unconnected - conditions. When we are negative, we tend to bring negative events into our life, because most of the things that we experience in life are those that come through mixing with other people. If we are surrounding ourselves with negativity, then other people will pick that up through their auras, and will feel depressed by it. This will change their attitudes - and indirectly their behaviour - towards us for the worse. Therefore, they are more likely to create negative experiences for us in our life.

If, on the other hand, we give out an aura of positivity, then others will pick that up and feel enlightened by it. They are then more likely to feel good about us, because we make them feel good about themselves - and

9: Synchronicity

the fact that they have a higher regard for us can eventually make them want to create positive experiences for us.

And this is what started to happen to Ann. She was feeling better about herself, and became less worried about her health - which started to make her feel more relaxed and stopped some of the health problems. The increased positivity was noticed on a psychic level by others, who began to change their opinions about her and treat her in a better way. When she remarked on this, I explained it by giving an example. I reminded her that 'like attracts like', and asked her to imagine that each of us has on his/her forehead a psychic label, which can be read (only on a psychic level) by other people.

If your label says 'I am useless', 'Treaty me badly' or 'Hurt me', then that label will show that you are in a period of your life when you are weak. Now no-one likes to be weak, and by advertising the fact that you are, you are inviting other weak people to take advantage of you; if they did, from their point of view, it would prove to them that someone is weaker than they are, which would make them feel better. From your point of view, it would reinforce the lack of self-esteem that you already have, so that it would make you feel worse.

But, if your label says, 'I am good', 'I am strong' or 'I can look after myself', this is also read by others, and it frightens away those people who are weak. After all, no one but a masochist would deliberately want a relationship with a person who was much stronger than him/her. However, the people who would be attracted to you would be the people who are already strong and feel positive about themselves, and so this would bring more positivity and more beneficial experiences into your life.

This question of relationships is always very important in everyone's life, and Ann was no exception. She asked on many occasions, 'When will Mr Right come into my life?' The only answer that I could ever make was, 'When you are Mrs Right'!

By the time that we got to the middle of 1994, Ann's life was definitely looking up. She had become far more confident, and her financial position was a little brighter. In fact, she was very good in her chosen career field, and with her qualifications now assured, she could look forward to starting her own little business working from home, and to a period of greater financial and social stability. But one day, when I went to see her son, she looked a bit perplexed. When I asked her what was worrying her, she said, 'Well, I am starting to lose all my friends'. I said that I was surprised at that, and asked her to give me an example.

'Well', she said 'take Joan: at one time she used to be popping in nearly every day, asking me if I could do a bit of shopping for her while I was in the town, or if I could pick up her son from school, and that sort of thing: but I haven't even seen her for a fortnight. I wonder if I have upset her?'

I pointed out gently that she had now changed the psychic label on her forehead, and it no longer read 'I am weak - take advantage of me'. It now said 'I am strong, and can look after myself'. Her friend Joan had recognised this change, and had realised that she could no longer impose her will on Ann - so had just stopped going to see her. Some friend! However, I asked Ann if she had had any other changes in friends, and she told me that she had met a lovely lady, some years older than herself, and they seemed to get on like a house on fire. This lady was a very strong person - so I pointed out that as Ann was now far stronger herself, she was able to attract stronger, more positive - and therefore more beneficial - people into her own environment.

There is a postscript to this discussion of positivity, and that is concerned with the negative effects which many television programmes have on us. If we remember that everything we see or hear has some sort of effect on us mentally, then the constant bombardment of TV images night after night must be a prime factor in forming our ideas. In fact, that is the sole reason for the existence of commercial TV stations, to give producers of products or services the opportunity of beaming their advertisements directly into our homes so that we can be brainwashed into purchasing them. If such advertisements didn't work, no one would pay for the privilege of screening them.

When we watch the daily news on TV, it seems that there is more and more bad news of all kinds, from wars or natural disasters to child murders - and that depresses us and causes us to wonder what the world is coming to. This atmosphere is compounded by the diet of sensationalism dished up as TV drama, always seeking to boost viewer figures by screening ever more lurid episodes of soap operas, police dramas or comedy series. Screening of films that seem to have no artistic merit apart from portrayal of violence, horror, sex and strong language

9: Synchronicity

adds to the mixture. The net result of all this is that we are continually bombarded by a stream of emissions that show human beings at their worst, and spread dark clouds of negativity daily. Is this really what we want to bring into our life? Or are we aiming for only the highest and the best? If the latter is the case, then we have a duty to ourselves to ask, 'What are we going to do about it?' (In many cases, the simplest and quickest thing to do is just to turn the rubbish off)!

Chapter 10: Affirmations

The use of Affirmations can also produce positive results in areas other than personal relationships - such as in a work situation. On one occasion, I had an interesting example of this that concerned my youngest daughter Penny, who at that time was managing a hotel in a famous seaside resort. The hotel was part of a Group, and Keith, the Area Manager was giving Penny a very hard time: he always seemed to be picking on her and trying to find faults in her performance; after several months of this, Penny was showing the strain. She phoned me up in tears one day, almost ready to hand in her notice, so I suggested a strategy she might use to bring about better conditions. I suggested that she used an affirmation along the lines of 'I am wonderfully happy in my job: I have a very good Area Manager who likes my work'. I also suggested that while she was saying this phrase, she visualised Keith bathed in rose-pink light. (Rose-pink is the colour of Love). She didn't hold out much prospect of success, but said that she would do it, as she had tried everything else.

Three weeks later, she phoned me up in a totally different mood - she was jubilant. She said, 'You will never guess what has happened today: we have just had a meeting of all the General Managers in the Area, and Keith has praised me and said that I am a shining example of how everyone should be managing their own hotels'. Strong stuff, these affirmations!

When one analyses this case, one can see that Penny herself had not changed Keith's behaviour: no one can change anyone else's behaviour. Rather, her own view of Keith had changed between the two telephone conversations: due to the original series of setbacks in her relationship with him, she had started to *expect* to be criticised, and had effectively created that forehead-label which said, 'Criticise me'. After three weeks of affirmations, she had changed that label to one that said, 'I deserve to be treated kindly' - and that is exactly what happened: Keith picked up on her new energy, and treated her completely differently for the rest of her time in that particular hotel.

When we realise the value of affirmations, we can experiment further with them, and as success breeds success we begin to realise that we are actually starting to change the conditions in our own life - in fact, changing our personal reality. Whatever area of our life we want to change, we can do so, and bring new conditions into our life: whether we want a new job, greater financial security, a better social life, health or even happiness - we can do it. It might take some time, but sooner or later, we can make it happen. However, what we are really changing directly are not the conditions themselves: these are merely the outward manifestations that we have drawn into our life. We are actually directly changing *ourselves*, and by doing that, we are bringing the new conditions in.

I spoke earlier on about Little Sue. When I first met her, she was in a dreadful emotional state: she was just coming out of the last of *eight* failed live-in relationships - and was still only in her early thirties. I introduced her to the concept of affirmations, and she worked like a slave on saying them. After some months, she had made great progress in her general attitude towards life (and her feelings about herself), so I asked her what specific area of life she would like to start working on now. She replied that she had no social life at all, as her previous boyfriend hadn't allowed her to mix socially with other people, so she wanted to work on that area. We discussed it and I suggested that she should make up her own affirmation - something like 'I have an excellent social life: I have some wonderful friends.'

A few weeks later, I rang her up and asked how she was getting on. 'Dreadful', she said. Rather surprised, I asked her why. 'Because there are not enough evenings in the week to take up all the invitations out which I am getting', she replied. Because of the positive way in which she now viewed herself, she had started to develop a vivacious character, which had made her a very attractive woman. She had also joined a Friendship Club, and had immediately become very popular with all of the members - male and female - and now had a full diary of social events to attend.

The next area that troubled her was her financial situation, which was not particularly satisfactory. We discussed her life history and she realised that, coming from a poor family, she had always *expected* to have to work very hard to even scrape through life, with little left for luxuries. I suggested that she should start to expect only the best out of life, and should visualise herself on the top of a cliff, overlooking the 'Ocean of Plenty'. Then, holding her arms wide open, she should say some affirmation like 'I have infinite finances: I am wide open to receive all the wealth of the Universe'. This she did, and made it part of her ritual of affirmations every day.

To cut a very long story short, she married one of the men whom she met at the Club, and they were very happy together. He is an Australian, and they emigrated to Australia to start a new life, sold the husband's house in England for a very good price, and were able to build their own luxury house in Perth.

I asked my inspirers on one occasion what the spiritual science behind the success of affirmations was, and was reminded of the saying in Physics that 'Nature abhors a vacuum'. I then remembered that on one occasion, I had seen a TV Science experiment where air was pumped out of a tin can and, when a vacuum was being created, the can was suddenly crushed by the force of the atmosphere outside it overcoming the strength of the metal holding it in shape. My inspirers said that if you say something which is not currently a fact, you will create a spiritual vacuum between the physical reality and what you are saying. The more you say it, the greater the vacuum becomes, until eventually your will overcomes the physical reality, which changes to become the same as what you have said in your affirmation. This is the origin of the phrase 'Mind over Matter'.

Now I have never met anyone who could move physical objects by thought at a distance, (technically called telekinesis), but I have read accounts of it being done, and seen pictures which purported to show it happening. And I do remember that somewhere in the Bible there is a quote saying that if one had faith enough, one could move mountains (which I must admit I found difficult to believe). However, my original scepticism was destroyed completely when I was part of one psychic experiment that proved that moving things by thought *are* possible - and this is how it came about.

My wife Sybil is a very powerful teaching medium, and over the years has trained many aspiring psychics, some of whom have become mediums or healers in their own right. On more than one occasion, I have been part of a group that has lifted a table, largely by the power of thought.

10: Affirmations

All the members of the group put one finger under the table, and then concentrated their thoughts in order to make the table rise off the floor - and it did. It might be said that a group of people could lift any small table by each lifting with one finger, but if so they would obviously show the strain of lifting - and there was no strain apparent - the table just seemed to float up by itself.

But to dispel all suggestion of natural forces applying, after the success of the first experiment the one that followed was impossible to fake: it involved one member of the group sitting on a chair, which was then lifted off the floor by four people in the same manner.

I have also seen pictures of people who were apparently able to levitate (rise from the ground by overcoming gravity), which is equally hard to believe unless one personally sees it happening. But if we are working in the finer realms of spiritual reality, I can quite understand that by the force of willpower alone we can create different realities in our own life, most of which will be as a result of changing our attitude about ourselves, and starting to use the power of positivity, rather than always living in negativity.

To refer back to Little Sue, she had one physical drawback that had dogged her all her life: she had enormous breasts. She tells the story that when she was at school, at the age of twelve, her mother had to buy her first bra, and it was size 34B. By the time I met her she was still size 34, but now a GG cup.

About ten years ago, she decided that she wanted a breast reduction operation, which would neutralise one of the complexes which she had always had about her own appearance and would also have a beneficial effect on her health. The only problem was that such operations were very rare under the National Health Service, and she couldn't afford to have it done privately. So I suggested that she might try affirmations once more, and so she did, saying something like 'I have had a successful breast reduction operation'.

A few months later, she heard about a lecture that was being given by a lady who was a plastic surgeon, on the subject of breast reductions. She attended it, together with many other women, and decided to apply to be considered for an operation. She was told that there were 200 women already on the waiting list, and that the surgeon was allowed to do only four a year on the NHS. Then started a long series of elimination interviews and tests, each more stringent than the last, until she got down to the last twelve, and was put on the formal waiting list. She was told that her operation would probably be done in about three years' time. This was not acceptable to her, so she decided to hurry matters up, and in January of one particular year, she started to say the affirmation 'I have had my operation before the month of May this year'.

One morning in early April, she received a phone call from the hospital: could she come in immediately in order to have her operation the next morning; the lady booked in for it had cancelled at the last moment, and none of the others on the waiting list could go in at such short notice. So she went, the operation was done leaving her with no visible scars at all - and she was out of hospital before May. She had changed the reality of her own life by the power of her own will - through using affirmations.

Chapter 11: Holiday

One of the problems with counselling someone else of the opposite sex is the danger of getting into an emotional relationship with them. In fact, in certain circumstances, an unscrupulous counsellor will take advantage of a vulnerable client and a sexual relationship will ensue.

In my case, I was already getting very fond of Ann - and to this day, I don't really know what sort of relationship I wanted with her. It certainly wasn't physical in any way, and could not ever have been. I was still too traumatised after the death of Eleanor to ever want another physical relationship. But as I have Libra rising in my horoscope, (Libra being the sign of partnerships,) I did have a desperate need of companionship, and looked forward to our weekly hour or so together after I had seen James. I suppose, as there was an age-gap of 25 years between us, it was more of a father-daughter feeling that I had for her rather than anything else - and I was quite happy for it to remain that way.

Then I had what seemed at the time to be a bright idea: how would Ann like to go away with me for the summer to the mobile home in Normandy. I intended going there at any rate, so it would cost nothing more to take her as well. She cautiously accepted the idea, despite the dire warnings of some of her friends, but said that she would go only if she could take her sister with her for the first week of the six weeks when we would be there. I was quite happy with that. It was a thirty-two ft long home, with two-bedrooms and the possibility of making up a settee into another bed, and as the ferry fare included passengers with the car, the sister would have to pay only her own return fare when she came back.

Both Ann and her sister were very excited about the holiday, as neither had ever been to France before, while I was also excited, as I always came alive when I went across the Channel. Whenever I went, I would remember the time when I lived in France for three years, while

A Practical Spiritual Primer

serving with NATO forces before 1960: I had become quite fluent in French during that time, as I often had to interpret for the families of British soldiers who were renting houses and had problems with the landlords. But without continual practice, one always loses fluency, so I always welcomed the opportunity to brush up on my French. Also, I am certain that I have lived at least three lives in France, as I have had flashbacks to previous existences there from time to time. But there was another psychological reason for my excitement: I am a teacher, not only professionally but also by nature, and can never resist the delight of showing people new things. In fact, as I have been going to France for more than seventy years, there is always a danger of me being a bit blasé about going over there, so seeing it once more through the eyes of newcomers is always a pleasure for me.

So I took them both over there, and the first week passed quickly. We went round to all the local sights, they had their first taste of snails and frogs' legs, and all went well. The sister was into walking at the time, and as the campsite was near the Orne Canal, we used to have a daily walk of about a mile or more along it and back. (When we talk about canals in this country, we are talking about waterways that narrow-boats go along, and they are usually not more than ten yards wide. This canal was totally different: it was almost eighty yards wide, and frequently had ocean-going cargo ships pass through it on the way to the Port of Caen, an inland port some ten miles away).

When the sister eventually left, Ann and I settled into a weekly routine of domesticity, where she did the cooking, I did the washing up and we both kept the place tidy. We had a weekly outing to visit some local place of interest - ranging from a cider- or Calvados-maker to a tanning factory or a horse-stud. We went round local towns, spent time on the beach or went shopping. As Ann had no money of her own, I gave her about £20 each week to buy cards and personal souvenirs, although I paid all our other expenses. I also advertised the fact that she was a trained masseuse, and while she was at the camp she made about £200 from giving massages to various people.

About halfway through the holiday there was a catastrophe: we had a major row. I can't remember what it was about, but what I can remember was that astrologically Mars and Venus were in difficult aspect to each other for about a week. This is a very stressful time in all relationships, and warns of severe tension between the persons concerned. To anyone in a sexual relationship there was the possibility of a final release of tension through passionate lovemaking, but we weren't - so without being able to defuse the situation the scene was set for arguments. Unfortunately, this coincided with the first anniversary of Eleanor's death, so I wasn't in the best of spirits at any rate - and it was then that we both learnt how small a mobile home could be, as we started to get in each other's way.

The last fortnight was not a happy time, but it eventually ended and we came back. I went into the bank on the way home and changed Ann's earnings from her massage sessions from francs into sterling, and when I dropped her off at home I said, 'Give me a ring, when you would like me to come round' - and that was the end of the holiday.

Ann didn't ring that week, or the next, or the next - and after several weeks, I realised that possibly she wasn't ever going to ring, and I became very emotional. The fact that the relationship had finally ended was brought back to me in a dramatic way about two months later: I had gone along to a local Spiritualist church, and in the congregation, I saw Ann. When everyone was having a cup of tea afterwards, I went up to her and said, 'Well, it *is* lovely to see you'. She looked at me in a strange way and replied, 'Well, it's *not* lovely to see you,' and turned away. I then realised that everything was finished - and I started to grieve.

In some ways, it was very similar to the grieving process that had taken place after Eleanor had died: there was total shock and numbness at the start, but then anger instead of sorrow, until finally I started being sorry for myself. But now something very remarkable happened: I started to cry for the loss of the relationship, and the fact that tears were finally flowing meant that I could start to grieve properly for Eleanor at last. And did I grieve! All the tears that I had held back for the last year were finally released, and I dissolved in regret, remorse and self-pity. The only problem now was that no one could understand why I was so emotional. After a bereavement, everyone expects that the bereaved will cry - and so makes allowances for it - but a year later, everyone had forgotten that, and could not understand that there is such a thing as delayed grief.

However, there were two other unexpected results of this grieving: one was that I started to become emotional at the slightest provocation, and this is still the case, some twenty years after the event. As an Aquarian who had been brought up with the idea that 'boys don't cry', I had always been too controlled to show my emotions, but now the barriers are down and I can - and do. One fascinating way in which this now shows itself is that whenever I read or hear anything that is of profound spiritual importance, I feel emotional - and this has become almost a way of gauging how important the texts that I am reading are for me personally. I suppose that another way of putting it is that the grieving made me more spiritually sensitive.

The other result was probably far more important on a spiritual level: when I had got over the main issue of having an end to my relationship with Ann, I tried to understand what had caused it, and I went back to my own astrological chart and studied it. I had learnt many years before that one should never try to interpret an astrological chart for a friend, as one sees only what one wants to see, and not what is there. How much more difficult is it, therefore, to try to read your own chart, and be totally honest with yourself about the traits of your own character.

So when I looked at my chart anew, the one thing I quickly realised, (which I had never done before,) was that I was a real control freak, and in Normandy I had been in a situation where I could control Ann. I saw that she had been in a no-win situation, where she was completely dependent on me for everything from food to pocket money - and could not have even got back home without me. I also realised that I had subconsciously capitalised on this to control her all the time we were there. As soon as I recognised this, I looked back in my life to other relationships, and particularly to the one with Eleanor, and I realised with horror that I had also controlled her throughout our marriage. But there was something even worse: I was still doing the same, and was either deliberately or subconsciously controlling everyone I met.

In a horoscope, the element of control is shown by Pluto, and wherever he is in the chart will show how the person perceives that he/she was controlled as a child. In my case, he is in the ninth house, which represents 'Further Education, formal Religion, Law and long journeys'. Well, I had been totally controlled by my mother in all of these, having been forced to go to Church three times every Sunday, and forced to go to University to study Law, which I totally hated. On the plus side, of course, she had sent me on my first trip abroad to France, and I have had a love affair with that country ever since.

11: Holiday

Now there are two stages possible in one's relations with Pluto. In the first place, most people perceive that they are controlled as children in some aspect of their life. (I emphasise *perceive*, because what actually happens and what we perceive to be happening can be two totally different things). This control normally continues during adolescence and into adulthood, and then one has two choices of how to react to it. Some people just accept it, and continue to be controlled for the rest of their life; others do the reverse, and fight against their original conditioning by doing the opposite, and controlling others.

However, whichever reaction we have chosen originally, when we are on a spiritual pathway we are sooner or later brought face to face with the whole issue of control, and have to decide what to do about it, and how to resolve it finally. In the ideal case, we decide to deal with the question of control once and for all, and to order our lives so that we neither control others nor are controlled by them, and at this stage, we start to release the spiritual power of Pluto. Although it is so very small - so small, in fact, that scientists no longer consider it a planet at all - Pluto is the greatest of all the planets spiritually, as it has the power of Transformation: we have only to realise that the element associated with Pluto is plutonium, the raw material for nuclear weapons, in order to recognise how powerful the planet is. It is said that it can turn a saint into a sinner or a sinner into a saint. So if we work with the beneficial side of Pluto, and are prepared to face up to - and overcome - our problems of control, we can not only transform our own lives but help others to transform theirs as well.

(In this context, there is a spiritual saying - 'Let go, and let God').
Note that I have said, '*help* others to transform theirs' rather than 'transform the life of others'. The latter is controlling, whereas the former is not. In fact, of course, no one can ever change the life of any other person. If that person is not ready to change, then nothing can make him/her change. The old saying, 'You can lead a horse to water but you can't make him drink' comes to mind. However, everything in life happens at the correct time, so if (or when) it is time to change then the person involved will do so, whether or not anyone is there to help.

I now realise, therefore, that the whole episode of my relationship with Ann was destined to change my life in ways I could not have imagined at the time, and that although there was a period of great trauma, the eventual outcome was very beneficial. I have said elsewhere that you never really forgive people at all until you can thank them for what they did: as far as Ann is concerned I can certainly not only forgive her for what she did to me. but I can also very sincerely thank her, from the bottom of my heart.

But apart from the spiritual kick-in-the-pants that my relationship with Ann gave me, it did one other major thing: it gave me the most vivid and detailed flashback to a past life that I have ever had. First of all, let me set the scene. I had known Ann for about two months when I had the overwhelming urge to help her financially - and I did. She was in desperate financial straits, so every week I took her shopping and paid the bill. There were 'no ifs or buts' and no conditions: we just went shopping like a normal couple and I paid. Cynics will say that this was just the actions of an old man trying to curry favour with a young woman, but if so, for what reason? I asked nothing in return, nor was there ever any suggestion of any sort of repayment.

This went on for several months, and even when we had come back from France I was ready to continue doing it - and part of the grief that I had about the end of the relationship was that I would no longer be able to help her financially. Weird! So I decided that the compulsion must have a Karmic origin, and I meditated on it, and got the answer.

In the 16th century, it was fashionable for wealthy philanthropists to become patrons of the Arts, and in 1544, I was a struggling young artist in Italy, specialising in miniatures. However, being desperately poor, I was often forced to choose between buying food and buying artists' materials. Then into my life came Signor Spinelli, a wealthy merchant, who took me under his wing. He made me a member of his own household, and provided everything I needed to continue my career. Most important of all, as I grew more proficient, he introduced me to members of his own circle who were all delighted to have a miniature painted of themselves or their children - and who paid me handsomely. In fact, after several years with him, I started to make quite a name for myself locally and became relatively affluent, and I vowed that I would repay all the money he had lavished on me over the years.

But then came disaster: one day, while at the docks overseeing the unloading of one of his ships newly arrived from a trading voyage, a heavy bale of cloth fell on him and killed him instantly - and I was bereft.

11: Holiday

In this present lifetime, that artist incarnated as me, and Signor Spinelli as Ann, which explained the obsession I had for helping her financially. And when finally it became obvious that the relationship had ended, I was told by my inspirers - whom I call 'those upstairs' - 'You have repaid your debt'.

***

I have mentioned this topic of forgiveness and thanks before; however, let me give the following little story to try to explain how it works:

I once went to a local Drama Society production of Oklahoma. This is the story of the bitter rivalry for the hand of the heroine between two cowboys, which ends when one of them shoots and kills the other. However, despite the fact that on stage there was absolute hatred between the two characters, every night after the show the two men concerned went and had a drink together at a local bar - the best of friends.

And that is symbolic of our own lives: before we come into life, we decide what we want to achieve and what lessons we need to undergo. We therefore decide what kind of experiences will be needed in order to give us those lessons. Now almost all of the experiences in life come through our relationships with other people, therefore we need to find others who are willing to play the part of those who will give us those experiences. If you decided that you needed to know what it is like to be bullied, then someone had to be found to bully you, or if you needed to be cheated, then someone had to agree to cheat you. Then later on in life, when your relationship with them is ended and they have played their part correctly, and either bullied or cheated you (or even both), if you can thank them for the experience then you are realising that everything that happened to you had its purpose - and was, in fact, *organised* by you originally.

This idea has a deeper significance, though: considering that we are all governed by the Law of Cause and Effect, when we play the bully/cheat role in someone else's life, we are accepting the inevitability of the same thing happening to us in a future life, so we are deliberately taking on 'bad' Karma in order to play our role in the other person's life-play.

I was once talking about spiritual philosophy with someone, and was asked who was the strongest among the disciples of Jesus. I hazarded a guess at Peter, as he was the one who had the job of holding the rest together after the Crucifixion, and eventually of spreading the gospel of Christianity after the Ascension. However, my colleague surprised me when he said that in his opinion the strongest disciple was Judas Iscariot! His role was foretold long before by the prophet Isaiah, and Jesus himself knew what was going to happen when he told Judas 'Go and do what you have to do'. If we assume that Judas took on the burden of the role before coming into his incarnation, and we agree that his name has been reviled throughout all the centuries since the Crucifixion, (in fact becoming synonymous with traitor,) we must accept that it took a super-human strength of mind to accept such Karma.

There are many, of course, who will totally ridicule the idea of such a pre-life agreement, but I had a very wonderful confirmation of it a few years ago. Whenever someone marries for a second time after having lost a spouse, there is always a nagging suspicion of doubt at the back of the mind, - 'Am I being unfaithful to... by getting married again' - and that will usually exist for a long time after the new relationship has started: certainly it did so for me. Now my second wife, Sybil, used to run Development Circles for young mediums, and one evening we were sitting in circle when a brilliant young medium who did not know me very well came to me.

She seemed fairly embarrassed, and she said, 'I don't really know how to say this', but we said 'Say it and sod it' - in other words say what you are impressed to say, and if people take exception to it that is *their* problem. She said, 'Well, I have a lady here who says that she is your wife'. (She didn't know that Sybil was my second wife). 'She says that she made an arrangement with Sybil before you all came into this life: she arranged that Sybil would take you over when she (your first wife) had finished her own earthly life'. She then went on to describe Eleanor, and gave enough evidence to prove that it really *was* her - as if the message itself were not enough. It was the loveliest spirit message I had ever had, and relieved me of any last niggle of doubt that my marriage to Sybil was perfectly right.

It was many months after I returned from the holiday with Ann before I made all the discoveries about myself, and even longer before I was able to forgive her and thank her. However, well before that finally happened a person came into my life who was to change it forever.

Chapter 12: Clare

The date was October 16th, 1994. I didn't know it at the time, but it was to prove the most important date in my life since the death of Eleanor - and probably one of the most important that there would ever be for the rest of my life as well. I had received a phone call from the Bookings Secretary of Bideford Spiritualist Church a couple of days before to ask me if I would be prepared to step in at short notice and take a service at the Church in place of a medium who had just cancelled due to illness. I hadn't anything booked for that date, so I had willingly accepted.

I wasn't doing much of a spiritual nature at that time: it had been more than twenty years since I had been involved in the running of a church, and so these days I just went along to services occasionally, either in Barnstaple or in Bideford - preferably the former, which was slightly nearer to my home in North Devon. Two or three times a year, each church invited me to take a service, but apart from that, I had little formal contact.

Spiritualist services are usually of a set format. First, there are prayers and an opening hymn, followed by a spiritual reading and another hymn, then a spiritual address. After a third hymn there is the part of the service which most people go there for - the clairvoyance, when the medium attempts to contact (or 'bring through') the departed relatives and loved ones of members of the congregation. When I did services, I had a slightly different format: as I wasn't clairvoyant, and hadn't developed clairsentience (clear sensing) sufficiently to give public demonstrations, I first gave a spiritual address and then I answered questions from members of the congregation on the spiritual philosophy that had been contained in the address.

This night was no different, and after the service had finished the entire congregation went down into the little Church Hall to have a cup of tea and biscuits, and to socialise a little before going home. On my way down to the hall, I was stopped by a lady who was sitting at the back of the church: she introduced herself as Clare, and asked if she might speak to me about what my inspirer had been explaining in his address. We talked for some time, and then she said that she was from Paignton, in South Devon, and invited me to come down to her house, so that my inspirer could speak to some of her friends on the same theme. I accepted and a provisional date for the visit was set for the beginning of November.

Looking back on that night, it was one of the most amazing examples of synchronicity that there has ever been in my life. Clare had once lived for a time near Bideford, and still had friends there. When she had heard that a close friend of hers from Paignton, who was a medium, was due to take a service at Bideford Church that weekend, she had decided to visit her friends for the weekend and then go to the church on the Sunday to support the medium. However, as he had cancelled at short notice, she didn't realise that he wasn't going to be there - and that is how we met. She was to prove the catalyst who changed my life completely - and I shall be forever in her debt for what she has done for me.

I went down to meet her friends, and my inspirer duly gave a spiritual address. Following that evening Clare and I became close friends, and I visited her every fortnight or so. I felt an intense rapport with her, and this confused me somewhat: many years before (possibly twenty or more), I had had a feeling that towards the end of my life I would be with a rather plump, jolly lady with a halo of light-grey hair. As Eleanor always had a very slim figure, and very fine bone structure of the face, I knew that this couldn't be her - and because I couldn't imagine not ending my days being married to her, I had dismissed the feeling as a figment of my imagination. But now the more that I saw Clare the more I felt myself being attracted to her, and this confused me, as *she* wasn't the lady I had seen either. I now know that Clare and I have spent many lives together (dating back to Ancient Egypt) in just about every relationship possible, and that in one life we were married to each other, so that was why I felt this intense attraction for her. However, at the time I didn't yet know this, so it was no wonder that I felt confused.

I found out that Clare was a Spiritual Healer and also a clairvoyant, and had a wide range of friends in spiritual and alternative therapy circles. She was a very mercurial person, who could be on top of the world at one

12: Clare

moment and down in the dumps the next. She was going through a very rough period in her life at that particular moment, so I offered to help her through counselling, using Louise Hay's book 'You can Heal your Life' as a base. On one of our evening sessions, I happened to mention that I had once been interested in Astrology, and she said that she would like to see if there was anything in her astrological chart which could explain the traumatic time through which she was going at that moment. So I got out my old books and did her birth chart. It was the first birth-chart I had done for almost twenty years. We discussed the chart and found out that it did explain a lot of the influences round her - and then one of her friends heard about it and wanted hers done also, so I duly did another. Before I knew what had happened I had started back into Astrology again, and I was drawing up charts in order to show people how their life had been pre-ordained, before going on to give them counselling sessions.

I had had a computer for several years - a BBC Model B - and had been programming in BBC Basic for some time. I then updated the computer and bought an Archimedes, which had much more storage but still accepted the same Basic language - and I decided to combine the skills of programming and Astrology, and started to write my own computer program to calculate and interpret basic birth charts. The work took place over several years, and when it was eventually finished, although it wasn't as good as some of the commercial programs which one can now buy, it was still very effective, and provided a good simple printout of the main characteristics in a person's chart. Regrettably, after many years of sterling service, the Archimedes computer gave up the ghost, and as it was not compatible with modern PC computers, I lost all the astrological and spiritual work I had done over the years that was stored on discs in Archimedes format.

Over the next year my visits to Paignton became part of my life, and from time to time I met one or other of Clare's friends, all of whom I found very interesting. I would occasionally go to the local Spiritualist church in Paignton, which was far bigger and grander than anything which existed in North Devon, and which was served by mediums from all over the country, not just from the local district. So I found myself being drawn into the life of Spiritualism once more.

Towards the end of 1995 I knew that there was a massive change coming into my life, due to the movement of my ruling planet Uranus into its own sign of Aquarius, and I knew that this would turn my life completely upside-down. The change had been heralded several months earlier, when I had been at the mobile home and had had problems when doing my morning walk along the Canal towpath, but now it was imminent. In addition, my youngest daughter Penny, who was at that time managing a hotel in a resort on the South Coast, had been to a Spiritualist church in September of that same year, and the medium had brought Eleanor through to her.

Eleanor had said, 'It is about time that your father stopped grieving for me - there's no need for it. Tell him that I am going to bring someone to him who will be with him for the rest of his life - and he will be in this permanent relationship by the Spring!' My immediate reaction when I had first heard this was 'Not ... likely!' There was no way in which I wanted to replace Eleanor with any other woman - I still loved her deeply. But I suppose that the suggestion must have had some effect on my subconscious. I remembered the vision which I had had some twenty years before, and I began to think that perhaps I might meet someone who was a widow, and who had lost her husband after the sort of idyllic relationship which I had had with Eleanor for the last seven years of her life. In fact, I remember asking Clare if she had a plump lady among her friends who had been widowed after a happy marriage - but she hadn't, so I forgot the matter.

For a while, Clare seemed to become more positive but then something happened in her life that really took her down to rock bottom again, and towards Christmas a year after I had first met her she was going through the worst patch yet. So in order to cheer her up, I suggested that she should throw a Christmas party and invite some of the wonderful people she knew, so that she would have something to lift her out of her depression (and also so that I would be able to meet even more of her fascinating friends). I told her that it needn't cost her the earth, as all the guests could be asked to bring a bottle and a plate of food. She agreed, and we set the provisional date for December 15th.

A couple of days before the date, she rang me up and said that there had been a change of plan. Her own house was not very convenient for throwing parties: there was very little street parking available, the house was at the top of a Close on a steep hill, and it also had forty-seven steps up to the front door. So she had gone round to one of her divorced friends,

12: Clare

Sybil, and had explained the situation; Sybil had agreed to have the party in her house in Torquay, which was on the level and had considerably more parking available. She said that she would put Sybil on the line to give me directions how to get to the house, and passed the phone to her.

Sybil told me how to get there, and then I started to chat to her, and in the process of doing so mentioned that I did Astrology. She said that she had never had her birth-chart calculated, so I asked her for her details (date, time and place of birth) - and she gave them to me. (Silly woman!) As soon as I had put the phone down, I went to the computer and put all the data in to calculate her chart. This meant that before I went to the party I knew all about her - and I liked what I had found out. I also ran the data through a program to find out our possible compatibility together, and the results were most interesting: a relationship between us would be either a total disaster from Day 1 or it would be one of enormous spiritual power. That sounded fascinating, so I looked forward to the party with a great deal of interest.

I had been going down to Torquay counselling Little Sue for more than a year by this time, and as my home in North Devon was more than fifty miles from Torquay I had arranged to stay with her overnight, so I went along to her house to take her with me to the party. I had baked a big Normandy apple tart as my contribution to the feast, and we went along together to the house. It was only a small house, and it seemed packed with people already, but Clare was there by the door, and she introduced me to the hostess, Sybil. I felt that I had met her already, as her face and appearance seemed vaguely familiar to me, but that was impossible, of course, as it was only through Clare that we could possibly have met. I got on very well with her, and we spent quite a long time talking to each other during the evening; in fact her daughter, Carolyn, was most amused every time she looked across the room and saw us deeply engrossed in conversation.

The evening was a great success: there was plenty of food and drink, as everyone had come well stocked with contributions, and although most people had never met they all seemed to be on the same wavelength and conversation flowed freely. I met some fascinating people, amongst whom were a Buddhist monk, a Past Life Regression expert, a Time Traveller, a Psychic Artist and many ordinary psychics, clairvoyants, channels and healers. Late in the evening, I happened to look into the corner of the lounge and I saw Sybil sitting there with a satisfied smile on her face, watching all the assembled throng conversing animatedly. I knew that she had the sign of Leo on the Ascendant of her birth-chart; Leo is the general, the organiser, the person who brings people together and then watches how they get on, and that was exactly what she was doing.

When it was all over, I went back with Sue to her flat and we discussed the evening. It was the first time that she had met anyone who was at the party, but she had had a whale of a time. She is naturally a very good mixer and a very attractive and vivacious young lady, so she had been much in demand all evening. She said that she had been particularly drawn to Clare and Sybil, and felt that there was some sort of a deep bond between her and Sybil. I agreed that Sybil was certainly a very warm and friendly person, (after all, she is a Libran, the sign of relationships) but I didn't think any more of it than that at the time.

The next morning I left Sue's flat, but when I got to the car I realised that I had forgotten to bring away from the party the large baking tray on which I had made my apple tart, so I went back to Sybil's house to collect it. To my surprise, Clare was still there: she had stayed the night (probably because she had been too 'squiffy' to call a taxi after the party) and she had just predicted to Sybil that I would be coming round to the house again, and also that I would be 'phoning her later that night. A few minutes later, I walked up the drive! I collected the tray and then offered Clare a lift home. We went in for a coffee, and she asked me how I had got on with Sybil. I said that I thought that she was very nice, and then started to 'tune in' to her psychically and sensed a bit of her future. I told Clare that she was about to get into a relationship, which would last for about three months, and then a second one which would be permanent. Alternatively, she would have two separate relationships with the same man, the first being a three months' trial, which would then become permanent.

Then Clare said five words that literally changed my life. She said innocently (Oh, so innocently), 'Could that man be you?' - and suddenly everything clicked into place. I knew why Sybil had seemed familiar to me when I first met her - she had been the woman with whom I had seen myself all those years before, and in occasional flashes of inspiration since. This was the big change which was imminent in my life, and which Eleanor had predicted in her message to my daughter. Everything fitted, except the idea which I had had about her being a widow after a very happy marriage - in fact she had divorced her husband a couple of years before, after a marriage which had eventually lasted 34 years but from which she had never received any emotional fulfilment.

I didn't know it at that time, but a few months before, Sybil and Clare had been for a joint reading with Dorothy Chitty, a very powerful West-Country medium, and Sybil had asked about the prospect of her ever having another man in her life. She had been told that there was a man already 'in the wings' waiting to come into her life, who was totally different in every way from her previous husband. That couldn't have been more correct. The previous husband had been a perfectionist in everything he did, was very neat and orderly, a very good tradesman - and a complete workaholic. In company, he could also be the life and soul of the party, but privately couldn't communicate his feelings, and certainly hadn't been able to make Sybil happy. I was exactly the opposite in every respect: I have never been very neat and tidy (in fact, I am rather scruffy), have always been a bit laid-back and lazy, and as far as being a DIY person is concerned, my idea of DIY is to do half of the job myself and then to pay an expert a fabulous amount of money to put it right. In fact, whenever I have done any woodwork, if a joint had a gap of less than a quarter of an inch between the two pieces of wood I have considered it a tight fit! These days, if Sybil sees me with any DIY tool in my hand, she tells me to go and lie down until the urge to use it has passed.

However, I excel in getting on with people: I have never really liked big crowds, but I have always had the knack of being able to talk to people in every walk of life and make them feel at ease. Finally, as far as relationships are concerned, I learned from those last idyllic years with Eleanor what makes a relationship really work - in fact, she taught me how to *love*. What I myself have always wanted in a relationship is to have the closeness and intimacy which is the need of my Libran ascendant, combined with the detachment and independence of my Aquarian sun - and that combination was what I was prepared to offer to anyone in a relationship. I realise that all of us need space, and that applies just as much to our partner as ourself. I also like to feel that I can be independent, and that means that I like to be on my own from time to time and 'have my own space', looking after and cooking for myself.

A Practical Spiritual Primer

Sybil had been told by Dorothy that despite (or possibly because of) the difference in character between her former husband and the new man, she would be very happy in her new relationship, and that in fact she and her man would fit together like two pieces of a jigsaw puzzle. She hadn't believed it at the time, but that is in fact how things have turned out. (Strange to relate, one of the joint interests we have is in doing jigsaws).

Following this question by Clare, I decided to 'take the bull by the horns' and to 'phone Sybil that same night. The call lasted two-and-a-half hours. The next night the call lasted three-and-a-quarter hours - and by the end of it, we were in a relationship, and all the basic details had been sorted out! We had agreed to give it a go for three months, and then to decide whether or not it was working: if not, we would cut our losses and part without recriminations, or else we would stay together permanently. Sybil said later that that was the most amazing phone call she had ever had in her life - and I don't think that it was any less amazing for me, either.

I took Sybil up to North Devon a couple of days after Christmas, when all my family were still there after the festivities, and she got on very well with them. It must have been an absolutely terrifying ordeal for her, as there were about twenty people there, all my children and grandchildren, son- and daughters-in-law, and (most daunting of all) Nanny. However, Sybil has a very warm and motherly air, and she soon charmed everyone, with the possible exception of Lesley, one of my daughters-in-law, who had always been very close to Eleanor, and who at first viewed Sybil a little suspiciously.

The rest, as they say, is history. We enjoyed each other's company enormously, and after only a month our friends were saying that we were already behaving like an old married couple. Then in the Spring we went to the mobile home in Normandy, and while in France, I took Sybil to Drancy, near Paris. We stayed with old friends there for a couple of days, and I showed her some of the sights of Paris. We went into the Sacré Coeur Cathedral, and sat in meditation in front of the huge representation of Christ; in that meditation, quite independently, we vowed our joint life to the service of Spirit. By the time we came back, we had decided that we were going to 'be an item' permanently - and that is how it has proved to be. As far as the astrological compatibility is concerned, we have now been together for twenty years and have never yet had a row, (which must be quite a record for a second relationship,) and we have enormous power when we are working together spiritually.

But just before that big change in my life, something else had happened that forwarded my spiritual education. I had met my third guru. I had gone with my daughter Ellie to a service in Barnstaple Spiritualist Church one evening, and the address of the medium had absolutely blown me away, as he had touched on things about which I knew nothing whatsoever. After his address, I turned to Ellie, and said, 'Wow! What did you think of that?' 'I don't know,' she replied, 'I didn't understand a word of it'.

I said 'That is the most amazing address I have ever heard in my life. I must talk to this man'. I found out that his name was Ron Buckle and that he was a homeopath who had a practice in Exeter, so I phoned him and arranged a consultation with him.

As soon as I walked into his consulting room I confessed that I was there under false pretences. I didn't want medical advice, but I had been at his demonstration and I wanted to ask him about the address. He didn't seem perturbed that I was wasting his professional time, and for the next half-hour, he gave me information that opened up completely new vistas for me. I learned of the cosmic connections to our world, and the fact that many human beings now in incarnation were originally 'Starseeds' who helped in the original colonisation of Earth by new life forms. Every time he gave me another fact, he said, 'But you know this already, don't you?' - and I found that I did. He was reminding me of information I already had, but didn't *know* that I had. He ended by giving me a list of books to read, which would reinforce and extend what he had said, and all too soon our half-hour appointment came to an end.

Ron was a lovely man, whom I saw only a couple more times during his life, and regrettably didn't have the opportunity for any philosophical discussion. However, 'by coincidence' I was soon invited to join a Cosmic circle, during which we contacted beings from other worlds, and I found out that all that he had told me was totally correct.

Chapter 13: Emotions

Every human being comes into incarnation with the aim of learning and undergoing lessons, and these lessons can only be obtained through having experiences. The experiences are usually gained by interaction with other human beings, and these interactions give rise to emotions.

Emotions range from the most positive of all, that of Love, to the most negative, that of Hate, and encompass the whole gamut of human life in between. There are many people who are afraid of their emotions, and some of the zodiacal signs are known for their dislike of showing them. Aquarius, for instance, is known for detachment, and Aquarians hate the thought of showing emotion, believing that it shows their weaknesses, through which they could be attacked. Pisceans, on the other hand, are notoriously prone to showing their emotions, and like nothing more than a good cry while watching a 'weepie' film. However, when we look at a horoscope chart we see that every sign is represented at some place or other in the chart, and so everyone is likely to feel emotion of some sort or other during the course of his/her daily routine.

There is nothing wrong with feeling emotion: it is the part of human life that distinguishes us from animals. However, the important thing is not how much emotion we feel or do not feel, but how we deal with the emotions that we *do* feel.

The emotional level of the aura is very close to the physical level, so if emotions are not dealt with in a satisfactory way then they can rapidly affect the physical body. One example is the emotion of anger: this is a very basic thing that affects all of us, and is associated with the hormone adrenaline, which is the 'fight or flight' hormone. When something is seen to be attacking us in some way, we may feel fear or we may feel anger - and there are two things that we can do about it. Either we can run away or we can stand our ground and fight. If the fear is predominant and we decide to run away, then the adrenaline gives us a boost of power so that our leg muscles are strengthened and we are able to run faster. If the anger is predominant and we decide to stay and fight, then the strength is expressed in the arm muscles, which allows us to hit the attacker harder. On a mental level, the brain is stimulated to work more quickly, either to decide where to run to and hide, or how best to attack.

Now there are two ways of attacking someone, physically or verbally. In our society, we usually choose to attack others verbally, although such verbal attacks may often develop into physical attacks as well. After the physical or verbal fight, when both parties have calmed down, the situation is cleared, and the perceived danger removed, so the body stops producing the adrenaline and returns to normal. However, where the anger has not been fully defused for some reason, then some adrenaline continues to be produced, and the 'normal' state is not achieved. In this case, the person is likely to continue to feel the emotion of anger, but be without the possibility of getting rid of it - and this can lead to either resentment or hatred (or both) and cause permanent damage.

Many people feel that they have no way of protecting themselves when attacked, and so submit to either physical or verbal abuse and don't do anything about it. But this doesn't stop the adrenaline being produced: it just means that more and more resentment and hatred is stoked up and more damage is done to them. In time, such feelings will start to have an effect on the physical body: either one can be one of the psychic causes of cancer - as in Eleanor's case - and eat away at the subconscious mind of the person, until eventually the body responds by starting to eat away at itself. Anger can be one of the causes of accidents if suppressed, and if it turns to bitterness, that can also affect the liver.

No human being enjoys harmful experiences, so when something stressful has happened to us we usually try to put it behind us and then get on with our life. There are some people, however, who have a sort of 'martyr complex', in which they like to hang on to bad experiences, and talk about them at the slightest drop of a hat. When this happens, the person, through re-living old negative experiences, is still surrounding him/herself with negativity, and is therefore more likely to draw even more negative experiences into their life - thus reinforcing their belief that they are among life's unlucky ones. In fact, there is no such thing as 'luck': everything has a cause and a reason for occurring, and we create our own 'luck' - good or bad - by our own actions and by the thoughts that we have about ourselves and about our ability to achieve success in the world.

Of course, this is only another example of the philosophy that 'what goes around comes around'. If we harbour thoughts of negativity of any kind about anyone, we will surround ourselves with negativity and draw to ourselves similar conditions, which sooner or later will manifest into our life. It is immaterial whether the origin of those thoughts came from the actions of others or not: they are *our* thoughts and we are responsible for them. (Remember that we have originally decided what lessons we want to learn, and so we have really brought the original actions into being). Therefore the question is not 'Who caused the original problem?' - but 'What can I do about it?'

If we are serious in wanting to do something, the first thing that we must do is to accept that there *is* a problem, and to bring it out into the light. Now this is not always as easy as it may sound, because very often we are unwilling to face up to the situation in our life at any given time, so we conveniently forget it, and bury it in the depths of our subconscious. (In passing, I note that the first thing that someone who attends a clinic for drink or drugs rehabilitation is urged to do is to accept that he/she has a problem. Until that is done, there is no possibility of starting the healing process). This same logic is always used whenever something goes wrong on a space mission. The first thing which astronauts are trained to say is, 'Houston, we have a problem'!

The difficulty with not accepting that there is a problem is that it never goes away, but just stays there and continues to hurt us without us knowing it. A very good analogy would be of having a thorn go into your finger and sink very deeply into the flesh. After a time it can no longer be seen on the surface, but it can easily become septic and make the finger swell up. In such a case the only solution is to have the thorn removed - and however painful that might be it is not nearly as painful as leaving the thorn to fester in the wound.

However, the dangers of leaving old emotional matters unresolved can be far more damaging than a thorn in the finger. They can be totally emotionally blighting, so that the whole of the future life of the person is affected. Very often, the person does not consciously know what is causing the problem, and goes through a succession of unrewarding relationships or - even worse - refuses to enter any sort of relationship at all, believing that

13: Emotions

any one would be doomed from the start. Of course, this sort of belief very quickly turns into a self-fulfilling prophecy, as the fact that the person shuns potential relationships gives others the impression that he/she is not a suitable sort of person with whom to explore a relationship.

So how do we start the process of healing hidden problems, if we don't even know that they exist? Sometimes it is fairly easy, as we meet someone from the past, see a photo or visit a place, or perhaps a friend says something - and this strikes a chord in our memory; then suddenly that past hurt comes back, and we briefly relive the past event, and feel the strong emotion which was associated with it. Let us just imagine that this has happened, and now we are faced with the feeling of total rage and helplessness that we had felt when the event had first happened. What can we do now?

The quick answer is that we have to do *something*: nothing happens without a reason, and the reason why we have been reminded of the original incident now is that we have come to a point at which we *can* do something. We can re-live the event, and do what we would like to have done at the time, had we only had the courage. In most cases, this means that we would have released our anger by verbally abusing, or using physical violence on, the person concerned, and we can re-enact this scenario. The original person is no longer there, of course, but we can *imagine* that they are, and take some sort of appropriate action - and this leads us on to think about Visualisation.

Many people will not have heard of visualisation, but everyone has heard of imagination, and the two words have almost the same meaning - bringing a person or situation into your 'mind's eye'. But when we talk of 'imagination' we are usually talking about 'daydreaming': it has no particular value, apart from giving us a few pleasant moments of respite from the boredom of our daily routine. For instance, we could start by saying 'What would I do if I won the lottery' - and then go off into a reverie, thinking of all the nice things which we would be able to buy, the places where we could go, the holidays which we could have, etc. However, visualisation has a much more serious purpose - we intend to use it to bring a spiritual change into our life!

So how can we use visualisation to help us in the particular situation which we are discussing now, where we are remembering - and feeling - the anger generated by some incident in the past?

A Practical Spiritual Primer

A simple way is to imagine that a pillow on a bed, or a cushion on an armchair or settee, represents the head of the person whom we associate with the past hurt. Concentrate on it, imagine that it is taking the shape and features of that person - and then recall the event. Recall it, re-live it, and feel all the anger and violence that the memory brings back. Think of what you felt like at the time, how you would have liked to shout and scream at the person, or physically attack them. Then *do* it: tell the pillow/cushion (representing the person) exactly what you feel, what you think of him/her, and what you would like to do to them - and allow yourself to attack it, hitting it as hard as you like and venting all your anger on it for as long as you want to. After a few minutes you will find that you stop, either out of physical exhaustion or because all your anger has disappeared - or a mixture of the two. Let yourself relax for a few minutes, calm down, and then resume your daily routine. To find out how effective the exercise was, try doing the same thing a few days later, and see if you can rouse the same degree of antagonism towards the person. If you can't, then 'you've cracked it', and the exercise has been successful. If there is still a bit of anger left, then do it again.

This, then, is a possible way of releasing the anger we still feel about old hurts we have identified. However, in most cases we don't know what the cause of our current problems was - all that we know is that we are not happy with our present situation, relationship, job, financial position, health, housing or whatever other problem we can identify - and we want to sort it out. But how do we start?

The most straightforward thing is to ask for professional help and go to a counsellor of some kind. All local authorities have a panel of counsellors to whom people may be referred, and asking at your local Town Hall or Civic Centre could be an easy way of finding how to contact one. The down-side of this is that although counselling is becoming quite common, in many cases there are long waiting lists to see someone on a one-to-one basis, and many people don't like to 'air their dirty linen' in a counselling group. In addition, private counsellors will normally charge a fee per session, which if you have financial problems is not a very palatable solution. Nevertheless, initially, a visit to your local Citizens Advice Bureau could be worth your while, to find out the details of help available in your area.

13: Emotions

However, whatever you decide to do, and wherever you decide to seek help, it is worthwhile realising from the start that no one can ever sort your problems out for you: you have to do that yourself! To go to a counsellor of any sort and expect to have your life changed without you having to do any work on yourself is similar to expecting to meet a fairy godmother who will wave a magic wand and make your life right immediately. It simply won't happen! (I used to teach French to adult students, and I always told them that if I could have instilled a knowledge of the language in pupils' minds without them doing any work I would have made myself a fortune and retired long before). I was never able to wave the magic wand for my students, and no counsellor can do it for you either.

Should you decide to 'bite the bullet' and start to work on your own, realise that it is going to be difficult - but the rewards will be proportionate to the amount of effort that you are prepared to put in. If - or to be more positive *when* - you eventually succeed, you will have the great satisfaction of having proved to yourself that you are far more clever than you ever thought - which will give an enormous boost to your self-confidence. I discuss how you can go about changing your own pattern of life in the next chapter, but let me remind you that whatever you do will be your choice; so before we go any further let us consider the subject of Choice.

All human beings have choices - in fact, in celestial circles the Earth is called 'the planet of choice'. The reason is that when we come into incarnation none of us has the knowledge that we are a spark of the infinite energy which is known by many names, but which in Western civilisation is known as 'God'. Therefore, each of us can choose which path we take, whether we wish to descend ever deeper into the realms of materialism or rise into the heights of spirituality. However, sooner or later that divine spark within us will start to steer us upwards - usually after hundreds of lives - until we finally make the conscious choice of wishing to be re-united with the Divine Essence, and start to work towards that end.

As an aside, I once asked my inspirers to explain the force that, sooner or later, makes us want to be reunited, and I was given this rather ingenious little example. I was told to imagine a large bonfire, which was roaring away and sending up sparks, sometimes as much as fifty feet into the sky. For a period of time, the force and heat of the flames will push the sparks up, and then, when removed from the vertical updraft, those same sparks will be acted on by the force of gravity and will gradually sink back to earth again. Naturally, the ones that have been sent up higher will take longer to come down, but come down they all will eventually.

So it is with all of us: each person carries within a tiny spark of the eternal Spirit, a minute fragment of the Divine. However far away that spark may travel from the Source, sooner or later the force of attraction (divine gravity, perhaps?) will bring it back to its origin. So however far we descend into the depths of materialism and physicality, sooner or later we will be inexorably drawn back to the knowledge of what we are, and make the journey back to the Source from which we all came.

We are also, at the same time, bound by the Law of Cause and Effect, which states that every action has an equal and opposite reaction - in a nutshell, 'What goes round, comes round', or 'As you sow, so shall you reap'. From our first incarnation on the planet, therefore, we made choices and when those choices affected others, we started to get involved with what is generally called the Law of Karma. This is the law which was designed for the human experience on this planet and says that what we do to others we shall have done to us by others - in other words, in its crudest definition, it is 'the Law of Retribution and Reward'. I have discussed this more fully in an earlier chapter.

In everyday life we are faced with choices - hundreds of choices, ranging from major decisions about where to live, what sort of job to do, etc. to simple things like what to eat, where to shop or what to wear. On reflection, sometimes the latter is not such a simple decision after all: any Celtic supporter who went into a pub full of Rangers fans wearing the colours of his team would find that his choice of clothing had dire, albeit predictable, consequences. Furthermore, there is more and more controversy these days about the values of eating different kinds of food, bringing in discussions about the dangers of various additives and the relative merits of eating organic as opposed to processed foods, etc. Then there is the subject of dieting, which has spawned a billion-pound industry led by food gurus who advocate this or that approach to one of the greatest problems of our modern age - obesity.

However, most of these choices pale into insignificance when we are faced with the major decisions in life. It is said that the most traumatic times of a person's life (apart from the death of a loved one) are moving house and divorce. Apart from these, there are many other situations that can be extremely stressful, and most of those revolve round the subject of relationships. This is not surprising, since the majority of our lessons in life revolve round the relationships we have with others, whether on a friendship, business or neighbourly basis - and most of all on a marital or partnership basis. So let us consider relationships.

First of all, we have to understand that many of the people whom we meet in this life have already figured in some way in one or other of our past lives - rarely in the same relationship, but almost always in the same *quality* of relationship. This means that if we have had a beneficial relationship with someone in a past life, and we meet again in this life, we are likely to see the person in a favourable light this time as well, and warm to him/her immediately; whereas if the past life has left us with unhappy memories then subconsciously we will probably be antagonistic to him/ her this time. However, one must also remember that there is a purpose in every relationship: if the latter case happens, and if we are fairly advanced spiritually, we may realise that the reason why the person has come into our life again is to help us to jointly resolve past problems, and that our being together represents an opportunity for us to grow spiritually. Therefore, paradoxically, we ought to try to give most love to the people whom we hate most!

The three most destructive forces in human life are Fear, Guilt and Shame, and from these three all other human problems flow. The greatest of these forces is Fear, which sets individual against individual, group against group, religion against religion and nation against nation. When we fear that something is going to harm us in any way, we react against it, and by the Law of Cause and Effect, that reaction itself causes its own reaction, and so on. If we think that someone is threatening us, we are likely to adopt some sort of defensive pose: that defensive pose may well be seen by the other person as *offensive*, so he/she will adopt an offensive pose, which in turn will make us even more fearful... and so it goes on, until the situation could well end in physical violence.

This is bad enough when viewed from an individual standpoint, but when nations are involved, it can become world-threatening. For instance, the mutual distrust and suspicion between the Communist block and the Western Powers led to forty years of the Cold War, which was finally defused only by one man's courage in accepting the right of other states to rule their own life and do things their own way. The world owes a great deal to Mikhael Gorbachev!

However, the aspect of Fear affects our life on a daily basis in far more subtle ways than just the perception of a threat of violence. Each of us wants to be accepted, liked, loved - and this basic desire means that we feel that we have to conform to the norms and standards of the group into which we want to be accepted. This is seen from a very early age: children want the same sort of clothes and toys as their friends, they want to be able to watch the same sort of TV programmes, see the same films and go to the same sort of places. The 'keeping up with the Jones' culture starts very early in life. Inevitably, since all families don't have the same sort of financial background, some children won't be able to have what the rest have - and will inevitably find themselves left out of the peer group - or at best find themselves on the fringe as hangers-on. Cliques form at a very early age in a child s development, and he/she soon learns the difference between the 'haves' and the 'have-nots'. It is a truism that children can be extremely cruel to each other, and it all starts in the primary schools.

Because we come into life with a pre-arranged schedule of lessons that we want to learn, we choose the experiences that will give us those lessons, and therefore choose the environment which will give us those experiences. Once this has happened, then things happen automatically, and predictably. Whatever experiences we have during the first few years of our life will make us into what we are when we first go to junior school, and the character we acquire there will then be reinforced by our passage through senior school - so that by the time we become an adult it will be so ingrained in us that it will have become second nature. What happens thereafter will depend on how much we realise what *has* happened, and why it has happened - but more importantly, it will depend on whether or not we realise what the object of the whole exercise was.

Many people never get to that final stage - and this is alright for them: they have decided, on a soul level, that they want to learn whatever lesson they are going through so thoroughly that they are prepared to continue it for the whole of this life, knowing that there will be many other lives to follow in which they can learn other lessons. However, many people come to a stage in their life when they rebel against the conditioning that has taken place to bring them to where they are - and decide to do something about it. The proverb 'Even the worm will turn' comes to mind at this

13: Emotions

time: however bad our situation, and however great the pressures on us, the human spirit is always capable of rising above the circumstances. The spur that causes them to want to change can range from total desperation - possibly when threatened by an apparently terminal illness or a hopeless dilemma - to being completely fed up with the daily round of a completely humdrum existence. In many cases, the pace of life has become so frantic that the person can no longer stand it ('Stop the world, I want to get off') and more and more people are getting out of the rat-race and moving to other parts of the country - or even the world - in order to find a different and more satisfying lifestyle

However, most people aren't in the situation where they can - or would want to - cut off all their ties and move to a different area or to 'foreign climes', and strange to relate many of the people who emigrate regret it afterwards. It is said that more than half of those who move to Australia from Great Britain come back, as they can't handle the reality of being separated from their families and friends, despite the fact that they may acknowledge that the standard and quality of living is so much better down-under! Nevertheless, everyone has the possibility of bringing change into their life - but how to do it is the problem.

Chapter 14: Changing

If you want to change your life, the first thing to do is to sit down and have a good look at yourself. This may seem surprising to many people: what they want to change is their situation, the problems they have, their job, the way their children behave, their partner - and a whole range of other things in their lives. So why do I say that if you are in this position you should start by looking at yourself?

(As an aside here, let me say that I am incorrect in using the word 'should': this implies that there is an obligation on you, and it also implies that there is only ever one way of bringing about change. The correct word to use is 'could', as what I am going to say is only a suggestion, a possible course of action - and it is up to you whether or not you decide to act on it. No one can live your life, and if you want to get other people to tell you what you *should* be doing then you are refusing to take responsibility for your own actions. However, in many cases this is what people do. They ask advice from all and sundry, neighbours, friends, family, colleagues, etc., get totally conflicting opinions - which is not surprising, as we are all individuals, and react in different ways to any given set of circumstances - and finish by being more confused than they were when they started).

So why do I say 'Start by looking at yourself'? In a nutshell, because that is where the problem lies. Once again, going back to first principles, you decided before coming into this life what experiences you wanted to have in order to teach you the lessons you wanted to learn, so here you are, having them. However, once you have decided that the lesson has been learnt, then you can move on into another phase of your life, which will be something different. As I often say to people, when you had learnt your two-times table in Infants school, you didn't just stay there repeating the same work over and over again - you progressed to learning the threes, then the fours, and so on.

14: Changing

When you decide to look at yourself, do it thoroughly - and honestly - going back to your early childhood experiences and analysing what you felt. Then continue through your life, thinking about each remembered experience and, most of all, how it made you feel about yourself. The process, if it is to be thorough, will take quite a lot of time, so don't rush it. You have taken all your life to get into the situation in which you are at the moment, so you can't expect to change things in a few minutes of reflection.

Whether or not you want to change your life, it is always a very rewarding spiritual experience to look back on your life and to see which memories come back to you. It is interesting to realise that most (but not all) of the things we remember are the moments of great drama in our lives, our greatest joys or our deepest tragedies. In many cases, these moments will be associated with turning points in our lives: for instance, it is only at the death of a loved one that many people are brought up against the greatest mysteries of life itself - what is it all about, where did we come from, is there any sort of life after death, etc. In fact, Death is probably the best recruiter for Spiritualism, as many believers first came into the movement after the death of a loved one. In other cases, of course, our memories are associated with periods when everything in the garden seemed to be rosy, when life was at its best.

However, the process of looking back on all these memories, whether of happiness or tragedy, brings us to the same conclusion: the situation we faced at that time, and the emotions we felt, came to an end! In the case of the loss of a loved one, this does not mean that he/she came back, but it does mean that we eventually learned to cope with the situation. The old saying that 'Time is a great healer' comes to mind. When our memories were of a period of great happiness in our life that also came to an end as the conditions changed. Many people have wonderful memories of their honeymoon, but how many are in the same state of rapturous love ten (or in many cases just two) years after their marriage?

However long the period which we are remembering lasted, there was an end to it, because as one famous agony aunt has said, 'This also will pass'. So we have to face up to one of the inescapable facts of life, that nothing lasts forever. How you react to this depends on what sort of person you are, how optimistic or pessimistic, how positive or negative. The pessimist will always see the bottle as half-empty, and will concentrate on the fact that no happiness can ever be permanent: the optimist will see the bottle as half-full, and will realise that no period of stress or sorrow is never-ending.

Astrologically, no moment in time is ever the same as any other moment, and therefore the conditions of that moment can never be repeated. There are of course cycles in our life, when similar types of situations are presented to us and we are forced to make decisions again about them. However, by that time, surrounding conditions will have changed, and we can decide to move on, using what we have learnt in the past cycle to help us cope with the new conditions. In fact, this is of great advantage to us, as we are given the opportunity to show that we have *really* learned the lesson, so that it doesn't need to be repeated in the future. However, in many cases when we look back at ourselves we see that when faced with similar situations in the past, we have made exactly the *same* decision, which has had the same or similar results in bringing us more hardship and problems.

In this context, it is very interesting to look at the problem of abusive relationships. In so many of these, people - usually women - will endure abusive conditions for a long time, until eventually it becomes unbearable, and they get out of it by leaving the abuser. But very often, they will enter into another relationship, which soon turns out to be just as bad as - if not worse than - the first one.

I once heard of someone who, after a messy divorce, described a second marriage on a slightly cynical note as 'a triumph of Hope over Experience'. Fortunately, all second marriages aren't the same.

Notice that I haven't said anything about 'making mistakes'. From a spiritual point of view, there are no mistakes in life. When I was a boy, I remember my father saying to me that the biggest fool in life is the one who pays twice for the same experience - so never make the same mistake again. However, as I have grown older - and hopefully a little wiser - I have come to realise that when one suffers a second time from having made the same sort of decision, the spiritual reason is that one *hasn't* learned the lesson the first time - and therefore it is necessary to have another *chance* to learn it properly.

This gives a truer perspective of the meaning of the Law of Karma. I said that the crude way to look at it is as the Law of Punishment and Reward - we are punished for the bad things we have done in the past and rewarded for the good. However, the more enlightened way of looking at it is to realise that through the Law of Cause and Effect, every action we take has an effect - and the Law of Karma is there to give us the opportunity of seeing both sides of the coin. It allows us to experience the effects of our previous actions, and thereby to make spiritual progress when we see the whole picture. Then we realise at last that the saying 'Do unto others as you would want them to do unto you' really means 'Do unto others what *will* be done to you'.

Of course, once we have progressed to the state where we realise what the whole picture is, then we have no further need of the Law of Karma, and we can formally renounce it for all future lives - providing that we can make sure that for the rest of this life we don't do anything else to create even more Karma for ourselves!

I had the fact that we are given repeated lessons until we learn them brought home to me very dramatically some years ago. When I was being brought up, money was always very scarce, so I soon learnt the value of thrift and even to this day, I hate the thought of any form of waste. In adulthood I was acutely aware of how much money I was earning - and soon realised that there were things called 'perks' which could enhance the value of one's wages. One of these was Expenses, of course, and I got into the habit of slightly inflating my actual mileage to gain extra payments, or of slightly overstating the amount that had actually been spent on legitimate outlay. Although it was dishonest, I suppose that it was nothing more than many other people in the same situation have also done over the years. However, I soon realised that something strange was happening: From time to time, I found myself losing out, and actually receiving *less* than I was really entitled to - but at first I didn't see any pattern in what was happening.

Then something really dramatic happened: I had been made redundant from one company, from which I had a protected company pension, and had moved into Teaching, from which I would get an automatic Teacher's Pension. In order to inflate that pension, I took the opportunity of transferring my company pension rights into the Teachers Fund, reasoning that this would give me a greatly increased pension when I reached retirement. That in itself wasn't either illegal or immoral, but it was another action from the mind-set of optimising my income. It was only later that I found out, to my horror, that the only funds that had been transferred over were those which I personally had paid in over the years, and that the bulk of the funds (what the company had paid in) had been excluded. This meant that in trying to be greedy, with a stroke of the pen I had signed away the equivalent of £80 per week additional pension for the rest of my life. The experience meant that at last, I had learnt the lesson not to be greedy - and thereafter I have gone to the opposite extreme, and pay very little attention to money, realising that I will always have enough for my *needs* - although not necessarily for my *wants*. And strange to say, since I did that I have found that all my financial needs are always met.

When you look at yourself, the odds are that you don't really like what you see. Very few of us are completely satisfied with who we are: we can recognise all sorts of faults in ourselves, ranging from the way we look to the way we feel, from the type of person we are emotionally to the way we behave in the company of others. In short, we don't like ourselves. Is it surprising, therefore, that we may well find ourselves in relationships with others that are less than satisfactory? After all, if *we* don't like ourselves, why should anyone else like us?

When we look at ourselves and don't like what we see, we become unsure of ourselves, and that brings in the emotion of Fear. We believe that other people won't like us, and try to do something to compensate for that and to give ourselves a better chance of being liked. We may try several different ways of doing it: some people try to agree with everyone whom they meet, so that they can ingratiate themselves into their company. Others will try to make themselves indispensable, with the thought that if the other person feels that he/she cannot do without them, that will be the basis for a relationship. Many try to show how good they really are by becoming the clown of a group, and doing silly things to make others laugh. Still others will put on a mask of bravado and show off, with the aim of trying to make others envious of how skilful or intelligent they are. The problem with all these ploys is that they are very rarely successful, and even if the person is able to make relationships, they are not likely to be very lasting.

In later life, someone who is unfulfilled emotionally may well adopt a pet and lavish love and affection on it, in the certainty that it will be returned, but this rarely happens with young people. However, there is one final avenue that may be explored by someone of any age who is not

14: Changing

successful in making relationships, and that is 'comfort-eating'. When people over-eat in order to compensate for a lack of emotional fulfilment, they are likely to put on weight - and this becomes a reason for them to believe that they don't have any success in attracting others into a relationship. So having now got something to blame, they can over-eat out of self-pity, which makes them even fatter (and to their own minds less attractive) - and so the vicious circle carries on. The mirror-image of this is often found with girls, many of whom are convinced that they are already overweight, and starve themselves in order to get model figures in order to make themselves more attractive - but often end up with anorexia, looking like skeletons. Interestingly, boys hardly ever seem to suffer from this syndrome at all.

However, let us go further, and assume that someone who doesn't like him/herself does actually manage to enter into a relationship, which leads in adult life to partnership or marriage. That does not by itself mean that the relationship will be successful. In fact, in many cases it is a good indication that it *won't* be. Usually, the relationship is relatively happy for the first few years, but then starts gradually to go sour. In the early stages of a deep relationship, people in love tend to put their partners on a pedestal, and shut their eyes to faults which may be only too obvious to other observers, but after a time the differences between the two people will start to show.

Traditionally, the time when marriages or partnerships come under strain is after seven years - the notorious seven-year-itch - and this is based on sound astrological facts. The planet Uranus has an 84-year cycle around the Zodiac, which means that every seven years it will aspect its natal position from a different house of the person's natal chart, and highlight the conditions that applied in the natal chart. If one considers the position of Uranus at the start of the marriage/ partnership, then seven years later the original conditions will be brought into focus, and if things weren't ideal in the first place, the differences between the couple will be emphasised. If any problems can be sorted out at that stage, all will be well, but if not, the relationship could well break up. However, even if they manage to patch up an unsatisfactory relationship they will face another crisis, which will arise seven years further on - if they are still together.

A Practical Spiritual Primer

When I discussed this with Sybil, she confirmed that in her own marriage there was a major crisis fourteen years before her divorce. It was patched up, but not well enough to stop it recurring seven years later. Once more it was patched up, but the problems were not totally resolved, so that the third time when they occurred they led to the divorce.

Although I have said that the original position is aspected every seven years, it should be understood that this is an *average* of seven years: it could be as short as six-and-a-half or as long as seven-and-a-half, depending on when the planet turns retrograde (appears to move backwards in the zodiac).

The most dramatic example I ever had of this Uranus cycle was many years ago, and it happened to close friends of ours. The two people concerned were Basil and Helen. It is a very long story, but I will summarise it.

Helen was a work colleague of Eleanor's, and over six years we built up a close relationship with both her and her husband. Every Saturday night we would meet, at one or the other home alternately, where the lady of the house had cooked a meal, and then after dinner we played Canasta into the middle of the night. I was in the early days of my study of Astrology, and I had done horoscopes for both of them.

One Friday Basil rang us up and said, 'Don't come round tomorrow, Helen has left me'. We were staggered: they had always appeared to be a very close, deeply loving couple, and we couldn't have predicted a break-up, but Basil explained that Helen had run off with another man, and asked me if it could have been predicted from her horoscope.

I looked up the chart, and was horrified by what I saw: Uranus, badly aspected, was sitting in the middle of her house of Marriage, a normal sign of doomed relationships. I *should* have seen it, but I had let my friendship override my astrological knowledge (a common danger when trying to do a horoscope for a friend).

I confessed my failing, but I said that the same sort of thing had happened twice before, 14 and 7 years previously; Basil became most upset, admitted that it was true - the first time, when they were engaged, she had had an affair with a fellow student, and the other, after their marriage, was an affair with her driving instructor; both had taken place long before we met them - and, ashamed that I had unearthed skeletons from the family cupboard, Basil never spoke to us again.

14: Changing

But that wasn't the end of the matter: I predicted to Eleanor that the same sort of scenario would repeat itself over and over again in Helen's life: she would break up a stable relationship every 7 years. We never saw her again, but we had a mutual friend who kept us up-to-date with her news for the next 28 years, and the prediction came true. We finally lost touch with our friend when we moved down to Devon in 1986.

If Helen is still alive, I hope that she has learnt her lesson of relationships, as she must be well in her eighties by now!

This basic seven-year cycle caused by the movements of Uranus is compounded by the cycle of another far weightier planet - Saturn. Saturn is called the Great Teacher of the Zodiac, and he gives us *exactly* what we deserve. The problem is that so many people think that they deserve nothing - so that is exactly what Saturn gives them. If we believe that we deserve only the best in life, then we are working *with* Saturn - and are more likely to get it. Now Saturn takes on average 28-and-a-half years to go round the Zodiac, so comes back to his original position when we are round about the age of 28 - usually known as the Saturn Return - and that is a really important point in the life of everyone. It is a time when we are forced to look at what has been happening in the first part of our life, to see where we have made our 'mistakes' and to make plans for the next cycle. (My first Saturn Return came at the end of my Army career).

Of course, when we consider most marriages or partnerships, this is also the time when things are very likely to go wrong. By the time that people come to their late twenties they have usually settled into some sort of routine, and the newness has worn out of any relationship into which they may have entered. It takes only something to go dramatically wrong - or even something small to blow up out of all proportion - to make them start taking stock of where they are, and what they are doing. If both partners are able to face up to the problems that have arisen in the relationship, all may be well. If the difficulties are only patched up and not sorted out properly, then they are likely to re-emerge later on, when further flash points in life occur at 36, 43 (another major one) and round the age of 50. The latter two are often times of what is normally called a 'mid-life crisis'.

However, the really big one will be the second Saturn Return, between the ages of 57 and 59. (The spread in the times is due to the separate movements of Uranus and Saturn). Often it all starts off with a sudden dramatic incident (the Uranian effect) which makes the person involved acutely aware that there is a problem, and this leads to a comprehensive review of the whole of the life and - in many cases - a determination to change that life for the future. (The decisions made now will last until the next Saturn Return - but then, at the age of about 87, it is a bit late to do much about one's life). In my own case, the second Saturn Return coincided with the death of Eleanor; that certainly meant that I had to review the whole of my life - although for some time I was unable to even contemplate what the future might hold, let alone take any actual decisions what to do.

So let us imagine that you have started the process of self-examination, and you have identified problem areas in your life. You have realised that everything was meant for a purpose, and you have seen that you are today the result of all the conditioning that went on in your life in the past (and has continued into the present). What do you do now?

One of the most positive things that you can do is to realise that once you have learnt the lesson, there is no further need to carry on learning it, so that it is possible for you to release the experience that formed the learning process from your life. The problem is that most lessons are tied up with the people who came into our life to help us to learn them - and every time we think of those people, we are taken back to the original time when we were having the experiences that were teaching us those lessons. Therefore, we have to release the people at the same time as the experiences.

Let me here make a distinction between releasing the people connected with the experiences and cutting those same people out of our life altogether. Many of those from whom we learn our early lessons are still important in our life - possibly members of our own family - and we could not bear the thought of getting rid of them. However, everyone changes over the course of the years, and those same people are now almost certainly different from what they were in earlier years, when we were learning lessons from them. So what we are aiming to do is to release the memories of the person who was associated with the experiences of that time, and leave our everyday relationship with the person untouched.

There are several ways in which we can release a person from our life, mostly variations on the same theme. Each one involves some deliberate symbolic releasing of the tie, sometimes cutting it by scissors or a knife, sometimes by untying a rope or other attachment. One of the easiest is the following procedure:

Imagine that you are standing with the person on the banks of a slow-moving river, near to a boat tied up to a post on the bank. Remember the person as he/she was when giving you the lessons, and put him/her in the boat, filling the boat with the colour pink, signifying Love. See him/her totally surrounded by this colour until the boat appears to be overflowing with it. Hold this vision for a minute or so, then deliberately release the rope holding the boat to the bank, saying 'I bless you with Love: I release you and let you go'. Then watch as the boat slowly edges out into the current and goes downstream, finally disappearing into the distance.

A slight variation on the theme is for you to put the person in the basket of a hot-air balloon, fill it with pink light and having blessed and released him/her cast off the rope holding the balloon to the ground, and see it float away into the sky.

I personally use a more complex way, which ties the person and the experience in together, but which uses a lot more wording. I stand on a seashore with the person, look them in the eyes from three or four yards away, and then say the following words:

'I forgive you for all that you ever did or said which hurt me. I realise that everything was done for my own benefit - although I didn't know that at the time. I can now not only *forgive* you for what you did, but also *thank* you, as you helped to make me what I am today. I love you. I bless you with love, I release you and let you go'.

I then direct waves of Love at him/her, imagining them to be like waves of the sea washing against a sandcastle, and see that with each wave the outline of the body becomes fainter and fainter, until eventually it disappears completely, and I have released the person.

You may have to repeat the process several times, as the person may well be associated with many different memories of difficult lessons, but persevere: the benefits you will receive from getting rid of all of the traumatic experiences will far outweigh the tedium of going through the same routine repeatedly. In some cases, the stress of re-living the memories may be so great that you feel that you can release only one memory in a session, in others you may find that you can go through a series of them without difficulty. Just remember that each experience that you release is one less to hurt you in the future, and that should help you to be resolute in practising your routine.

From time to time, it will be of value for you to test yourself and see how successful you have been. You do this by thinking of people who have hurt you in the past and asking yourself how you feel about them now. If you do not feel any animosity, try to deliberately remember an incident in which they hurt you, and now see how you feel about them. If there is still no animosity, then you can reasonably assume that you have cleared out the problem: if, however, there is still a bit left, just clear that particular memory again.

After having successfully cleared out many of your past experiences, you should start to feel much happier, and considerably more sure of yourself as you face the future. After all, it is the equivalent of having carried a heavy rucksack full of stones on a journey, and then halting and deciding to take the stones out and throw them away, one by one, before you go forward again. Just think what a relief that would be physically, and translate it into spiritual terms.

Chapter 15: Bill's Journey

I was once talking to a client who was at a crucial stage in her life, and she mentioned the subject of predictions. She told me of a medium who had predicted some dire event to a member of her family if he ever bought a red car. Her son had just bought a new car - a red one - and she was terrified that the predicted event was now imminent.

I explained that we are continually creating our own future, and that whatever path we are on at the moment can be changed by a conscious effort of our own will. We are continually making choices, and depending what choice we make, a different set of conditions will come into our life. A medium can only see what is the most likely of these conditions *at that moment of time,* and say what he/she has seen, but if the conditions change then the original predictions become invalid. I am reminded of the story of Jonah in the Bible: Jonah was told to go to Nineveh and preach the destruction of the city and the death of all of its inhabitants, if they did not follow the word of God. However, the citizens did repent of their evil ways - and the city was not destroyed.

In the Bible, Jonah became very annoyed with God, because he felt that he had been made to look a fool. He had preached death and destruction and it hadn't happened. However, God explained that because the citizens had changed their ways, new conditions now existed, and the prediction had been invalidated.

When I was meditating this morning about this subject, I was given a simple little story to illustrate the same principle. It is about the journey of a man, Bill. (His sister, Jill, also made a similar journey at a different time, but for ease of writing, and to avoid having to say he/she and him/her continually, I will concentrate on Bill's journey).

A Practical Spiritual Primer

***

Bill lived in the countryside, and had had a very hard life. One day he said to himself, 'There must be a better way of earning a living than this: I am going to make my way to the Big City and seek my fortune'. So he sold all his possessions, put the money he had accumulated over the years into a big bag, and started out to walk to the Big City, which was a long way away. He had not gone very far when he met one of his old friends, who asked him where he was going. Now this old friend had a local reputation of being a wise man, and when he heard that Bill was going on a long journey, he warned him against it. 'Don't go across any fields', he said, 'or else you will be gored to death by a mad bull in one of them'. Bill was quite disconcerted by this, but he had now sold up all of his possessions and it was a bit too late to turn back, so he carried on.

At first, Bill was very aware of the prediction, so he made a point of not crossing any fields, and just walked on paths round them. Then the paths ended, and he was totally surrounded by fields, so he had to make the decision either to cross one or to go back. Well, it was too late to go back now, so he crossed the field in front of him, looking nervously round all the time to see if there were any bulls in the vicinity. However, all went well, and he reached the other side of the field without any problem - and there he was faced with another field, and the same decision.

A little reassured by the fact that he had survived so far, he set off across this field, then the next - and so on, getting a little bolder each time, until eventually he had almost forgotten the prediction. Finally, he saw a big field in front of him at the other side of the hedge of the field he was crossing, and as he went out of the gate of the field he was in, he found that there was, in fact, quite a broad path leading down, in between the two fields. By now he had had enough of walking across fields, which was hard work, so on the spur of the moment he decided to take the path, which seemed to lead in the general direction of where he wanted to go - and in so doing he avoided a dangerous bull which was dozing in the shade, at the other side of the field which he would have crossed!

It was a lot easier walking on the path, and even easier when it widened into a farm track. He started to make good progress, but suddenly met an old woman, who asked him where he was going. He explained that he was on a journey to seek a better life, and she warned him not to go this way, as he would be run down by a tractor and killed if he did. This upset

15: Bill's Journey

him at first, but he remembered that the original prediction about the bull hadn't come true, so he took heart and went on his way. After a while, he came to a small village, and when he was on the outskirts, he saw that the track seemed to turn away from the village at a corner a hundred yards in front of him, and not go through the centre. However, twenty yards before the corner there was a small path which led off to the right and appeared to go into the village, so on the spur of the moment he decided to take it - and turned off just in time to escape a large tractor, which came round the corner at great speed, and which would almost certainly have killed him had he stayed on the original track.

When he got into the village, he found that there was a small shop that sold bicycles, so, as he had tired of walking, he decided to buy one, and set off happily down a lane. He hadn't gone very far when he saw a gipsy lady, who asked him where he was going. Bill told her, but the lady said, 'Don't go anywhere on a bicycle, as I can see you being knocked over by a car and killed'. Bill wondered what to do, but as he had already bought the bicycle, it seemed a pity not to use it, so he rode off resolutely down the lane.

He was joined by another cyclist after a while, and they chatted happily as they rode along together, side by side, until they came to a fork in the road. They debated which way would be best, and the other cyclist decided to take the road to the left. Bill however decided to go to the right, so they said their farewells and parted. Bill was never to know that the other cyclist was killed, half a mile further on, by a car which came round a bend towards him and skidded onto the wrong side of the road.

After a time Bill came to a small town, and rode past a used car company. By now, he was feeling a bit saddle-sore, as he hadn't ridden a bicycle since he was a lad. Cycling to the big city didn't seem as good an idea as it had done originally, so he wondered whether he would have enough money to buy a used car. He went in and spoke to the owner of the company, and ended up by handing over his new bicycle and a large amount of money to buy a decrepit-looking old car. Just as he was about to drive off, an old man saw him and said to him, 'If you go onto the motorway in that car, you will be killed in an accident'. However, Bill was used to predictions like this not coming true, so he just ignored it and drove off up the road. He did keep to ordinary roads for a while, but then saw a sign for the motorway and couldn't resist turning in that direction, reasoning that it would be far quicker than just going along the ordinary roads.

He made good time along the motorway, but suddenly heard ominous noises coming from the engine, and realised that something was seriously wrong. At the next exit, he turned off the motorway and went into a small town. He never heard of the thick bank of fog a couple of miles further up the motorway, which had caused chaos and many deaths in multiple accidents that day when drivers ran into it, slowed down and were hit by cars or lorries coming up too fast behind them.

Bill was told that the car wasn't worth repairing, so he decided to go to the Big City by train and went to the local station. As he was waiting for the train, he got into conversation with a lady, who told him that she often had prophetic dreams, and a dream the night before had warned her about riding in the front carriage of a train. She was told that the train would be involved in an accident, and all the passengers in the front carriage would be killed. When the train came, it was packed - apart from the front carriage, which was half-empty. The woman went to stand in one of the carriages at the back, but by now Bill scorned all predictions, and went to sit in the front carriage.

After an hour or so, the train stopped at a station, and Bill decided to get off while the train was waiting at the platform and get a newspaper and a coffee, but there was a long queue in the snack bar, and when he got back to the platform, the train had just left without him. Round the next sharp bend in the line, the front carriage of the train came off the rails, and an express coming the other way ran into it, smashing it to pieces and killing all the passengers riding in it. None of the other carriages were harmed.

Instead of waiting for the next train, Bill decided to travel the last few miles to the Big City by bus, and this he did without incident. He was fairly successful in the city, as he soon found a job, met a lady of his own age whom he eventually married, and had a fairly happy life. Many years later, in old age, he happened to be talking to a clairvoyant, who told him that he was a very lucky man. 'No I'm not', said Bill, 'I have never had the slightest bit of luck at all in my life. And don't you try making any predictions for me, as they never come true'!

Chapter 16: Death

One of the most abiding mysteries of this human life of ours is the age-old question of 'What happens after Death?' This is linked to questions like 'Where did we come from before this life?' and 'What is it all about anyway?' but the latter two do not seem to have as much effect on us as the first. The second is less important in our minds because anyone can accept the fact that we *are* here, so it doesn't really matter anyway, whereas it is only at times of stress in our lives that we are likely to ask the third.

Apart from the passing of relatives, I myself have had several personal experiences of the mystery of Death, one of which was the following: Joan was a very dear old lady, who was a good friend to Sybil and myself, and was one of the most spiritual people whom I have ever met. She had had a bout of a kind of 'flu, and appeared to be recovering well from it, so much so that when her daughter went in to see her one Saturday night she said that she was looking forward to being up and about soon. The daughter left, saying that she would phone her the next morning, but Joan said, 'Don't phone before 10 o'clock, as I am going to have a lie-in'. In fact, when the daughter phoned the next morning, there was no reply, so she contacted the landlady, who lived on the same premises. The landlady went in to check on Joan, and found that she was dead in her bed. Her doctor thought that she must have had a heart attack in her sleep, as her face was totally peaceful and showed no signs of distress. It was a wonderful way to go, but a great shock to all of us who had no inkling that it was even a possibility.

A comforting sequel to the story is the fact that Joan was a very powerful healer, and has already made her presence felt to several of her mediumistic friends, one of whom saw her at the wake following the funeral. She was going from group to group, listening to everyone saying nice things about her - and appeared to be quite frustrated because she (literally) couldn't get a word in edgeways.

In a previous chapter, I have mentioned the subject of how soon a person can come back after the death of the physical body, but for purposes of emphasis, I will now enlarge on the theme. The time that it takes someone to come back after their physical death will depend on two things: the first is their state of physical and mental/emotional health (how *ill* they are) up to the time of death and the second is their state of awareness of the fact that they are immortal. Let me expand a little on those two things:

There are many ways of meeting death, some of which are very slow and painful, and others that are extremely quick and - relatively - painless. Just take the example of someone who has been bedridden for many years, during which time not only the physical body but also the mind has grown progressively weaker, and this has been combined with the emotional despair which has set in. When such a person eventually leaves this physical life he/she will need a prolonged period of rest and recuperation before being ready to 'wake up' and start to enjoy the benefits of the new life in what is often called 'the Summerland'. This period will be needed not for the body to heal, but for the soul to heal, and may last for weeks or months of our time - although time as we understand it does not exist on the other side of life. Eleanor had been ill for almost a year before she passed, and the last few months must have been absolute Hell for her, knowing that despite the efforts of everyone the end was inevitable. So, although she was certainly spiritually aware, it did take six weeks before she was able to come back fully.

Compare that with the case of someone who dies without any apparent physical illness being present at all before the event. This is more common than most people recognise: accidents of all kinds happen every day, particularly road accidents or accidents when people are at work or while travelling by train or aeroplane. Daily we hear of disasters somewhere in the world, some natural and some man-made, which cause death to many people. Some deaths are horrific, but some are very peaceful, such as cases of families going to bed at night and being all killed by a blocked flu in a gas central heating system, which caused a build-up of lethal carbon monoxide.

16: Death

In addition, from time to time we hear of 'Sudden Adult Death Syndrome' cases, where apparently healthy adults, including many who were athletes or sportsmen/women, have suddenly died without warning and without any known illness at all. In all these sorts of cases those concerned do not need any prolonged period of rest and recuperation - they are immediately aware of their surroundings.

A good example of this was my late father-in-law (from my second marriage): he was sitting up in a hospital bed talking to my wife and her daughter, when suddenly he gave a little gasp - and was gone. Sybil had often talked to her mother about spiritual philosophy, and from time to time the old man had listened in, but as a down-to-earth working man from Burnley, in Lancashire (born under the earthy sign Capricorn), he had never had any truck with life after death or all that rubbish - so he was certainly not prepared for what happened. However, as befitted a very practical man, he found a way to come back to my wife through a medium after only about a week, and said, 'One minute I was sitting up in bed, talking to you, the next I found myself above the bed, looking down on myself and wondering why the devil you were both crying'.

Another example is that in 2012 my mother-in-law, a wonderful woman whom everyone loved dearly, died following a fall in which she broke her hip. She was in hospital for only a week before eventually succumbing to pneumonia. The next night she appeared in a teaching circle run by a friend, who is one of Canada's leading mediums, and gave the message 'Tell Sybil that I have arrived and I am alright'.

In most cases, however, the fact that someone does not need a period of rest and recuperation doesn't mean to say that they realise what has happened - that depends on their level of spiritual awareness before they died. Let us imagine the case of two separate groups of people: the first group is completely aware of the reality of the survival of the soul after the physical death, and realise what has happened almost immediately after they pass over. They already know that their loved ones on the other side are there to greet them, and in their final conscious moments they walk towards the Light and many joyful reunions take place. The only thing that is now necessary for such people to do is to find out how to make contact with the loved ones back on Earth in order to comfort them and assure them that they (the dear departed) are still all right. There have been very many documented cases where such people have actually attended their own funeral and have tried to lighten the suffering of grieving relatives (as did my mother-in-law, who was seen with two of her sisters - long-deceased - doing a 'Three Degrees' dance routine in front of the coffin)!

In the other group, the people have no knowledge of the possibility of survival, so after the physical death they find that they still exist but have no idea of what has happened to them, where they are or why those to whom they speak take no notice of them. They may remember the events leading up to their death, but nothing else. In fact, they don't realise that they are dead at all (which of course, from a spiritual viewpoint, they aren't). Sooner or later, of course, they will realise it, when they are able to see those loved ones who have gone before, who are there to welcome them and to take them away into the Light, where they can be taught how to cope with this new existence.

The fact that our loved ones on the other side are waiting for us when we pass over was shown to me dramatically when my father died in 1974. Eleanor and I had been sitting by his bedside, when suddenly I heard the names of people being called out. The only one that I could recognise was that of his mother, Susannah, although I verified those of the others later. Then I realised what was happening: someone was calling the roll of those who were gathering to welcome him back home - and I became very emotional. However a voice said to me, 'No tears - only joy'. Then a feeling of utter peace came over me, and my father's tortured breathing calmed down. A few minutes later he passed. I remember going out into the dark starlit night and being absolutely ecstatic, looking up at the stars and feeling that I was completely at one with the Universe - and that all was well: everything was happening exactly as it was meant to happen. It was perhaps a strange reaction, but such an intense experience that the vivid memory has remained with me to this day, forty years later.

Some of the saddest cases of all are the people who are so convinced that physical death means the complete extinction of the personality that they refuse to accept the loved ones who come to help them, and remain in a sort of grey limbo, a prison of their own making, until they can be helped by the prayers of others to gradually come to a true understanding of what Life and Death are all about. Many Spiritualists, as a labour of Love, undertake to help such people and sit in what are called 'Rescue circles' to help them to move on into the Light. I have sat in many such circles, and have experienced the joy that such poor souls feel on being released from ages of torment. In common speech, they have been in Hell - but the Hell has been only the state of their own mind.

This is not to be taken as implying that such people are wicked. They have been in that self-imposed Hell because of their own pre-conceived ideas that that is where they would be, separated from any form of contact with anyone else, and effectively 'dead'. In the physical world, thoughts are slow to manifest as facts, whereas the next phase of existence is in a dimension where thought becomes fact almost instantly. So therefore, having created the 'nothingness' of their own private Hell they then *live* in it, until they realise that they are able to move on.

I am reminded of a story told to me by a friend who is a powerful medium. It might be regarded as amusing, if it were not for the fact that it is so tragic. This friend was in Malta when she saw a funeral procession going into a local church and went in to join the congregation. Now normally, whenever there is a funeral, while all the mortal loved ones of the deceased gather in the church to pay their respects, they are also joined by the loved ones from the other side, who are welcoming the deceased 'back home'. However, in this particular case there was no one from the other side at all!

Curious to know why this was, my friend went psychically into the crypt of the church, and found a group of souls clustered round one who had obviously been a priest. She asked them why they were there, and was told that they were afraid to go anywhere else, as they were dead. She urged them to make their way into the Light, as there was no longer any need for them to stay on the earth, but when they consulted the priest, he said that it would be better if they stayed where they were until they had confirmation from the local Archbishop that it was all right to move on. So stay there they did! I hope that the Archbishop was a bit more enlightened when he finally passed, so that they could be released from their own self-imposed Hell.

A similar thing happens to those who are so tied to their physical possessions in this life that they cannot bear to be separated from them on death - so they remain in the same house, which eventually gets the reputation of being haunted. Most of these souls are harmless: they remain there, not realising that they are no longer of this world, but getting more and more frustrated when they see other human beings using and enjoying the things which they still think are 'theirs'. However, in some cases they start to disturb the new inhabitants, and then they have to be dealt with.

Clare, Sybil and I have often been called out on 'ghost-busting' missions, (properly called 'rescue work',) to try to rid a building of the presence of someone who is upsetting the family now living in the haunted house. The vast majority of souls who are earthbound are still here simply because they do not realise that they have passed, and/or they do not know that they have the power to move on when *they* decide to. In these cases, Clare contacts them, explains what has happened and then directs them towards where their loved ones are invariably waiting to take them away into the Light, where they will learn how to adjust to their new life. In some cases all that is necessary is to tell them to turn round and look towards the Light: when they do so they always see the loved ones waiting to welcome them.

In other cases, the souls realise what has happened, but are quite happy to remain where they are and take pleasure in watching the activities of the new families in the house - particularly when there are young children there. We were once called to a house where the family had felt a presence in several rooms, and in the kitchen we found the soul of a lovely old grandma type of lady. We found out that she had never been able to have any children of her own, but had always loved having children round her - and was now enjoying being with the six children in the family of the present inhabitants of the house, several of whom could 'see' her. In another case, the former owner of the house was fascinated with electrical devices of all kinds, and particularly mobile phones, which he used to spirit away. He was also very fond of switching electrical appliances on and off. He had to be told that there was no longer any need for him to remain attached to the house, and he could move on if he wished: however, if he chose to stay then he was told quite firmly that disturbing the resident family was not acceptable behaviour.

There are occasionally some souls who are actively upsetting the household out of pure malice, and these have to be removed in a more forcible way. It is usually Clare - as a fully-fledged medium - who does the exorcism, while Sybil and I generate the spiritual power to help her - and I have been present at many battles between Clare and souls who refuse to release their hold on their house. They have to admit defeat

16: Death

eventually of course - the power of Light will always prevail against every form of darkness.

It may be strange to read of loved ones from the other side welcoming back someone who has just died - but that is exactly what happens. So let us examine the whole subject of Birth and Death at the same time:

Let us start at the stage where a soul has decided to incarnate again. It has decided what lessons are to be learnt in the incarnation and what sex is most appropriate for it to assume - and has sorted out the parents and environment which will be appropriate to give the experiences to teach the lessons. All that needs to be done now is to bid farewell to all the friends and loved ones in that other dimension and make the journey into the foetus already growing within the chosen mother, in time for the birth to take place.

At this stage, I must tell an amusing story which was once told to me by a very famous medium. She had been called to the hospital bedside of a young mother-to-be, who had been in labour for two or three days, and despite all the efforts of medical staff the actual birth process could not be started. My friend was asked if there was anything she could do. She contacted the incoming soul (a male) psychically, and asked him why he was giving his future mother such a hard time. He replied that he was having such a good time with all his friends at his leaving party that he wasn't ready to be born yet. So my friend told him that if he wasn't very quick, they would put a pair of forceps into the womb and would drag him out by the head, which would be very painful. The message must have got home, because two hours later he was born with no problem whatsoever!

Now when we come into incarnation in this world, we are actually coming into an existence where we are severely limited and restricted in our abilities, compared with those that we had when we were still in the other dimension. In that dimension, we had only to think that something existed and it immediately came into being, or ask how to do something, and we would know immediately!

In our world, of course, there is a huge difference between thinking of what we would like to happen and actually being able to make it happen. Just think of the problems you might have if you were put in the seat of a machine of some sort - and had to learn to drive it without any instruction manual. Such problems are simple compared with the ones a soul faces when coming into the body of a baby. Not only that, but in this life we have to undergo all the lessons and experiences which we have chosen, some of which will be traumatic. So for the incoming soul it is really similar to going away to a sort of Boarding School (many Spiritualists call this world 'the schoolhouse of learning') and leaving all our friends and relatives behind.

As far as those friends and relatives whom we are leaving are concerned, there is not a lot which they can do while we are away learning our lessons, apart from sending their love to us and, if we are spiritually aware, giving their support and encouragement by coming to us either directly or through a medium from time to time. However, when we get to the end of our life on this planet, they are there to welcome us back home, and they celebrate the date of the homecoming in the same way that we on Earth celebrate the date of our original birthday. This is why Spiritualist mediums often talk about an anniversary being celebrated, and make no distinction between what we would consider a happy anniversary (a birthday or wedding day) and an unhappy one (a death).

I have said that we choose the lessons we wish to learn in this life, but there is a corollary or flip side to this: we are *not* allowed to go back home until we have learnt all those lessons. I had a very dramatic example of this in my own life:

It was Christmas Eve 1984, and I was in my mother's flat. Every Christmas season after the death of my father ten years before she had come over to stay with us for four or five days, and I had gone to get her as usual. However, this time she said, 'I have decided that I am going to stay here this Christmas, instead of coming to you'. I was a bit surprised, but not unduly worried: after all, she had everything she needed in the flat - she always kept enough supplies in to last for at least a fortnight - so I just stayed for half an hour or so and chatted to her. Just before I left, she said something amazing: 'I have been thinking, you know: perhaps it wasn't *all* your fathers fault'. I couldn't believe my ears: for the last fifty years of my life she had impressed on me, at every opportunity, that all the problems in her marriage had been caused by my father - and now she was saying that perhaps they weren't. I left her, promising that I would look in to see her at some time after Boxing Day.

When I got back home, I told Eleanor what Mother had said. 'Don't be stupid', she said 'You must have misheard her'. And despite my protestations, she remained unconvinced. The morning after Boxing Day

16: Death

I had a phone call from my sister, to say that she was at Mother's flat, and that Mother was very ill. I dashed over and found her slumped on the settee, almost falling off. Sylvia had called an ambulance, and I cradled Mother in my arms, where she died before the ambulance men arrived.

Looking back on her death, I believe that she had *had* to come to terms with her relationship with my father before she was allowed to go home. She had frequently felt his presence psychically during the time since his passing, and presumably had been able to reflect on all the things that had happened during their long marriage (a few months short of fifty years). So during those last two days she was able to make her peace with herself, forgive him and at the same time forgive herself. Then, once she had reached the moment when she was able to say to me that it hadn't all been his fault, she had shown that she had learnt that last lesson, and was *allowed* to go.

Looked at from a purely spiritual viewpoint, the object of any soul ever coming into incarnation on this planet is to experience what it is like to be bound into a physical existence, with all the limitations that entails. Therefore, in order to prepare ourselves to be able to tolerate such an existence, we deliberately close down our memories of what life is like in the perfection to which we have been accustomed in our previous existence, and allow ourselves to be convinced that life in the physical body is all that there is. We therefore get into the strange position of believing that Reality is the temporary state in which we live on this planet, rather than the permanent state of our true existence.

Furthermore, if we want to experience what human life really is, we have to experience all of it, the good and the bad, the pleasant and the unpleasant. This means that during the overall period of our earthly lives (several hundred of them) we will explore the extremes of delight and despair - and everything in between. How can we ever truly appreciate 'light', when we have never known 'darkness', or 'happiness' without ever having known what 'sadness' is? There is even an old saying, that 'You never appreciate what you have got until you lose it'. Conversely, of course, once someone has suffered greatly in early life, and things start to become better later on, they are more able to enjoy what they have than someone who has never known hardship at all.

As we get further on through our spiritual journey we have had more and more experiences, and become more able to recognise what other people are suffering in their own lives. Whenever we are very strongly affected by the sights or stories of the misfortunes of others, we are *empathising* with them. This is not the same as *sympathising*: sympathy is feeling sorry for someone, empathy is putting yourself in their place - and you can only ever do this if you have been in that position yourself, either in this life or in a previous one. However, never fall into the trap of saying to someone, 'I know how you feel'. You don't! No one ever knows how another person is feeling: although we may have been through an identical experience, our physical, mental and emotional constitution is unique, and can never be the same as anyone else - so therefore we cannot know *exactly* what they are suffering at any one time.

The idea of choosing our lessons in life causes a great deal of difficulty for some people. 'Why', they say, 'should I have ever wanted to choose such a miserable existence as I have now, if I had had the choice originally? I might have just as well chosen to be rich or famous, whereas now I am poor and a mere nobody'. Well, let us consider the following analogy:

Imagine that you have a burning ambition to be a doctor, for which you need an 'A' Level in Chemistry, amongst other subjects. You take your exams at school and fail dismally at Chemistry, but do very well at Art, which is your favourite subject. You now decide to enrol at a College of Further Education what would you apply to study, Art or Chemistry?

Well, there wouldn't be much point enrolling on an Art course, would there? However much you like the subject, and however good you are at it, it won't be the slightest good in helping you to achieve your ambition to be a doctor. So, although you don't really like the subject you decide to enrol on a Chemistry course, and to stick at it until you have the appropriate level that will allow you to start studying for your medical degree. It may take several years of very hard work to do, but the final result will bring you a great deal of happiness, and the satisfaction that you were able to achieve what you set out to do.

So it is with our personal life-plans. We have had the benefit of being able to see all our lives to date before we came into this incarnation, and based on that information *we* have made our choice. The fact that now, from a human viewpoint, we can't remember those past lives or even remember having made the decision in the first place, doesn't mean that it hasn't happened. Of course, as we progress spiritually, we are

16: Death

progressively more able to understand what has gone on, and looking back, more able to realise that what we did has worked out for the best. As I have said before, it is often only long after the traumas of our lives that we realise that things did eventually work out to our advantage.

Having said that, though, there are some things that as human beings we can never be expected to forget and forgive, and the most horrific of these is where another human being has taken away the life of someone we loved dearly. Such was the case with the hundreds of people who were affected by the deaths of the victims of Dr Shipman and of the victims of any murderer. However spiritual we may be, some actions are so non-human that we are at a total loss to comprehend how they could happen. In such cases only someone at the Christ level of consciousness, or at least at the Saint level, could be capable of forgiveness - and there are not very many people in the world who are at that level yet.

Chapter 17: Children

It is a strange fact of human nature that when we talk about spiritual philosophy, we tend to forget all the rules when it comes to children. However much we know, and however spiritually developed we are, the logic doesn't seem to fit - and there is nothing more likely to 'throw us' than when we are faced with a child being hurt, or even worse, losing his/her life.

We may well understand that we all come into life with a set number of experiences in mind, each of which will teach us certain lessons, and we may even accept that when things are really rough in our lives we are going through the learning process which we ourselves have decided on. We may be able to look back on our lives and see that we were conditioned in childhood to start the pattern of behaviour which has dogged us all our life, and accept that it was all done for a purpose. However, if we see a child suffering, then we immediately start to question the whole process, forgetting that we were once children ourselves.

This feeling may be triggered by TV images of starving children in the Sudan, Syria or other crisis parts of the world, by pictures of children wounded and maimed in war-torn countries or by the filming of children with special needs, handicapped physically or mentally, such as we see during some of the programmes connected with the annual 'Children in Need' appeal. Television has the immediate visual effect that gives it the edge over radio or newspapers: there is nothing quite as moving as watching footage of natural disasters, war-torn areas or appalling personal tragedies while you are sitting in the warmth and comfort of your own home. We are affected deeply by seeing the images of children who have been subjected to extreme cruelty (sometimes leading to their deaths) at the hands of parents or step-parents, the very people who are supposed to be looking after them. Finally, possibly the most traumatic of all, we follow the daily dramas of children who have been lost or abducted from their homes, and grieve with the parents when, all too often, those children are later found dead. At times like these, we are often driven to ask the age-old question, 'How can there be a God, if He allows such things to happen?'

Let me say first of all that there is never any excuse for hurting children, much less deliberately torturing them, and to take the life of a child is one of the worst of all crimes. Those who do this are showing that they do not realise that whenever they harm others, either directly or indirectly, they will suffer the same at the hands of others, whether in the current life or a future one - and by taking advantage of the vulnerability of a child they will also be harmed when they themselves are at their most vulnerable.

When we talk about choosing what happens to us in life, it has to be continually emphasised that the choice is *not* made while we are acting out our lives as human beings, but long before we came into incarnation - and unless or until this distinction is made and understood then every attempt to explain tragedies which happen to children is totally futile. No child will ever consciously and deliberately choose to be hurt, any more than an adult will, and even those adults who are very spiritually advanced, and realise that everything which happens has its spiritual purpose, would hesitate before actively seeking torture and/or death. That is why the lives of so many Saints who have died rather than renounce their faith are so remarkable. So what are we saying when we talk about making the choice?

Let us go back to first principles, and say that each of us is a glorious spiritual being, and a mature spiritual being at that. We were before we came into incarnation, and we chose the conditions of our life that would give us the experiences we need, in order to learn the spiritual lessons we have chosen for the stage of development at which we are. When we come into incarnation, only a minute part of that glorious spiritual being actually enters the human body as the soul: the entity which is the majority of it remains in the Higher Dimension from which the soul came, directing the events of the life, and we call that entity the 'Higher Self'.

The soul is then born into the body of a baby, because that is how life begins for all humans. (There is actually one exception to this rule, but I will leave discussion of that until later). So however spiritually advanced we are, we all go through the same process of being babies. Most of those who come into incarnation as babies will, of course, grow up into human adults, but some of them will have chosen to be in incarnation for only a short time, in order to carry out specific tasks: the shorter the physical life is, the more likely it is that the tasks are to give the *parents* particular experiences, rather than for the children to have experiences themselves.

Now none of us knows the spiritual path of another person, nor can we possibly know, unless we are one of those highly advanced beings who are able to read the 'Akashic Record' of another. (The 'Akashic records' are kept in the next dimension up from us, and are records of everything which has ever happened in the history of the world. The record of an individual will tell the complete story of that person's journey through all his/her incarnations: it is therefore not surprising that the only beings who are permitted to access those records are the ones who are already so advanced spiritually that they would never consider using access for any non-spiritual reason. None of us, therefore, is ever likely to be able to know what the purpose of any soul was when it came into this incarnation, why it chose the lessons it wanted to undergo or what it wanted to achieve. On a spiritual level, that would be the equivalent of reading someone else's personal mail - and so is definitely taboo.

If the soul decided that its purposes could be achieved in a short incarnation, who are we to say that it was wrong? We are looking at the situation with merely human eyes, and making a human judgement about a spiritual matter. We somehow equate long life with spiritual value, and if a human life is cut off in its prime, we deplore it as a waste. In truth, however, the situation is usually the opposite: when we hear people talking about a child whose life has been cut short in any way, whether by illness, accident or by the deliberate action of another human being, we very often find that the child is described in glowing terms as an 'angel', 'lovely child', or as someone who 'brought happiness to everyone who met him/her'. In fact, such children are very advanced souls, who have been able, during their short life, to touch the hearts of many others, and to leave them with happy memories. Someone once described this as 'leaving footprints on the hearts of others'. In this context it is interesting to note that in the part of the West Midlands where I was brought up there was - and probably still is - a saying that 'The best go first and the worst are left to mend'.

17: Children

From a spiritual viewpoint, we come into incarnation with our agenda of what we want to do, and once we have achieved all our goals *we are allowed to go back home*. This applies whether our earthly journey is one of a hundred years or only a hundred minutes. By the very act of coming into incarnation, we change the reality of many lives - and in some cases that is the sole objective of that life.

Many years ago there was a series on television called 'That's Life', which ran for so many years that it seemed that it would be a permanent part of the television scene. In one of the episodes, the tragic story of Anthony Nolan was told. Anthony had a very rare disease, and his only hope of a cure was by means of a bone marrow transplant - if a suitable donor could be found. Regrettably, there was no existing organisation that could be called on to provide a bank cf bone marrow samples to be used for comparison with Anthony's own marrow, in the hope of finding a perfect match. We all watched with horror over the months as Anthony, a beautiful little boy, slowly became more and more ill, and a whole nation mourned with his parents when he finally succumbed to the disease.

However, his death was not in vain: spurred on by the lack of facilities which led to it, an organisation was set up to provide a 'National Bone Marrow Bank' of samples, and this in turn led to the situation where today the chances of another child surviving the disease which Anthony had (and also many other similar diseases) have been dramatically increased. So this remains a permanent memorial to a very brave little boy, who achieved more in his few years of life than most human beings ever achieve, even if they live to a ripe old age.

A particularly poignant occurrence from a human point of view is when a baby is carried to term by its mother, but is then stillborn. This happened on one occasion in my family: David, my youngest son, and his wife Lesley already had a daughter and were looking forward to the birth of their second child, a son; on the date the baby was due Lesley hadn't started in labour, so she was sent back home for the weekend from hospital, and told that the labour would be induced, if necessary, on the following Monday. However, when she went back to hospital on Monday it was found that the baby had died in the womb over the weekend - and Lesley had the trauma of having to go through labour knowing that the baby was already dead.

A Practical Spiritual Primer

It is difficult to know what the spiritual objective in such circumstances would be. The soul did not in fact incarnate, and hardly touched the earth at all, so it could not have gained physical experience from the event. It is probable, therefore, that it was all to do with the spiritual progression of its parents, both of whom were 'Born Again Christians' - possibly a test of their faith? As I said, we cannot evaluate the reason for such an event within the life of another - we can only send our love to those concerned in their hour of need. However, in the case of my son and his wife, where others may have been put off the thought of trying to have another child, they went ahead, and Lesley gave birth to another lovely baby girl who brought light and love into the lives of all whom she touched, and is now a very beautiful and gifted young woman.

I mentioned that there is one rare set of circumstances in which a soul does not incarnate in the body of a baby. This is called the phenomenon of 'Walk-in', and happens when a very advanced soul wants to come into existence in this world as an adult, usually to do some high-level spiritual work that will benefit humanity. In the 'Cosmic Clearing House' where Higher Selves are arranging the patterns of life of future human beings, an arrangement is made in which one soul will come into incarnation and live a normal life, then will leave it at an appropriate time. However, rather than the body being abandoned and then dissolving into its constituent parts, as normally happens on death, it is used by the advanced soul, who 'walks-in' and takes over the physical body, while retaining all his/her own spiritual attributes.

The most convenient time for such an event to take place is when the first person is faced with a life-threatening situation, either through an accident or an illness, and relapses into a coma, during which he/she makes his/her transition. Then, during the comatose state, when the body is still alive, although there is no mental or emotional human activity, the second soul can make its entrance and has a certain length of time to acclimatise before the body is eventually resuscitated. Not surprisingly, when this finally happens, the new soul is not likely to recognise any of the friends or relatives who congregate round the bed - and has to start from scratch getting to know his/her new family.

There have been hundreds of documented 'walk-ins', and all of them follow a similar pattern, telling the stories of people who find themselves among strangers and have to start to get to know the whole

17: Children

history of their life from scratch, before they can be integrated into their new human family. Just imagine what it must be like to have to step down your own personal vibrations, accept the limitations that come from being in a physical rather than a mental world and entering an alien body *as an adult*; imagine having to learn how to control this body's various physical functions and then in a short time having to learn the names and relationships of a whole lot of new people, all of whom appear to know you already. But so many people have done it - and remember it - that there is now an International Society devoted to maintaining contacts between people who have had such experiences. It is called 'Walk-ins for Evolution', and has its own web site for those interested in learning more about the subject. The most famous modern 'walk-in' was an American woman called Ruth Montgomery, who wrote a book about her experiences. Another man who wrote a series of very influential spiritual books about fifty years ago was a Tibetan monk, Lobsang Rampa; he also had a comparable experience, which he describes in detail in one of his books.

When we talk about premature deaths - or what we consider as premature, as they happen before the age when people normally die - the shock of losing a loved one is not confined to those who lose a child. When there are natural or man-made disasters, many people of all ages are killed, and the grief felt by their relatives is just as great as that felt by those who lose a child. However, looked at from a spiritual perspective, what has happened in that case is that an opportunity has occurred for the soul to make its transition back home - and it has taken it. Once more, the decision of the soul has nothing to do with a conscious decision of the human being, who may well have been in the full flush of adulthood with the prospects of a splendid and fulfilling life in front of him/her. The soul has responded to a reminder by the Higher Self that it is time to go back, as it has finished the tasks for which it came into incarnation - and it has done so.

When such a thing happens, and an 'untimely' death takes place, we are all reminded of the frailty of human life, and are brought back with a shock to a consideration of what our priorities are. A biblical story puts this in context, and tells of a man who was making great plans for the enlargement of his farm by building new barns and storehouses, not realising that he would be dying that very night. How many times have we been faced with the shock of the sudden passing of a loved one, and have regretted that we did not spend more time with, or express more love to, the person concerned? As the pace of life seems to become ever more frantic, and we all become more materialistic, perhaps we are in danger of forgetting what the object of it all is - to interact as human beings with those whom we meet during life, and by that interaction to learn what it is like to be human. Perhaps we need the occasional shock of losing someone whom we know or love to bring us back to reality.

Perhaps we could set aside some fixed time in the year (and why not Christmas?) to remember that none of us will be on this Earth permanently, and as we don't know how long any of our family or friends still have to live before making their transition we could for a short period do everything we can to express our love for them - including patching up old disputes and differences. In that way, when they are no longer there, we would have less guilt and remorse to cope with.

I end this chapter about children on a more positive note. On numerous occasions over the last fifty years, I have been in the congregation of a Spiritualist Church when the soul of a child has made him/herself known to the parents, or to someone who could take a message to the parents. Whatever the circumstances that led to the child's passing, the message has invariably been 'I am alright now. I have lost all my pain and I am happy. Please don't cry for me any more, as there is no need to do so'. So many times when this has happened, there has not been a dry eye anywhere by the time that the child has finished speaking. Often the child comes back after many years, just to remind the parents and/or friends that he/ she still loves them. However, I have never heard any child (or for that matter any adult) *ever* say that they would wish to be once more living their life in the physical world which we all believe is the true Reality.

Spiritualist philosophy tells us that all of us are in this life to learn lessons and to carry out certain tasks and duties, and that when we have finished - at whatever age - we are *allowed* to go back home. Perhaps that simple creed will help people who are devastated by early deaths to come to terms with their loss.

Chapter 18: Guides and Inspirers

For those who are not familiar with the concept of guides, I should give a little explanation. According to Spiritualist philosophy, each of us has one main guide who volunteered to help us before we came into incarnation, and who stays with us throughout our life until we go back to the place from which we came originally. Apart from that one guide, whom many consider as 'the still small voice of conscience', telling us what is the right thing to do at any time, we have other guides (sometimes called helpers or inspirers) who come to help us to develop specific spiritual gifts. This means that the more developed a person is spiritually, the more he or she is likely to have several guides, each one moving in to help at the appropriate time, when needed or called upon. There is never any rivalry between guides: on their plane of existence, they have gone beyond human concepts such as precedence, importance and jealousy: each one accepts when the help of another might be more appropriate - and just steps back to let that other take over.

I have on occasions worked on the platform at a Spiritualist meeting (meaning that I have conducted the service). I have never been clairvoyant enough to give messages in a service, but I used to give an inspired (channelled) address, and then follow that with a question and answer session about the philosophy that had been expounded. On such occasions I always had three guides with me: the first led the prayers, the second gave the address and the third explained the philosophy behind what had been said. Each took their turn and moved in at the appropriate time to do their bit. The same system applies when a person advances spiritually and is able to understand a higher level of philosophy: the existing guide just moves out and the new, more advanced, guide takes over.

I carried on contacting my own guides, and I was continually asking questions about all aspects of spiritual reality. I found that whenever I asked a question, an answer would come into my head - but how was I to know whether that answer was coming from Spirit or was just a figment of my imagination? That problem was solved in a very ingenious way. I found out that whenever I had asked a major question and had apparently received an answer, I would 'by co-incidence' read an article, pick up a book, or hear an address dealing with that particular question - and invariably the answer which was given was the same as the one which I had mentally heard.

Let us now look at the subject of Guides in more detail. First, let me state that the whole universe works on Love - in fact the very building blocks of it are Love - so in any other dimension but the one in which we live everything is done with the intent of showing Love - and the way that it is shown is through Service to other beings, particularly those who are lower down in the ladder of spiritual evolution.

Before we come into incarnation we make the choices I have already outlined, and agree with all the actors in our personal scenario what parts they will play. However, there are some actors who do not have a physical role, and those are our Guides. The first of these is our Personal Guide. This is an advanced being who has formerly had many lives in the physical body and has no further need to incarnate. However, he/she takes on the role of spiritual advisor/ mentor/ friend to us, and accepts to be with us throughout our earthly life.

Some people may think it unlikely that a spiritual being would bind him/herself to the service of another without reward for what may be up to a century or more, but that is looking at things from an earthly perspective, where time is a factor. In the next dimension, time as we know it does not even exist, so a century is no more than the flick of an eyelid. A famous Christian hymn puts it into perspective: 'A thousand ages in Thy sight are like an evening gone'. In addition, as far as reward is concerned, the reward is in doing the job well - a concept that is a little too advanced for most human beings to accept.

Our personal guide is with us all the time, so close to us that if we only ask a question of him/her we are likely to get some sort of answer which comes into our minds immediately. In most cases, we know subconsciously what is right from what is wrong, and what we should or should not do. In the wonderful children's story 'Pinocchio', Jiminy Cricket was the personification of Pinocchio's conscience, so it is possible for us to think of our personal guide (a little irreverently) as our own Jiminy Cricket.

The next being who binds him/herself to us for our whole life is known as 'The Gatekeeper'. His/her job is to act as a spiritual bodyguard to us, and not to allow any harmful psychic influences into our aura, where they might affect us badly. Usually when they are seen by psychics, the personal guide and the gatekeeper are standing behind us, one on our right hand and the other on the left. The gatekeeper is unlikely to ever be recognised as being needed, unless we are doing some sort of spiritual work where we voluntarily open ourselves to being influenced by beings from that next dimension (as happens in some forms of mediumship). In that case he/ she organises and keeps those beings in order, so that they can influence us and work through us in the most effective way. For instance, very often when a medium is working from the platform, (taking a service,) he/she will speak to a member of the congregation, and the loved ones of that person, who are on the other side, are so excited at the opportunity to make contact that they all try to come through and say 'Hello' at the same time - and therefore need to be kept in order. I suppose that we could think of the gatekeeper, once more a little irreverently, as being similar to the bouncer in a nightclub, who lets in only those who are prepared to behave themselves.

Then we have our individual guides who come in when we need help with one or other of the spiritual disciplines that we are learning or practising. For instance, a speaking guide will come to help us to give philosophy, a mediumship guide for clairvoyance, a healing guide (usually a doctor or some other former member of a medical profession) will come to help with healing, etc. Then, to complicate matters even further, new guides will come in as and when we are able to accommodate their energies, and not before. Spiritualists normally refer to others who come to help them, who are not associated with a specific gift, as inspirers or helpers.

As I have said, there are no human-type ideas of precedence in the next dimension: when a lower-level guide sees that we are ready for the next step up, he/she just bows out gracefully and lets the new guide take over. In Sybil's case, she is a wonderful healer, and for many years, has had a neurosurgeon as a healing guide. She was told some time ago that there was a new guide, a Chinaman, who was ready to bring in a higher healing vibration, and she has now begun to feel the buzz of excitement as this new guide comes closer to her aura.

When I first started to channel, back in the early 1970s, my speaking guide was a very humble craftsman, who called himself 'the potter'. After some years he was replaced by a Buddhist monk named Chang, but I was told that there was a high-level Confucian guide who was waiting in the wings, who would come in only when I was ready. He could not use me at that time, as if he did, his vibrations would burn me out. If there are any electricians reading this book, they will know that the result of putting a high amperage through an ordinary appliance would be to blow the fuse (at least, if not burn out the whole appliance). This is exactly what would happen on a spiritual plane if an entity with an energy that was too high tried to use some instrument who was not yet ready. (In fact, that would never happen in practice, as the spiritual entities who wish to use us are very much aware of our limitations, and would never even try to use us until we are totally ready).

After about ten years Chang himself disappeared, giving way to an Arab philosopher, but now, some thirty years later, I have been given a psychic drawing (portrait of a spirit entity) of a Chinaman, who says that his name is Mao Chung; with the portrait came a message which says that the Confucian is ready to start to use me - and I await this with not a little awe and trepidation.

I was once asked why we needed to change our guides at all, and if we could always be certain that what the guides said was the total truth. To understand that I give a little analogy, that of learning Mathematics (as I was once a Maths teacher). Let us take the case of three Maths students, one at Primary School, one at Secondary School and the third one at University. All would be learning Mathematics - but that would be the only similarity between them. Each would be at a different stage of understanding, so the style of teaching and the language used to teach them would also be different. It would be just as unrewarding (both ways) for a University lecturer to try to teach a primary pupil as it would for a Primary teacher to teach a University student, and the secondary pupil would fare just as badly with either teacher. Therefore, as we progress in our knowledge and understanding of Maths, we get more and more advanced teachers - and exactly the same process holds true for all those who are striving for spiritual progression.

18: Guides and Inspirers

As far as the second question is concerned, the same reasoning applies. If we asked a Primary teacher about calculus or higher algebra, it is likely that we would get a reply of only limited value, whereas if we asked the University lecturer he/she would be able to tell us the full story - and so it is in the spiritual realms also. Two human beings on different levels of understanding may be discussing a spiritual problem, have different views, and each may possibly quote his/her inspirer as an authority for those views. However, it will usually be the more evolved one who will have the more evolved guide. Therefore, each human being will have been given information at the level that he/she could understand: neither of the guides was wrong - just right at their own level of understanding. (After all, guides are still progressing spiritually in their dimension, just as we are in ours).

This leads us on to the question of Truth. One of the fundamental questions to which Mankind has never yet found a satisfactory answer was asked in its simplest form by Pontius Pilate who, when questioning Christ asked, 'What is Truth?' In our everyday life, all of us are certain that we know the truth about everything from the price of food to world politics, etc., but to what degree is that actually correct? Our knowledge of anything can never be more accurate than the latest information at our disposal. If we are discussing the price of a particular food item, we might not know that it is a heavily discounted permanent loss leader at a local supermarket that we never visit, so our information could be wrong. As far as world politics are concerned, dissent has been raging about the Iraq war ever since it was even discussed as a possibility in 2002 - and most people now have doubts about the authenticity of the Intelligence information used as a basis for declaring war in the first place.

Throughout history what was considered as indisputable truth by one generation has been queried - and in some cases ridiculed - by following generations. What happened to the theory that the Earth was flat, and that if you sailed too far you would drop off the edge into a total void? We smile knowingly at that ridiculous idea now, and yet it was firmly held for many centuries. In the year 1600 Giordano Bruno was burnt at the stake for daring to suggest that the universe did not revolve around the Earth, and yet now even the dullest secondary school child knows that the Earth is only one of a group of planets which revolve round the Sun - and many children know that the Sun itself is only a second-rate star towards the end of one of the arms of a whole galaxy. A hundred years ago, astronomers were convinced that the stars were simple balls of fire. Now we know that the majority of stars are actually distant galaxies - and the number of galaxies has expanded from possibly twenty during the last century to billions today. In fact - with the information coming from the latest update in the Hubble space telescope - even that estimate may soon be proved far too low.

In the field of medicine, similar advances have been made over the centuries, to the level where some doctors are now claiming to have the ability to clone a complete human being, as the famous sheep Dolly was cloned some years ago. It is a far cry from the level of knowledge of the 19th century, when cholera was considered contagious and bacteria, microbes and viruses were totally unknown.

So in both of those fields, Astronomy and Medicine, (and in many other scientific areas,) what was truth in past centuries is now dismissed as ignorance and even today's truths may well be superseded tomorrow.

If then it is impossible to define truth in the physical world, where we have an increasing array of sophisticated devices and gadgets at our disposal, how much more difficult is it to define Truth in the abstract world, where the only tools we can use are our own observations and the revelations of various human beings over the centuries, purporting to be of divine origin. I do not deny the possibility of Divine Revelation, but I just comment that it has to be channelled through human beings, who are rooted in the particular social and economic framework of their time. Such revelations are then commented on and interpreted by all the following generations. and inevitably, distortions creep in over the centuries. For instance, Biblical scholars have identified up to a thousand changes in the original text of the New Testament, (based on changes of style and language within the text) and some go as far as to state that there is not even one verse of the Gospels which is totally untouched by later alterations.

When things that were appropriate in one past civilisation are applied strictly to modern conditions, then problems are bound to occur. For instance, much of the Jewish moral code concerning sexual matters was very relevant when it was first established: there was a need for the population to grow rapidly, so anything that lessened the possibility of pregnancy was to be avoided - and therefore masturbation and homosexuality were proscribed. However, some millennia after the code was written - and long after the need to increase the population rapidly ceased - the same taboos are still in force in the Jewish, Christian and the Muslim religions alike, causing both religious and political problems.

In the face of all the truths claimed by different religions, creeds or ideologies in the world, what is a sincere seeker to do? I believe that the only way to make spiritual progress is by us personally going back to the source of all knowledge - in whatever way we understand the term - and then by creating our own personal philosophy and code of morals and ethics for our own lives - and this is where we can be helped by our guides. Remember that a guide is never there to tell us what to do. No guide can live our life for us, nor would any one even try, but as they are always there when we want to consult them, they can help us to make our own way through life, and to make the best decisions for ourselves (best meaning the most appropriate at this particular stage of our life). In this way, we will achieve our own Truth, which may not be valid for anyone else, but will provide us with our own personal code by which to live.

This simple code of living means that when someone else tells us what he/she believes, we should accept it as Truth *only if it resonates with our own Truth.* If it does not, then to accept it would be to violate our own freedom of choice, and would be to allow someone else to impose (directly or indirectly) his/ her own will on us. I am reminded of the famous quote from Shakespeare, where Laertes is counselling his son: after giving him all sorts of good advice, he says, 'This above all, to thine own self be true. And it shall follow, as the night the day, thou canst not then be false to any man!' Wise words indeed, which we would do well to study. To what extent in our own lives do we allow others to rule us? I suspect far more than we would willingly accept.

This concept also applies to you, the reader, here and now: if what I am saying strikes a chord in your mind, then it is resonating with your Truth, and can be taken to be (at least in part) valid for you. If it does not, then disregard it, put the book down, pass it on to someone else or even throw it away - it is not for you! One of my aims when writing the book was that it should serve as a practical exercise for me and should discipline me into looking back on my own life (while I still have the mental faculties left to do so) to see how I arrived at my present state of spiritual awareness, (without trying to compare this level of awareness with that of any other human being). The other aim was that I should pass on whatever information I have received from any source whatsoever to others, who may or may not find it of interest or value in their own journey towards spirituality.

It is quite possible that you read this book and you find that you already know everything about which I have been writing. In that case, all that I have done is to help you to remember consciously what you have already learnt in the accumulation of your past lives - and which is already in your subconscious mind. However, if you read it and you are not too sure about what to think, possibly this is the time to see if you can contact your own guides and try to get confirmation (or otherwise) that this is correct for you. All that you have to do is to sit quietly by yourself, close your eyes and just ask the question, 'Is this right for me at this moment of time?' Concentrate on the question, and see what happens. If you feel easy, happy or relaxed - or exceptionally if you hear something mentally like 'Yes' or 'O.K.', then go for it. If however you feel at all uneasy or disturbed, then it is definitely not for you.

If you already have a strong religious conviction which explains adequately to you what we are doing in this life, and helps you to understand all the mysteries of Life, Death and so on, then the book is most definitely taboo. However, if you are of this persuasion, it is unlikely that you will have picked it up in the first place.

When I look back on my years teaching Map reading in the Army, I remember that we used compass bearings very extensively, and these were used to pinpoint certain positions on a map. Just imagine that you knew that the position you were seeking was on a particular map-bearing from the point at which you were standing: by locating where you were on a map and by drawing the bearing on the map from that point, you could be certain that the position you wanted to locate would be somewhere along that line. But where?

The question could be answered by being given a bearing on the position from a different place, ideally at some distance and direction from the first; then, going through the same process again and drawing the bearing on the map, the two bearings would cross at some point - and that point would show you the position you were seeking. If you wanted to be absolutely accurate, you would choose a third spot some distance away

18: Guides and Inspirers

from both of the other two and request a bearing from there - and so would be able to confirm the position without doubt.

If you imagine this idea as a field exercise in locating a particular position in a wood in the middle of a large field, the first bearing might be taken (say) from the North of the wood, and would give a general direction. The second might be taken from the East, and would given a very good estimation of where the position was. Finally, a third taken from (say) the Southwest, would confirm the position without doubt.

Perhaps one could find the position of absolute Truth - if such a thing exists - by a similar method. By looking at the question from one religious viewpoint one would get an idea of the general position, then by studying the same question from another one, there would be a different idea. Likewise, if one studied it from a third, fourth or fifth viewpoint, etc., all would produce different ideas. However, amidst all the contradictions which would be exposed, there would be a certain amount of consensus of opinion, which would be free of all the specific dogma associated with the different religions - and this consensus could provide a reasonably accurate idea of the position of that Truth.

To finish off this section on Guides, from time to time I have spoken about inspirers. These may be a whole host of people, ranging from our own guides to some of our loved ones who are on the other side and who have sufficient knowledge to be able to advise us on spiritual matters. In my case, one of my own inspirers is probably Aunty Margaret, who is almost certainly still watching over me to make sure that her 'spiritual son' does not go too far astray.

Chapter 19: Love

In the last chapter I spoke about guides helping us out of Love and service - but what do we mean by Love? It is one of the most misused words in our modern vocabulary, so let us study it for a moment through the eyes of different people to see if we can find what it really means.

The Young Adult.
'I love you: I want to go to bed with you'. This sentiment will cover probably more than half of the times when the phrase 'I love you' is said. There is nothing wrong with sexuality: after all, it is a natural mechanism which ensures the survival of our species - but let us not call it *Love* - its true definition is *Desire*.

The Collector.
'I love you: I want to add you to my collection of rare or precious objects (anything from jewels to cars) so that I can show you off to my friends'. This sentiment has nothing whatsoever to do with *Love* at all; it is nothing more than *Possession*.

The Owner.
'I love you: I want to be able to rule you, make all your decisions so that you become totally mine and do what I want immediately without question'. This has just as little to do with *Love* as the last one, being a simple example of *Control*.

The Weakling.
'I love you: I want you to look after me, support me, tell me how good I am and make me feel good at having such a wonderful person to boost my own self-esteem'. This is a little closer to *Love*, but not

19: Love

much: although it accepts that the other person is wonderful, it is really not *Love* but *Need*.

The Martyr.
'I love you: I want to put you on a pedestal, devote my whole life to you, do whatever you want and never query the fact that you will always be right'. This is often thought of as *Love*, but the person who has these sentiments is more 'in love' than loving - so really it is a case of *Infatuation*.

Let me in passing say a little more about the emotional difference between 'to be in love' and 'to love'. In the first case, the person concerned is so besotted with the object of affection that no fault can be found in him/her. It is a totally irrational feeling, and in fact shows that the person loving has lost control of his/her emotions. Compare this with the second case, where the person knows all the faults of the other, but can still feel the same affection regardless. He/she is still in control of the emotions and can take a conscious decision to love.

The Bargainer.
'I love you: at least, I am prepared to love you if you will love me in return'. This is not *Love* at all, it is simply a *Contract*.

The Parent.
'I love you: I want to raise you, look after you, and lavish all my affection on you so that I can fulfil my natural role in life. I want to make you what I think all children should ideally be. I want to make you what I wanted to be myself, when I was a child'. This is very close to what most people will accept as *Love* - and indeed, it may well be exactly that. However, the last sentence is definitely a case of *Manipulation*.

Although I have made 'The Parent' the title of the 'Manipulation' kind of Love, this is not to be taken that I believe that all parental Love is manipulative - it isn't. In fact, the job of parenting must be one of the hardest jobs in the world, and the one for which most people are least prepared. I realise that in these modern times, parenting courses are springing up in certain areas, but most of us (and certain the middle-aged generation and older) have had to learn how to be a parent by example, probably the example of our own parents. Now since my generation (the children who were born either just pre-war or just post-war) were brought up fairly strictly, that is how most of us brought up our own families. When our children were brought up, in the 'Swinging Sixties' and the Seventies, conditions were becoming far more lax, so our children were more likely to rebel against the discipline which they received and - most importantly - decide to bring up *their* children in a far freer and easier manner.

Government legislation has played its part by progressively banning overt discipline such as caning in schools and smacking children at home, and even giving children in Care homes the right to walk out as and when they want to, as staff no longer have the right to physically restrain children. This has led to a generation of children now who have a lot of freedom, very little discipline and even less respect for authority in any of its forms, from police to teachers and - most of all - for parents.

The final two things that have combined to make the role of the parent intolerable are the rise of our Consumer Society and the creeping menace of drugs. As far as the former is concerned, children are continually bombarded with advertisements for all the latest clothes and gadgets. In fact, one Christmas I read of a single woman with three children, living on benefits, who spent about £1,500 on Christmas presents bought on a credit card, which would take her until the next Christmas to pay off. To my mind, this is just a case of indulging the children by buying them off with presents, rather than doing the hard thing and showing them the value of the old adage 'Cut your coat according to your cloth' or 'Buy only what you can afford'. Teaching children that sooner or later everything has to be paid for, and if you can't afford something it is better to go without, rather than buying it and putting a millstone round your neck for the future, would be a far greater show of Love than giving them the idea that they can have everything they want, when they want it.

However, most parents have an ideal in their minds of what they want their children to become, and in most cases, they succeed fairly well. But there are a large number of parents who want to make their children either into clones of themselves or who want to turn the children into what *they themselves* wanted to be when they were that age; in this, they are effectively re-living their own lives through the children, regardless of what the child really wants to do in life - and this is very definitely 'Manipulation'.

Well, we now know some of the things that Love isn't, so can we have something more positive and find out what Love really is? Now that is what used to be known as the 'Sixty-Four Thousand Dollar Question'. (There I am showing my age: these days it would be the 'Million Pound Question'). I think that the first thing that must exist in order for any sentiment to be Love is the quality of Altruism.

This is by definition doing something for the benefit of another person, without necessarily receiving anything back in return. The Martyr has something of this in his/her makeup, as has The Parent, but in the first case there is a lack of rational thought in the belief that the object of the Love will be always right, and in the second there is the desire to mould him/ her to the ideal which exists in the Parent's mind. In all the other cases cited, the object of the Love is only secondary to the main intention of providing a service to the person who is loving.

The second thing that must be present is for the person loving to *do* something that shows Love. If there is no physical, mental or emotional action on the part of the person loving, it is difficult to see how Love can exist. Nevertheless, within that framework there are very many ways of expressing ourselves: we can take some physical action, say something of value, or even send a prayer of healing or of comfort.

In many cases, there is the willingness to do everything for the benefit of the person served, to the exclusion of one's own personal interests - for instance, where a son or daughter devotes his/her life to tending and caring for an aged and infirm parent. Such a person often finds that his/her own life has been on hold for so long that, after the parent passes over, it is very difficult to start living for him/herself again, because he/she is now in their late thirties or early forties. This is a case of true martyrdom, in the best sense of the word, because all the decisions to devote the life to the parent will have been taken in the light of cold reason, fully understanding the possible consequences - and therefore it is an example of Love at its highest level.

A similar kind of Love is seen where the parents of a physically- or mentally-handicapped child build the whole of their life round the needs of that child, to the total exclusion of their own wishes or plans. As I have said before, it is only those who are already very spiritually advanced who can enter into contracts for this kind of relationship.

The final element of Love must consist in a permanent benefit of some spiritual kind to the object of the Love. For instance, the gratification of that person's desires would not necessarily qualify: giving drink to an alcoholic or drugs to a drug addict would not produce any real benefit in their life at all, any more than giving matches to a child who wished to play with them would help him/her. Of far more value would be to try to help each of the first two to kick their habits, and to explain to the child why playing with fire is not a good idea. However, some actions are far more difficult to classify. When does a genuine attempt to help a person stop helping and start hindering them? I have a wonderful friend, a Cancerian mother, who until a few years ago was still doing all the washing for her bachelor son aged 27. Was that helping him - and therefore Love - or hindering his own development - and therefore Control? (As an aside, Cancerians have great difficulty in letting go of the reins, and will often carry on mothering - or perhaps a better word would be 'smothering' - a son or daughter long after that child has become an adult).

It is a difficult decision when to stop helping those in need and to start encouraging them to stand on their own two feet. The problem very often arises when people start to help others, and then find that the others attach themselves and becomes more and more reliant on the helpers, who becomes almost obliged to carry on helping, through a form of emotional blackmail. Providing a set of crutches is all very well if they are a step towards the people walking again, but of no value at all if they completely replace their desire to walk by themselves.

We have discussed what elements must be present in order for Love to exist, so can we now pull them together? One of the most famous of 20th century psychologists, M. Scott Peck, wrote a book called 'The Road Less Travelled', which became an instant best-seller and was the forerunner of many more, all of which are still very good reading. He defined Love as 'the willingness to exert oneself with the intention of furthering the spiritual progression of another person, or of oneself'. This is a brilliant way of bringing together all these separate elements - but many people will query the final three words. Don't they contradict

19: Love

the Altruism element, which says that the benefit should be mainly for the recipient?

Well, once we learn how the Law of Spiritual Interest works, it gives us more incentive to use it to our advantage. We are more likely to do things deliberately to bring us credits than we are to bring debits. In fact, after a time, we can start getting a kick out of doing good deeds just for the fun of it, realising that we are going to be repaid in kind, at some stage or other in the future! I once heard this described as 'divine selfishness', where we do things with no desire for an earthly reward, but knowing full well that we will be rewarded eventually, either in this life or in a future one on this earth. Perhaps that was what M. Scott Peck meant when he added *or of oneself* to his definition of Love.

Many years ago I asked the same question of my own inspirers, and I was told that this was all part of a divine paradox: the more that you do for others without thought for yourself, the more spiritual benefit you will receive, whereas doing something of value to someone else with the main intention of benefiting yourself will bring you some, but far less spiritual benefit. The parable of the Pharisees comes to mind, in which Jesus said that those who do good deeds and let everyone know about it 'already have their reward'. So it all comes down to intention: being a professional do-gooder with the object of furthering your own welfare is of less value than doing the same thing for the love of it - and for the love of the people whom you help.

I once met a man who claimed that he could almost gauge the amount of spiritual benefit he would receive from doing any act of charity. While I would strongly dispute the possibility of that, I would even more strongly doubt the spiritual value of such a mind-set. Compare it with the members of the Salvation Army, who carry out a wide variety of social work without thought of personal benefit of any kind, immediate or deferred: I think I know which approach I would prefer. Personally, as an Aquarian I get a great kick out of helping others, in whichever way I can: I know that it helps my own spiritual progression, but that is not a real issue for me - I just do it for fun. I have not yet reached the state where my own spiritual progression is of paramount importance to me: perhaps if I ever do so I will start to worry more about *why* I am helping others - rather than just doing it and enjoying it

A Practical Spiritual Primer

As far as the definition of Love is concerned, I have reached my own conclusion. In my philosophy, Love is the act of recognising the divine spark in another person - and reacting to it. It involves the acceptance of the idea that each of us contains that divine spark, and therefore that each of us, at one level, is a part of every other human being - and, indeed, part of every other being in the universe. When we are able to relate to others and see our own divine spark reflected in them, then we can truly say that we love them - and this applies to whoever those others may be (family, children, friends, partners or just acquaintances). In fact, Jesus said that we should even love our enemies - although that takes a lot more effort to understand (and certainly far more to carry out).

The concept of loving others does not imply that we should subordinate ourselves to them, or them to us: it accepts that each of us is on his/her own personal path - and that our path is different to that of everyone else. It knows that we will be together for only a short time in this life, and that we come together to achieve certain aims and learn certain lessons from each other - and then move on. In fact, to use an old expression, we are all like 'ships that pass in the night'.

We may move on at the end of our joint lives, or after only a short period together. Whichever it is, it will always be at the most appropriate time, the time that we, as individuals, have already jointly chosen on a spiritual level. Once more, this has nothing to do with the decisions we make on a conscious, physical level. If we fully understand that the process of life is perfect, it makes many of our everyday decisions so much easier. For instance, if we come to a parting of the ways with our current spouse or partner, and we can part in Love, this makes the difficult decisions about splitting up shared assets, custody of children and the like so much easier. Those who have had the spiritual vision to achieve this have often ended up as far better friends apart than they ever were as partners together. However, without that understanding the parting takes place in acrimony, and every decision becomes a matter of principle which must be fought over, very often in the courts, which benefits no-one at all (except the lawyers) and just leaves bitter memories in the minds of all concerned.

One particularly difficult question regarding Love is that of how someone can love another person after the death of a dearly loved spouse or partner. Isn't there an element of unfaithfulness to the memory

19: Love

of the departed loved-one when the one left behind starts up another relationship? The fact that the question is asked at all echoes the question asked of Jesus in the Bible, where the same woman married seven brothers successively, each time after the death of the previous brother. Jesus was asked, 'When she gets to Heaven, whose wife will she be?' The answer, in simple terms, was that 'in Heaven there is no marriage or the giving in marriage' - and when we ask the question, we are trying to apply earthly customs to an existence in another dimension. Therefore even asking the question shows how little we understand what Love is all about.

In a previous chapter I have told how Eleanor said that she would bring me a new partner, and did, and she was seen by one of our grandsons with both Sybil and me at our wedding. I have told how she came back and explained that, long before we all came into incarnation, we had jointly decided that I should marry Sybil after her (Eleanor's) death. I still love her just as much as I ever did while she was on Earth, and nothing can ever replace that Love, which itself can never fade or die. That Love existed - and still exists - because I could relate to the divine spark in her, and still do. Each person has a unique energy pattern, and my energy pattern at that time fused with that of Eleanor and created something unique and immortal, which will last until eventually we are both fused into the Energy from which we originally came.

Sybil is a very wonderful woman who radiates love to all and sundry. She is a great healer and a spiritual powerhouse. She also has a wonderful energy pattern, which is naturally totally unique and very different to Eleanor's pattern - not better or worse, but different. As all of us choose our own pattern before we arrive on Earth, and that pattern is continually evolving, it can never be compared with that of any other human being. So what about my Love for Sybil? How does that compare with the Love for Eleanor? Well, there is no comparison at all, nor can there ever be, and to even ask the question is a nonsense. How can you compare a superb piece of music with a sublime painting? Is Handel's Messiah better or worse than the Mona Lisa? How can you compare a Cordon Bleu meal cooked by the most famous chef in the world with the feeling of a new mother as she first touches her baby? My relationship with Eleanor was perfect - as is my relationship with Sybil: there is no possible competition or comparison between them.

My present energy pattern is still evolving, as is Sybil's, so the combination of the two is evolving even more, as we are continually sounding new depths in the concept of Relationships. I 'did my apprenticeship' in relationships during my long life with Eleanor, so I was able to get off to a very good start when Sybil and I became an 'item'. This means that the fact that I was so much more spiritually developed and understood what Love was really all about by then has avoided the difficulties of the usual period of adjustment that characterises most marriages or partnerships - and particularly second relationships.

When we live our lives on Earth, the concept of Love between two partners is usually bound up with that of fidelity, and is therefore one of Exclusion. Any form of sexual activity with another person is seen as a betrayal of that Love, and is therefore taboo. We love someone to the exclusion of everyone else or we don't really love him/her at all. This concept was challenged in the 'Swinging Sixties' by the 'Flower People', who promoted the idea of 'Free Love', in which sexual encounters with all and sundry were held as being totally beneficial. The idea had a rapid setback when the plague of Aids started, but now, with the advocacy of 'safe sex', it appears to be having a comeback. In many cases, when two young people meet for the first time, the only appropriate question is 'Your place or mine?' - it is an automatic assumption that sexual activity is going to take place. This, however, has nothing at all to do with any concept of Love - it has far more to do with lust.

In the next dimension, we learn that Love is a relationship of Inclusion. Having experienced the sublime emotion on Earth, we are able to apply that same emotion to our dealings with *all* those whom we meet. At that level, we are able to see and understand the subject to a far higher degree, without the complications of human sexuality being an issue. Which brings us back to where we were in a previous chapter, and explains why guides are able to attach themselves to us, work with and support us throughout our entire earthly lives - out of Love, in the truest meaning of the word.

Chapter 20: Predestination

Sybil and I were once at the home of a young friend whom we were helping, whom I shall call Michelle. She had had an appalling life, and at one time had almost been on the verge of ending it all by committing suicide, as she was so depressed and physically ill at the same time. Fortunately, she didn't, and we used to meet her regularly and introduced her to a number of our friends. This served to widen her circle of positive contacts, which was previously woefully lacking - if not totally absent. We had been talking about everything happening at the right time, when we are ready, and she could relate to this. She said that a few years ago, when she was at her lowest point and everything seemed to be totally negative in her life, she had got down on her knees and prayed that something would happen to end her state of misery. Soon afterwards she was introduced to a lady who gave her enough hope to be able to carry on and who - just as important - was the one who was instrumental in her coming down to Devon.

When things seemed even bleaker after one Christmas, she knelt down again and prayed either to die or to be relieved of her pain, only to 'coincidently' meet Jean, one of Sybil's friends. Jean then introduced her to Sybil, who is a very powerful healer and also a very wonderful motherly woman. Sybil took her under her wing and afterwards Michelle made enormous progress, not only physically but also in her understanding of spiritual matters; in fact, she went from being afraid of any mention of spirituality to taking a lively interest in it. Every time we met her, Sybil gave her healing and we both discussed spiritual philosophy with her. She is an Aquarian, the same as me, so much of what I said to her about spiritual philosophy struck a chord within her, as though it was something she knew already, but hadn't previously remembered. She was actually a brilliant psychic, but for most of her life had been told that she was mental when she said anything about what she had seen, so had come to dread the occurrence of any sort of psychic phenomenon

During our discussion together one week, she said that she couldn't understand why we had come into her life at the particular time we did, when she was in so much need. So I asked her if she had been surprised when we arrived on her doorstep that evening. She replied that she hadn't, as she had arranged the time for us to arrive with Sybil only a few hours before - so I pointed cut that this was exactly what had happened to bring us into her life. As she didn't understand, I explained it further.

When each of us comes into life, only a tiny part of our whole spiritual being actually 'comes into incarnation' (a spiritual term for 'being born'). The remainder of us, our real self - or as it is called, our 'Higher Self' - remains in the dimension where we were before we started life here, and is always watching over us, and making sure that we are following the path we chose before we were born. To those who are not familiar with this idea, the idea of a Higher Self is not much different from the idea of having a 'conscience' which tells us what we should or should not do - and most people have heard of their conscience at some time of their life or other. However, thinking of it as our conscience is only a step towards understanding the Higher Self, as it is closer to us than our conscience: It is literally part of us - or perhaps it would be more correct to say that we are literally part of it.

Now our Higher Self knows us better than anyone else, and whenever we sincerely want to bring a change into our lives, the Higher Self is the entity that organises things. I have spoken already of the decisions we all made, and the agreements that we entered into, before we started this life - but they didn't end there. We carry on making decisions all through our lives, and depending on the decisions we make we are continually bringing positive or negative conditions into our lives - and the mechanism through which it is all done is that of the Higher Self.

If we look at how this works in a slightly irreverent way, we can imagine a gigantic celestial sorting office, manned by seven-and-a-half billion Higher Selves all sitting at computer screens, watching over their respective earthly counterparts. Two of these are watching over X and Z. Z is quite spiritually aware, and always tries to be positive, no matter what the problems in life, whereas X is just the opposite. Then, because his/her

20: Predestination

life is going more and more 'pear-shaped', X makes a conscious decision to change direction and to abandon the road that he/she was on which was leading into more and more negativity. So X's Higher Self calls out to Z's Higher Self, (mentally, of course, as in this higher dimension verbal speech is not necessary,) and they make an agreement that Z will 'coincidentally' meet X and introduce him/ her into a group of people who are all positive; this will then open up a totally new world of possibilities and take him/her in a completely different direction.

But things can't happen immediately in our world, as they would in the higher dimension, where action and reaction are almost simultaneous. It takes some time for the conditions around the lives of X and Z to be changed, and many other Higher Selves may have to be contacted and asked for permission to vary slightly the lives of their charges, so that a series of 'co-incidences' can take place which will eventually lead to X and Z meeting.

Of course, in the above scenario, the original decision might have been to do something that would lead X *towards* more negativity instead of *away* from it. The process would still have been the same, but instead of X meeting Z, who was surrounded by positive conditions, he/she would have met Q, who was surrounded by negativity and negative friends, who would have the effect of drawing X deeper and deeper into negative conditions.

Theologians have argued for centuries about the conflict between Free Will and Predestination. Supporters of the first maintain that each human being has the power of deciding his/ her own destiny, and that we are not bound by any over-riding celestial plan in our lives. Those who support the second say that 'God' (as they understand the term) knows everything, and therefore knows the future as well as the past. As each person's destiny is already planned before he/she starts life, there can be no Free Will for anyone.

In my personal understanding, each of us is a spark of the Divine Creator (expressed in whatever form our mind-set can understand), and we come into incarnation in order to show the power of that Creator through living a human life. Every individual is totally unique, and there has never been a double for any one human being since the start of life on the planet, nor could there ever be before the planet itself dies. So before we are born, we choose the conditions into which to be born, we choose our parents, our environment, the lessons we want to learn, our skills and weaknesses and our general pathway through life. We have then used our free will to set the pattern - and once we have set the pattern we are predestined to follow it.

But just imagine that we achieve what we want to do years earlier than planned and so we decide to take on further challenges and change the overall timing - or even the direction of our life: what happens then? Well, since we are a part of that divine creative force, we can change the scenario, and so we plan something else. We don't need to deliberately contact our Higher Self, as we are always in permanent contact with it. All that we have to do is to express the firm, conscious intention to change, and the Higher Self knows. As it is always ready to do anything we decide, it starts to bring into play the conditions that will allow that change to take place. Within the overall predestination of our life, we are exercising our free will to create new conditions - but once those new conditions are created the force of predestination takes over again and our lives carry on as before - but now going in a new direction.

I believe that once we realise what is really going on, the old arguments about free will and predestination become reconciled into one large overall picture. In this picture the original act of free will creates predestination until, nested within that condition, there is another act of free will creating more predestination, and so on until the end of our lives. And this idea of individual acts of free will and predestination nested within each other interminably explains the conditions of human life a lot more easily than any other philosophy. If you want a practical analogy of what happens, all that you have to do is to think of a series of Russian dolls: inside the outer one there is a smaller one, and inside that one even smaller, etc. So having originally chosen our main life plan, we are predestined to follow it until we realise that we can choose to vary it and make another choice, and so on.

I was once asked to explain this whole concept in simple words to a friend, and asked my inspirers for the best way to do it. I was given the example of a playwright who is writing the scenario of a new play in which he/ she is going to take the leading role. He/she sits down and writes the play, and then looks round to find actors to play the parts. Once all the roles have been allocated, there is the grand opening of the play, which is one of those mammoth productions lasting several nights. But after the first night, the playwright gets an idea of a new twist in the plot: so he/she sits down and writes a new scene which will add to the play's depth and complexity, and has to get the cast to hurriedly learn new lines (or even has to hire new actors) before the next night's episode. Then, if he/she has any other ideas for the plot, the same thing happens again - and this re-writing carries on until the last night of the play

This is very similar to human life: we have all written our own plays, and are now in the process of acting in them; but if we want to change the scenarios and bring in new actors, or write out existing ones, then we are at perfect liberty to do so - after all, *we* are the playwrights. But an additional interesting complexity is that while we are all taking the lead in our own plays, our friends/ neighbours/ colleagues and many others whom we contact during life are also acting in our plays - and we are simultaneously acting in theirs. Therefore, if we decide to write someone out of our play, then we have to be written out of their play at the same time, and in the same conditions. Fortunately, we don't have to arrange all that ourselves, as we can leave it to the respective Higher Selves of all those concerned to do the work.

This idea of a moving script is really not so surprising after all: it is continually happening in every one of the 'Soaps' we see on the television. The most dramatic example of it was when Bill Owen (the beloved 'Compo') died in the middle of a series of 'The Last of the Summer Wine' - and had to be hurriedly written out of the script. The only difference between the soap plots and the plots of our own lives is that the writers of the soaps don't act in their own plots, whereas we do.

So we came into Michelle's life at exactly the right moment, some four to six weeks after she had prayed for help. (As an aside, it seems that this is the standard lead-time between somebody asking for help and the moment when some person comes into their life to help them. Certainly it is the lead-time for all those people who come to us for help). About a year after we first met, her health became considerably better, and she was able to face the world in a way that she had not done for many years in the past. She started to attend a Centre for adults of all ages who have psychological problems, and found out that she was coping with the experience of mixing with other people far better than she could ever have dreamed possible. Not only that, but she made friends who are very beneficial to her, and started to have the beginnings of a social life.

After a couple of years or so she disappeared from our life. We never found out what had happened: she may have moved away out of the area, as she had relatives in another part of the country, but we still remember her with affection and are proud that we helped her to turn her life round in such a positive way.

Chapter 21: Religion

I have had no personal contact with any of the major religions apart from Christianity, so what I say about others is only a general opinion. However, as far as Christianity is concerned, I have explained that I was steeped in it from an early age, and so it has formed the background against which much of my later spiritual philosophy has evolved. Therefore, these few comments must be understood to be in that context.

I have no problem with anyone who is a sincere believer in any religion, no matter which. All forms of religion are only ways which Mankind has accepted to try to come to an understanding of what life is all about, and all adherents to any religion believe in some sort of 'Supreme Being' who was the initial 'Creator' of the whole Universe. Most religions rely on an initial 'divine revelation', which was given to some historical or mythical human being, who was gifted with a very high degree of spirituality. My difficulty with most organised religion is that over the centuries this revelation has been commented on by generations of men, who have succeeded in applying human judgement, values and criteria to what was the original divine inspiration, so that it has become more important for followers to obey the *letter* of the Law rather than its *spirit*.

However, if one is discussing a supreme being, then by definition it must be far greater than anything that the limited intellect of human beings can understand, and so even by the very act of trying to *understand* it, humans are automatically *diminishing* it. By the same reasoning, even the naming of the being is a diminution of it. For instance, in the Christian tradition it is usually referred to as 'the Father': this makes Christians subconsciously think of their own father, and all that he meant to them. It also immediately gives the being the masculine gender and by implication denies that it can have any of what we normally consider 'feminine' attributes. In actual fact, the being itself must be far greater than the concept of every human - and since there are more than seven-and-a-half billion of us on the planet, it must be greater than the collective wisdom of all those people. So if some religious people say that it is not... (whatever does not fit in with the accepted dogma of their religion), they are saying that it *cannot be* that particular thing - which is to deny the *ability* of the Supreme Being to be just that, and therefore to diminish its power.

Much of this applies to Christianity, with its roots in the history of Judaism. Jesus himself was, of course, a well-documented historical person; but once one goes beyond that truth, one then has to interpret the meaning of the mission of Jesus - and this is where the problems start. They started, in fact, immediately after the Crucifixion, where the disciples were faced with the apparent end of the mission; then, after the Resurrection they were given instructions to 'Go and preach the Gospel' - and became apostles - a Greek word meaning 'those sent out'. This was all very well, but what were they to preach? They now had to decide what the mission of Jesus had really been all about - and the arguments started.

In ancient times, the personality of a messenger and the content of the message that he brought were often confused in people's minds. Being a messenger could be a very rewarding occupation: if he brought good news he was often highly rewarded with great honours and wealth. However, it could also be a very dangerous occupation: a messenger bringing bad news was often beaten, or - if the news was really awful - put to death.

This same confusion between the messenger and the message arose just after the crucifixion, because there were two ways of understanding what the mission had meant. The first was to concentrate on the messenger, and to say that the mission was all about Jesus being divine, and that all that anyone had to do was to believe in him and be saved. The other way, concentrating on the message, was to say that Jesus was a man, who became a 'son of God' once the 'spirit of God' came onto him at his baptism, and therefore he was showing that *all* humans have the ability to become what he became, *provided that they followed the path which he advocated.*

There is a great difference between the two interpretations, and even the followers of Jesus could not agree which was the correct one. Some, like Peter, preferred the first, while others, like Nathaniel, Thomas and James the brother of Jesus, followed the second. For a while the debate raged, until eventually Nathaniel went off to found the Eastern Church, Thomas went down to India, and both preached *their* interpretation, while Peter led the majority of the flock in the opposite philosophical direction. James the brother of Jesus remained as the head of the Church in Jerusalem, the then centre of the new religion. The split became final when Paul (who never even met Jesus during his life) came down on the side of Peter, and through his travels eventually founded the Church of Rome.

Then, when the new religion had become the established religion of the Roman Empire some three centuries later, the official dogma began to be created, but more and more confusion regarding what the religion was all about arose. Commentaries and interpretations of the gospels proliferated, and original texts were changed, until it became uncertain what the wording of the original texts had actually been.

I have noted elsewhere that Biblical scholars have identified hundreds of amendments to original texts. How they do this is by studying the language and style of a particular passage and identifying words or phrases which do not fit in easily with the bulk of the text. (As a crude example of this, if one picked up a supposedly ancient text and found that it contained words like 'random access' or 'diesel', or phrases like 'street-wise' or 'emotional abuse', one would immediately begin to suspect that the original had been considerably doctored)! As far as the Bible is concerned, the final result of such changes is that no-one today can say with certainty what the original wording of the gospels was - and when one is reading about what Jesus himself *said* one does not want to know what an unknown commentator on his words believed that those words *meant*, particularly if that commentator is trying to justify his own beliefs.

The result of this proliferation of texts meant that some sort of standardisation of doctrine had to be carried out, and this was done at the first Council of Nicaea, in 325 AD. The assembled bishops considered a minimum of 270 books (some sources say up to 4,000) which told the story of the early Church, and they decided to let God choose which books should be accepted as representing the 'true' faith. One contemporary observer said that all the books to be considered were put on the floor in a large room, which was empty apart from one table. The room was then locked, and the assembled bishops outside were asked to pray all night that the correct books should be put up on the table in the room. When the room was opened the next morning, there were 27 books on the table, and these 27 were chosen as the authentic books that were acceptable, and became the New Testament. 'By coincidence', all these books were those for which the young Bishop Athanasius had canvassed. All the remaining books were burnt. As a footnote to the story, it is not recorded who kept the key to the room overnight!

In the middle of the 20th century the Dead Sea Scrolls were found, and also the hoard of scrolls at Nag Hammadi, dating from the 4th Century AD, which together give us the titles and much of the text of a further 29 of the lost books. Not surprisingly, the general attitude of the Church is that they are 'of dubious authenticity and add little to existing knowledge'.

As the Church grew in influence, it became an enormous *political* power, and inevitably the political and the spiritual became confused and led to wars which were waged about differences in religious faith (e.g. the Crusades and particularly the one which led to the extermination of the Cathars). In addition, temporal corruption led to spiritual revolt, and the growth of the Protestant movement, which in its turn led to more wars of religion.

However, the adherence to Peter's and Paul's view of what Jesus' mission was all about has meant that whatever sect or faction of Christianity believers may adhere to today, the basic idea about the divinity, and therefore the worship, of Jesus is still the cornerstone of the faith. From that point of view, I am definitely not a Christian, as I have never found any reference in the gospels where Jesus says 'I am divine - worship me'. In fact, there is even one occasion when he specifically compared himself unfavourably to God. Someone had called him 'good Master' - and he replied 'Call no-one good but the Father!' I consider that the quote 'I and my Father are one' is highly suspect, as it does not sound at all like the style of Jesus: throughout his life he referred to himself originally as 'the son of Man', and then - after his baptism - as 'the son of God', so the use of a phrase in which he apparently identifies himself as the equal of God has a good chance of being either a later amendment or an addition. Perhaps it might be more likely if it were something like 'I and my Father are *at* one'.

In one way, however, I could be considered as a Christian, and that is because I follow the opinion of Nathaniel, Thomas and James the brother of Jesus, and believe that the mission of Jesus was to show that we are *all* sons and daughters of God, and by following the example which he gave we can arrive at a state of 'salvation' - or whatever the appropriate term is in each person's own mind-set. I therefore accept Jesus as an 'Ascended Master', one of those exalted beings who are working to help humanity to evolve spiritually, and I try to live my life in accordance with the spiritual principles he proposed.

I note that there are many of the spiritual gifts which are practised today which were mentioned in the gospels, for instance the gifts of clairvoyance (talking to Moses at the 'burning bush'), 'healing' (on numerous occasions), and 'speaking in tongues' (at Whitsuntide). I note also that Jesus said, 'These things shall ye do also - and greater than these!' Healing has now started to be given in some Christian denominations, and 'speaking in tongues' is being demonstrated in some Pentecostal churches. It is probably too much to hope that one day we may even see clairvoyance or trance channelling in churches - but I suppose that one can always hope that some of the ignorance and antagonism which exists against such gifts will one day disappear.

One example of that antagonism is the attitude towards getting information from another dimension. If this happens to a Christian, it is considered as 'divine inspiration': if it happens to anyone else, it is considered as 'the work of the Devil'. The same sort of reasoning is used when the subject of healing is discussed: healing in the confines of a church or chapel (provided it is not a Spiritualist church) is a miracle, and shows the power of the 'Holy Spirit': healing anywhere else, or by anyone but a Christian, is definitely either impossible or done through using the forces of Evil. (If I remember correctly, this was the charge levelled against Jesus himself by the Pharisees - so perhaps we can say that non-Christian healers are in good company!)

As I have been writing this section, I can look back on a remarkable case of spiritual healing within my own circle of friends. Several years ago, Sybil and Clare went together on a round-the-world tour, and much of their time was spent in Australia, with my family. However, three days before they left Clare suffered an accident in which she badly tore a ligament in one of her legs, and was put on elbow-crutches, in excruciating pain. We immediately called on healer friends and acquaintances from this country and all over the world to send healing to her, which they did. She had an appointment with her consultant two days later, and when I went round to her house to take her to the local hospital I found that she had no pain whatsoever, and although still using her crutches she was able to stand on the leg for short periods of time. I took them both to the Coach Station the following day and, although still using crutches, Clare was walking almost normally, with very little trace of even a limp. Such is the power of spiritual healing!

Whatever may be our view of religion, in the final analysis every human being is exactly where he/she needs to be at this moment of time. If we need the strong framework of an organised religion and we feel comfortable when some authority is telling us what we should or should not do or believe, then so be it. If we are able to accept that there is some truth in all religions, and we pick out what we feel is the core of truth from each and use it to form the blueprint by which we can live our lives and understand the purpose of life itself, then that is right for us. If we believe that the ultimate in human achievement is to live in total harmony with the natural world, as practised by some Aboriginal tribes and by North American Indians, then that is what we should do. The main problems arise when we are so convinced that we are right that we believe that everyone else is wrong, and try to convert others to our own particular brand of thinking - particularly if that conversion is done by threat or by force - or, even worse, by killing them because they do not follow our faith.

In that context most religions in the world (except perhaps Buddhism) are guilty, as all have at one time or another tried to spread their faith by means of the sword. This is not to deny that there have been many great missionaries who have taught by example - Albert Schweitzer and Mother Theresa in Christianity are two who come to mind immediately. Yet even now, in India, there are attacks against the Christian minority for trying to corrupt Hindus - and even the 'foundation of nuns' which Mother Theresa herself set up has been attacked for supposedly using their social work as an excuse for making converts to Christianity. Perhaps there will come a time in the history of the world when people will be judged by what they do for others, rather than by the creed or philosophy that they profess or do not profess. After all, didn't Jesus himself say 'By their fruits ye shall know them?'

As I write this, I have been listening to the news of a series of co-ordinated bombings in Iraq, which have obviously been aimed against the Shia majority on their holiest of days. It reminds us that although in

21: Religion

Christianity there is hatred between two factions of the same religion (Catholics and Protestants), the drama of which was for many years played out in Northern Ireland, this is not the only religion affected by sectarianism. Historically, in Islam there was discord between the adherents of the new religion some decades after the Prophet Mohammed died, regarding who was to be his rightful successor. The Shiites followed the claim of Ali, Mohammed's son-in-law, to be Khalifa whereas the Sunnites followed the claim of Omar, believing that he was Mohammed's adopted son - and therefore rightful heir. This led eventually to war between the two factions and the defeat and execution of Imam Husein, grandson of the Prophet, in the holy city of Karbala. The religious rites commemorating his death have been the targets of the bombers, and there are some commentators who suggest that the bombings in Iraq had the aim of turning the internal strife between the Shiites and the Sunnis into open warfare. With murderous hatred such as this between two sects of the same religion, is there any hope for an eventual reconciliation between all the differing religions of the world?

Re-reading this script two years on, when we are hearing of atrocities by the 'Islamic State', in which murder, rape, slavery and oppression of every religion or sect which does not conform to the strict fanatical interpretation of Islam preached by the 'Caliph' take place on an almost daily basis, the only thing which can possibly give us hope for the future is the analogy of the pendulum. The more it swings towards its highest point, the greater the force acting on it to stop and reverse that swing. How much longer now before the moderating force of opinion of ordinary, peace-loving Muslims is able to stop - and reverse - the movement causing so much damage to the religion, and so much Islamophobia against its adherents?

Chapter 22: Soul Mates

Many people spend much of their life looking for their 'soul mates', beings with whom they are supposed to be so compatible that, having met them, they will be instantly transported into the realms of physical, mental and emotional bliss, which will last for the rest of their lives. In most cases, of course, they never find these mythical beings, and just have to put up with whatever partners comes into their lives - or more correctly, whatever partners they themselves bring into their lives. But do soul mates exist, and if so how does one make contact with them?

My own personal philosophy is that they do, but not in the way that most people think about them. When they talk about soul mates, most people think that there is only one perfect person in the world for each of us: is it very surprising that we so rarely find that one person? After all, there are some seven-and-a-half billion of us on earth by now.

Spiritual philosophy tells us that we are all sparks of the divine creative force, and I can certainly understand this. However, in the higher philosophy, that force split off from itself an infinite number of parts, each of which is known as a Monad. Each part in turn split itself into twelve souls, and each soul split itself into twelve soul expressions. That means that there are 144 soul expressions in each monad. Now since each soul expression is a *part* of a soul, which in its turn is a part of a monad, this means that each soul expression is connected, directly or indirectly, to 143 others. They are not actually *part* of the others, but are allied with them. As an analogy, think of the different parts of the body: the legs, arm and head are all parts of the body and are connected with each other, but are not actually part of each other. However, each soul expression is part of its individual soul, in the way that each finger is a part of the hand, or each toe is a part of the foot.

22: Soul Mates

The object of the splitting up of the monads is to gain a larger amount of experience at the same time, so the individual soul expressions may be scattered around the universe at any one time; they may be on different planets, perhaps on the Earth, or perhaps not in any form of incarnation at all at the moment. However, many will be in incarnation on Earth at the same time as others in the same monad.

A further complication is that originally, when this planet was first being brought into physical shape, a call went out throughout the universe for volunteers to come in and help with its formation, and the formation of all the different species on it, including our own. So groups of volunteers from all over the Universe came down, and all the individuals in those groups (sometimes called 'pods') had the same characteristics, as they all came from the same planet in one or other of the parent constellations. So when they started to work on the Earth they stayed fairly close together, and have remained close together throughout all their incarnations ever since. Although the conscious memory of who was in our individual pod has long since been erased, it is quite likely that when we now work in a spiritual discipline in very close harmony with another person, we were originally members of the same pod.

So from all that, we can see that there are many different people with whom we may have a deep spiritual relationship: other soul expressions within our own monad, and those from our part of the universe who originally came to work with us on Earth as members of our own pod. My own inspirers tell me that there are at least 60 different people on Earth at any one time with whom each of us could have a totally harmonious relationship.

Having said that, one must remember that the object of all human existence is to have experiences, and through those experiences to learn lessons - and the majority of lessons that we learn will be through problems of some sort with other people. So if we are in a totally harmonious relationship with someone else, it is unlikely that we learn very much from each other.

However, it is often said that the best foundation for harmony in a partnership is where both partners have a common aim, which they can pursue together, and perhaps that is what we are really meant to look for in life. Perhaps all those lonely people in the world would be well advised to join clubs where they can meet others who share their own interests, whether in dancing, chess, gardening, literature, music, drama, country walking or anything else. In my own case, apart from the desire to do spiritual work, healing and teaching which Sybil and I both share, we also have a common hobby of doing jigsaw puzzles - a mundane enough activity, but one in which we can both work together in perfect harmony. Curiously enough, before we ever met, Sybil was told by a medium that we would fit together like two pieces of a jigsaw puzzle, each one complementing the other - and this is so: my weaknesses are covered by Sybil's strengths, and vice-versa, and although we work in different ways when we are giving healing to or counselling clients, we form a very powerful team when working together.

Carrying on the theme of soul mates, perhaps the true soul mates are those people who have lived together throughout a lifetime, have managed to survive everything which life can throw at them, have gone through the good times and the bad, and have made it to the end together. Possibly those are the ones who are far more successful than the people who meet their perfect partners and live happily ever after - or at least until the end of their days. In former times, of course, the majority of marriages were like the previous sort; there was no easy way out of a marriage when divorce was difficult and expensive and when marriage breakdown leading to separation incurred considerable social stigma. The prevailing motto in those days was 'You make your bed and you must lie on it'.

In this context, I am reminded of my own parents: they were totally mismatched in temperament, and fought each other verbally for most of their married life - in fact until their last ten years together. By that time, although only in their sixties, they were so mentally old and tired that they just gave up fighting - and as a result moved into a period which proved to be the happiest of their life. They became almost 'Darby and Joan' figures, and after my father's death (my mother outlived him by ten years) anyone listening to her talking about him would have thought that they had had a perfect marriage. Perhaps, then, they could (in retrospect) be considered as soul mates - they had taught each other the lessons about relationships which they had come to Earth to learn!

In these modern times, however, when time itself seems to have speeded up, so many people are unwilling to put in the work which is needed to make a relationship succeed: they seem to go for the 'quick fix' and expect instant marital (or extra-marital) bliss - and when it doesn't happen they simply break up the relationship and try again with someone else. In this context, although divorce is so much easier and less expensive (comparatively speaking) than it used to be, it is still a hurdle to be overcome when a relationship is ended; this means that now fewer and fewer people are even getting married in the first place, which must have some effect on the commitment which they have to each other from the start.

Paradoxically, in the case of many relationships in which the partners live together and then decide to get married after a number of years, that very fact seems to introduce tensions between them, leading to eventual estrangement and even divorce. So perhaps commitment itself can be seen in two different ways, one as the desire to work together to overcome all difficulties, and the other as a harness into which each person is put. Is this another example of the difference between a positive and a negative approach?

Chapter 23:
The Law of Spiritual Interest

L ong ago I asked my inspirers to explain the mechanism of how 'What goes round, comes round' works, and it was explained to me, but I found the explanation very complex and difficult to understand. However, I recently asked the same question, and was given a much simpler explanation - they have obviously realised that human beings cannot understand the complexities of human life as well as they can. The explanation was as follows:

When you go to your bank and make a deposit of money, you expect to get interest on it. When your account goes overdrawn, you will pay interest. This is so much a part of everyday life that you don't even question the system.

Now as a human being, you have an account in the Bank of Life, but the conditions are different from those in a normal bank. For instance, you can't merely offset debts that you incur against credits that have already accrued: they are kept in two separate sections. Next, everything is immediate: things start to happen and interest (positive or negative) accrues immediately anything is paid in or taken out. Finally, it is a Bank that rates you, not by the value of the money you have in your account, but by the value of the experiences you have provided for others.

Positive experiences are actions that enrich the lives of others in some way; they may be only small or they may be large, and vary from a friendly smile to a stranger to befriending someone who is at the lowest ebb in his/her life. The merits that you get for these are placed in the Credit section of your account, and immediately start to earn a high rate of interest, which has to be paid to you in the same way that it originally was earned, i.e. through positive experiences. However, since the rate of interest is very high, you will always be paid more - and in some cases far more - than the value of the original deed.

On the other hand, when you inflict a negative experience on anyone through some action that harms him/her in any way, that is placed in your Debit section, and in a similar way starts to incur high interest charges from the start. Once more, it depends on how negative the original action is: it might range from a scowl or a derogatory word spoken with the intention of hurting another person to a course of action - possibly over years - that bring someone down to the gutter or destroy their self-esteem. The original action was negative, and it must be repaid in kind. It could eventually incur interest - in the form of negative experiences - which seems totally disproportionate to the original action.

The interesting thing about this explanation is that there is no mention of the other person at all. Some people believe that Karma, the so-called 'Law of Retribution and Reward', works only between the two people involved, but obviously, it isn't absolutely necessary: whatever you do to one person can attract reward or retribution from another. This, after all, is only logical, else otherwise any two people who had been involved in any Karmic incident would be locked together eternally in tit-for-tat exchanges. Having said that, of course, where the positive or negative exchanges have been exceptionally extreme in one life, it would not be surprising if the parties agreed to have another round of relations together in a subsequent life in order to emphasise past harmony or to clear away all past problems.

In our everyday life we make a conscious decision when we shall put money into or take money out of our account. We do the same in our spiritual life - but in a slightly different way. When we go to a hole-in-the-wall cash-point to take out money, we need to key in our code number before the machine will give us anything. In our spiritual life, we need to make the conditions right before we can release any of the credits we have accrued - and we do this by creating a positive frame of mind. This is the 'code' that our spiritual bank needs before we are repaid what we have earned, in the form of positive experiences. On the other hand, if our frame of mind is negative, we are 'keying in the code' for the negative section of the account, and are more likely to reap its reward by starting a chain of events which bring some of our accrued debits back to us, giving us negative experiences.

A Practical Spiritual Primer

So there are significant similarities between our everyday and our spiritual banking systems. There is, however, one major difference - and that is in what happens when we leave our current incarnation. In the physical bank, we lose everything physical when we die - and the most that we can do with the assets we have owned is to arrange who shall have them after our death, by means of a will. In the spiritual bank, we take our accrued assets with us! This is the only case that gives the lie to the saying that 'You can't take it with you'. In fact, if we are talking about spiritual assets, not only *can* you take them with you, but you *do*. There is, of course, Biblical evidence for this, because we are enjoined 'not to lay up treasure for ourselves on earth where moth and rust corrupt but rather to lay it up in Heaven, where moth and rust do not corrupt'.

So the spiritual assets which we accrue in our lives are carried over from one life to the next (to carry on the comparison with earthly life, we 'bequeath' our assets to ourselves in our next earthly incarnation.) They won't usually change the overall pattern of that incarnation, but they may well bring into it pleasant experiences which we might otherwise not have had. However, if we consider the assets as including gifts and talents, we may well find ourselves remembering those gifts and talents that we have used in former lives as we make spiritual progress in the current life.

I have already spoken of one of the reasons why we may find ourselves reacting badly to someone whom we have only just met for the first time - we may be subconsciously remembering a difficult relationship in a past life. However, there is another very good reason why we react badly to another human being, and that is when we have something in our character of which we are ashamed, and we meet someone who reminds us of that trait. It is often said that the people whom we meet hold up a mirror to us, so that we can see in them our own characteristics. If we like those characteristics, we are likely to get on with the person. If not, then we will dislike them from the start.

Many people will ridicule this concept, as they cannot relate to any of the characteristics of someone whom they dislike at all. But this denies the possibility that these were traits that have been brought forward from past lives, which are presented to us so that we can finally dispose of them. I once had a dramatic instance of that in my own life.

I have a son who is a 'Born Again Christian', with whom I used to have many philosophical battles. I remember one family gathering at which there were five of us arguing about religion and spiritual philosophy until five o'clock in the morning - and going to bed without being a single step nearer to reconciliation. These days I am much older and - hopefully - much wiser, and realise that each of us is on his/her own pathway, which is totally right for us, although it may be totally wrong for anyone else. So I tend not to discuss religion with anyone at all, unless I am within my own circle of people, all of whom are on the same wavelength as me - the old adage of 'Like attracts like'.

The one thing that always incensed me more than any other in my discussions with my son was when 'the Devil' was mentioned, as I am of the mind-set that believes that the greatest problem of human beings is fear. Fear breeds negativity, which in its turn breeds evil. When there are enough humans around creating evil they make an 'egregor' (or 'thought form') which is personalised as the Devil - and the more that this egregor is spoken about, the stronger it becomes. Therefore, whenever Born Again Christians talk about the Devil, they are in fact helping to perpetuate it.

(As an aside here, the idea of 'egregors' is well-known in Buddhism, although they are given the name 'tulpas'. It is said that some Lamas in Tibetan Buddhism were so powerful that they could create tulpas that could actually be seen by less advanced human beings!)

Things came to a head some years ago, when I met a Born Again Christian Minister, whose extremist views made those of my son seem mild by comparison. For him, the Devil was everywhere, and in everything, and when he noticed the slight tremor in my left hand, he said that it was because I had the Devil in me. The facts that the tremor is possibly a mild form of Parkinson's Disease, and that I am now approaching old age, when things like that happen, were brushed aside - it was definitely the Devil. I extricated myself from that conversation as soon as I could, but for several hours afterwards I was still seething with rage, which was totally out of character with my Sun-Aquarian detachment and my Ascendant-Libran balance. So I decided to meditate to try to find out why that accusation had 'pressed my buttons', and had had such an effect on me.

I concentrated on the mirror-effect, trying to find out what was within me which I disliked so much that it had caused such a violent reaction - and I was taken back to a life in mediaeval France, some seven or eight hundred years ago. In that life I was a Christian extremist, (possibly a member of the Spanish Inquisition) who had the job of rooting out unorthodox beliefs; over a period of many years I sent hundreds - if not thousands - of people to their deaths on the pretext that their beliefs 'showed that they had the Devil in them' - and I had never forgiven myself for my actions in that life. Once I had identified the problem I could take steps to remedy the situation, and forgive myself, knowing that everything I had done at that time had been pre-arranged - and so I was able to not only forgive the Minister for what he had said to me, but also to thank him mentally for having given me the opportunity of clearing out another problem from a past life.

Earlier, I said that the interest earned on a negative action might appear to be totally disproportionate to the original action, and this may seem to be contradictory, if the object is just to balance up the account. But let us consider the matter a little more closely. Just imagine that you have, in one life, committed the ultimate sin against someone - you have killed him/her. Who have you affected? Well, obviously, you have killed that person, and to balance up the account you will in turn be killed, in similar circumstances But that person could have had parents, brothers or sisters, a spouse, children, and friends - and all of these will have been affected by your action, and so you will eventually have to atone for the harm that you have done to them as well. Therefore the final repayment will be many times that which the original action seemed to have warranted.

Of course, the same thing will apply when you have shown a kindness to another person, in any way. That person may also have had many others who were concerned about his/her welfare, and by helping that one person you will have indirectly helped all those others, by easing their mind about him/her. In addition, of course, your single kindly act may have helped the person to become more cheerful or confident - which could, in extreme circumstances, have helped to change their future life - and all of this will be repaid to you in interest, which may appear disproportionate to what you did for them.

Chapter 24: Stephanie

Another milestone in my life came in late 1996, when I met my last guru. A friend of ours wanted to go to an international conference of 'Walk-ins for Evolution' in Street, Somerset, and had no transport. Sybil and I volunteered to take her there, as it was only about 75 miles away. However, at the last moment we decided that we would like to attend the conference ourselves, and as accommodation was already fully booked, we went in our camper-van.

I have rarely met such an interesting group of people in my life. There were about 80 of us altogether, some of whom were scientists (one Swedish man had invented an engine powered by water), and many who were international names in their own fields of psychic research - colour therapists, past life regression experts, counsellors, channels, psychic artists, writers, mediums and lots more. One lady even claimed to be from the planet Venus - and said that she went back up to her spaceship every night to watch over her sector of Earth. We found out about her unearthly activities when Sybil complimented her on her blouse, which was a silvery-grey, silky sort of material, of a kind that I had never seen before. She replied, 'Yes, it is nice: I chose it because it looks very much like the material of my space suit'. How about that for one-upmanship!

On the last afternoon, there were some 5-minute slots in the programme, which had been created for anyone who wished to stand up and have their say about any spiritual matter. The last one was taken by a small lady with long black hair, who started off her talk by saying, 'Do you realise that the last time we were all together was in Atlantis?' To say that this was a conversation-stopper would be an understatement - everyone was 'gob-smacked'. She went on to say that in Atlantis, the scientists did not understand the religious people, and vice-versa - so that in this incarnation both parties had come together to finally resolve some of the issues which had existed and which led to the destruction of the Atlantean continent in that long-forgotten time. I hope that this time round, those issues will be resolved and by a *common* effort, some of the problems with which Mankind is faced in the world at large will be considerably mitigated.

We both found the whole weekend fascinating, and made some very interesting contacts. On the last night, just before we left, we went to an impromptu birthday party for 'Lady Venus', and someone there demonstrated a spiritual device which consisted of a couple of coloured glass spheres, which were put on the floor about six feet apart, one just above the head and the other just below the feet of a person lying down. The sensations one got by lying in between them varied from person to person, but all felt some sort of energy or other passing through them.

The week after we had come back, we were contacted and asked to come to a meeting at which we would discuss the possibility of setting up a Devon branch of 'Walk-ins for Evolution', at the house of the lady who had spoken about Atlantis. We found out that her name was Stephanie - and she was to become my last guru. The branch was never formed, but most of the people contacted stayed in touch with each other over the years. However, for me, events took a quite unexpected turn: I was talking to Stephanie one day, and she said that *she* was the person who had introduced the energy spheres; she was now receiving a lot of channelled information from various sources, and as she personally was a triple-dyslexic (reading, writing and speaking) she was not able to reduce what she had been given into recognisable grammatical English. As I had very good fluency with both the spoken and the written word, I volunteered to proofread all that she had produced to date - and thus began a very productive relationship, which lasted for over nine years.

I found that Stephanie was channelling material from 14 Ascended Masters: Ascended Masters are spiritual beings, most of whom have had many lives on Earth before achieving the status of perfected human beings, and therefore have no further need to carry on with human incarnations. These 14 beings who channelled through Stephanie represented all the main religions of the Earth, past and present. Some of them are household names within those religions, for instance the Christ Energy, Gautama/ Sakhyamuni Buddha, Pallas Athene, Kwan Yin and Melchizadek; others, like El Morya, Soltec, Hilarion and Djwahl Kuhl are

24: Stephanie

less well known - and some (Ashtar, Nada, Kla-la, Elys and Yuminale) were totally unknown to me.

Little did I know what I was taking on when I accepted to do the proofreading. For a start, the level of language was incredibly high, and the subject matter so complex that I could not read and correct much more than a couple of pages in a night. That, combined with the mass of information which was coming through, meant that I was stretched to the limit to produce the finished product; not only that, but my mind was being stretched at the same time, and faced with concepts on a spiritual and scientific level far beyond anything I had yet imagined, let alone understood.

Stephanie is multi-gifted, a member of the Institute of Crystal and Gem Therapists, a Healer, a Shaman and one of the foremost Psychic Counsellors in the country. She has a large telephone counselling clientele and is one of the most amazing psychics I have ever known. To give an example, one day I mentioned the name of one of my daughters, who lives in Australia: Stephanie had never met her, but immediately linked into her, looked in her aura, saw a man there (my son-in-law), jumped over to his aura and gave me a reading on his character. I have never before known anyone who was capable of doing that within the space of about 15 seconds.

Stephanie is one of the most amazing human beings I have ever met, and her own life story, showing how she achieved success after the most un-promising of childhoods, would make an incredibly interesting book! She and I are really at opposite poles in most ways: I am a mental person, who has always prized intelligence and any sort of mental occupation very highly. She is an intuitive person, who has always had to rely on her psychic faculties to get her through life, because of her originally poor level of education. I have always been a 'male chauvinist pig', and a true control freak - whereas she has suffered so much with male chauvinism that she can be reasonably described as a 'rampant feminist'. I have three professional qualifications to my name, whereas she has none - and yet I am the first to admit that she has more knowledge about a wider variety of practical and spiritual matters than I will ever have. She has a fascinating way of learning from books: she just picks up the book, puts it under her pillow at night, and by morning has assimilated - on a psychic level - its contents. She also has more commonsense than I do: in fact she couldn't have less - as I have none at all.

Stephanie introduced me to the concept of vibrational spiritual energy, which prepared the way for my current study of Metaphysics, and we travelled together for many years to 'Mind, Body and Spirit' fairs around the country, selling her vibrational energy products; this in turn introduced me to a large number of people, all of whom specialised in one or other of the many spiritual disciplines, alternative therapies, etc. - which enlarged my knowledge of the variety of branches of spiritual science which exist, and which were at that time unknown to me! Over the years when we were working together, I learned an enormous amount from her - and I will always acknowledge the huge spiritual debt that I owe to her.

Chapter 25: Stages in Life

I have said that approximately every seven years Uranus causes a change in our lives - and in my case, this has always meant either a change of employer or a change of job within that employment. This started at the end of 1954, when I went into the Army for the first real job of my life, and it has continued with amazing regularity ever since. The last time it occurred was early in 2010, when I wrote my new book so at the moment I am in an in-between period, digesting and developing the new knowledge which I was given in that channelling . I am looking forward to late 2016, or early 2017, when my next change of occupation will come. At the moment I have no idea what it might be, as I am 'getting into my dotage' now, but I am sure that it will be as interesting as the rest of my life has been!

As five of my children are now permanent residents in Australia, with Australian citizenship, I hope that quite a part of my future will be spent in that wonderful country. Although I have no prospect of being able to get a residence visa at the moment, I will certainly want to spend several extended holidays down-under. It is interesting that I had never had the slightest interest in visiting Australia for the first 66 years of my life, until my daughter Ellie and her family emigrated there and invited us to visit them at Christmas in 2000. However, as soon as I stepped off the plane at Perth Airport I immediately felt at home. There is a wonderful spiritual energy about the country, which is so beautiful and varied in climate and vegetation, and the people are so amazingly open and friendly that it is hard *not* to feel at home there. In addition, about 60% of the population of Perth are of British origin, which gives one the feeling of being in Britain with a far better climate. So far I have been to only Perth, in Western Australia, and to Sydney, in New South Wales, but I have no doubt that the same applies everywhere in that vast continent/country.

A Practical Spiritual Primer

So I come to the end of my reflections on my own earthly journey over more than eighty years. Looking back over my life, I have realised that there were many separate stages in my own spiritual development, which were as follows:

The first was my introduction to the possibility of prediction, as shown by Aunty Margaret's predictions about Eleanor and me living together in Tutbury. Then, six years later, when I had almost forgotten that first event, she introduced me to Spiritualism and to services in Spiritualist churches.

Learning about the fact that when a person 'dies' it is not the end of them as a personality is a major step in most people's lives - and it certainly was in mine. Many people never get to that stage, but without a firm conviction that the end of physical life does not mean the extinction of the person completely there is very little to alleviate the suffering of those who are bereaved. Orthodox religion is not much help either: it is not much comfort to someone who is bereaved to know that their loved one is 'asleep', and will remain that way until 'the trumpet will sound, and the dead will be raised'. It is even less comfort to be assured that 'Christ, in his mercy, will look after the souls of all those who have died, believing in him' - if the dear departed was not a believer or, even worse, was a convinced atheist. If it can be shown that all the 'dear-departed' *still exist* after the death of the physical body, and that regardless of their religious beliefs - or the lack of them - they can still contact those who are left on Earth, then the sense of permanent loss which we have after their passing can be diminished, or even after a time completely disappear.

It took me many years to become convinced of the truth of the personality surviving the death of the physical body, but once I had got to that state I was able to meet my second guru and to learn about how spiritual beings can use us as 'instruments' in order to channel spiritual philosophy.

This then prepared me to enter into the life of a Spiritualist church, where I practised sitting in circle, learnt how to channel and also found out that I had a gift of healing. I was introduced to the possibility of Reincarnation while sitting in circle, and also started to learn about Rescue - where the souls of those who have departed this life and who have not made a full transition into the Light can be helped to move on from their own private Hell. Some of those whom we helped were just lost, and needed to be told only how to face the Light. However, many had lived lives that would normally be thought of as 'wicked', and so had created the situation where they had deliberately separated themselves from the Light - and were in fact afraid of going into it. The state in which such souls exist is sometimes known as 'Limbo' but is more commonly known in Catholic circles as 'Purgatory'.

Of course, Spiritualism has been condemned as evil since its inception over 170 years ago. It has been accused of raising the souls of the dead, dabbling in the occult, necromancy, deceiving the gullible and other such hideous crimes. This is not surprising: if the truth about what happens after death - that the *real* person survives, although living in another dimension - were generally known and accepted throughout the world, there would be a lot of clerics of all religions who would be out of a job!

Then, because of an incident that upset the harmony of the little Spiritualist Church, I was taken away and made to do my own thing - and found that I was drawn to various books that broadened the scope of what I had so far only touched upon in the realms of spiritual philosophy. I now know that everything that was happening to me during that long period of time (about twenty years) was synchronicity. All that I knew at the time when it was happening was that every time that a question or an idea came into my head about an aspect of philosophy, 'by co-incidence' I found a book which dealt with that particular aspect in a certain amount of detail. One of these was the book about the life of Edgar Cayce, which was only the first of a series of books that I read about the concept of Reincarnation. I think that it was only when I started to study this concept that I started to be able to make any sense at all out of the manifest inequalities and injustices of human life on our planet.

Next, after the death of Eleanor, I met my third guru, who introduced me to the idea of the Earth being only one element in a chain of Cosmic consciousness, and the possibility of being contacted now - and having been contacted in the past - by beings from other parts of the Universe as well as by those from other dimensions. I learnt of the possibility of the forerunners of Mankind coming originally as 'Starseeds' from other star-systems in our known Universe. Following this, I was 'co-incidentally' invited to sit in a Cosmic circle, where from time to time beings from other star-systems channelled through sitters.

At about the same time I learnt about Ascended Masters, enlightened beings from backgrounds of many different religions who may or may not

A Practical Spiritual Primer

have lived out a series of lives on the Earth, and who are now involved with raising human beings to the spiritual level at which they can 'ascend' into the next dimension whilst still being in a conscious state. This is connected with the Ascension of the planet herself into that same dimension. There has never been a simultaneous ascension of a planet and of all its inhabitants before in the history of the galaxy, so there are beings from all round the Universe who are watching with interest to see what will happen here within the next few years. We are told that they are all anxious to get ringside seats for the great spectacle!

Another dramatic event at this time was when I was drawn to Louise Hay's works, and the concept of Positive Thinking, which so helped me to sort out my own life and then gave me the knowledge to show others how to help themselves as well.

Meeting Clare and then Sybil gave me an entry into a group of people who are all on a very high spiritual wavelength, which has allowed me to discuss and expand my own spiritual philosophy, while giving me the grounding and emotional fulfilment which is invaluable for anyone seeking to 'do their own thing'.

Then, of course, I met Stephanie, my final guru, who taught me about 'vibrational energy'. This gave me a completely new concept of 'God', which I now see as the creative power behind everything or, perhaps more accurately, the creative *Energy*. I have come to realise that we, who contain souls - sparks of that creative power - are capable of 'co-creating with God', and able to change Reality - the reality of our very lives - and create our own futures. I realise that we are able to work with the elements, with Nature with the planet itself, as well as with various Angelic and Devic entities, in order to further the work of Spirit (which in my vocabulary is synonymous with the Creative Energy). In fact, as we are energy, we can relate to the energy in everything else on the planet, whether living (other humans, animals and plants) or non-living (minerals, stones and crystals) and work with it in order to further creation by showing the absolute harmony of everything created.

Everything in the Universe, ourselves included, is energy - and as energy is non-destructible and immortal, we ourselves are indestructible and immortal. The human body, of course, is very frail and ephemeral, and at the end of our earthly life breaks down into its constituent minerals - but the soul, the *real* us, the spiritual part that the body contains, can never be destroyed. It was split off from the creative Energy at some unimaginably remote time in the past, has assumed many different temporary forms in different star-systems over its long existence, and will continue to do so until eventually it is re-united with the source from which it came, at some unimaginably remote time in the future. During the course of hundreds of lives on our planet, where it has been learning to cope with the density of physical matter, it has had many changes of personality, each associated with one particular incarnation.

Many of the different religious systems in the world teach us that we are weak, sinful and in need of divine approval in order to survive this life. One of the lines of an old hymn of the Church of England comes to mind: 'Have mercy on us, worms of Earth'. We are constantly being urged by clerics of all denominations to 'Repent of our sins' - else we will not enter into a state of blessedness which is reserved by their divinity for only the faithful who have followed the teachings of their particular religion to the letter. They maintain that all who do not are outcasts, should be scorned and/or shunned (and even, in some mind-sets, killed) - all in the name of Religion. They talk of the Last Judgement, when 'the wheat will be separated from the tares'. What is more, they state that we have only this one life in which to reach the stage of perfection required for the ultimate Paradise.

(In passing, I note that most Eastern religions are far more tolerant, particularly those that accept the doctrine of Reincarnation as part of their faith. As I have said earlier, it is difficult to condemn someone for not following your religious tenets in this life if you believe that you may incarnate as a member of *their* religion in the next).

I explained that I was brought up in the confines of a strict Church of England tradition, and many of my memories of the prayers used emphasise the state of worthlessness of Mankind. Phrases like 'Have mercy on us miserable sinners' and 'We are not worthy so much as to gather up the crumbs under Thy table' come to mind. Is it any wonder that Church attendance is diminishing so rapidly? After all, if going to Church makes you feel totally unworthy, when continually compared with the perfection of the life of Jesus, then it is not surprising that so many just give up.

When reading a newspaper recently, I saw a cartoon showing an empty church by the side of a cinema, which had long queues of people waiting to go in to see the film 'The Passion'. Whether one thinks that the cartoon is funny or tragically sad, it is difficult to understand how the Christian Church could have managed to create such apathy about its main message in the modern world.

In my understanding of what it is all about, nothing could be further from the truth than the absolutism of most Western religious thinking. I see the purpose of life for us as being that each of us is here to 'co-create with God', to produce new complexities in the story of human development on this planet. Marianne Williamson is a famous American authoress and self-help guru, who has written many books. In one of these, 'A Return to Love' (1992), she says that the thing of which we are most afraid in life is not that we are too weak - but that we are too strong. We are afraid of being able to change the world by the very force of our personalities - and that fear does not serve either our own purpose or the purpose of Humanity at large. If only each of us would use the power we possess in order to create the life we want to lead, free of any thoughts of controlling or dominating any others, what a world we could create! Could any wiser words ever be spoken?

Having already exceeded my allotted span - the three-score-and-ten years of the Bible - by more than ten years I do not know how long I have to live now before I am allowed to go back 'home', nor do I know where I will end my days. However, I know that I will always be wherever I am meant to be, at the right time to experience whatever I am meant to experience. I don't know what will happen in the future: all that I know is that the future is going to be very interesting, as we approach the end of this major cycle in the history of the world. In fact, as I am always saying to my friends, 'All is well'. The process of Life is always perfect, and whatever is *meant* to happen in my life - what I have already decided on a spiritual level should happen - *will* happen, and will be for my eventual benefit, although I may not realise that at the time. The worst thing that can ever happen to me is that I will die - although that is inevitable anyway: it is just a question of when and how it happens. However, even Death will signify that I have done enough in my life to be allowed to go back 'Home', having fulfilled all the contracts and learnt all the lessons which I had undertaken to do before I came into this life. So therefore I will just carry on 'going with the flow', doing whatever I am inspired to do at any time and knowing that in the overall scheme of things I cannot make a 'mistake'.

I am still curious to know what my 'great work for Spirit' will be: although I always try to do my bit to make the world a better place in my little corner of existence, there is nothing in my life so far which is likely to have repercussions outside the circle of my family and friends. What I do know is that Humanity is now past the end of the world cycle, which was forecast by the Mayan Calendar hundreds of years ago to occur on 23rd December 2012, and a massive change of consciousness is becoming imminent. Physically, the latest buzzwords are 'global warming' - and scientists are discussing how this will affect the Earth in future. Not only that, but they have already detected changes in the magnetic fields of the Earth around the Southern Pole area: perhaps that is the forerunner of the dreaded magnetic reversal of the Poles, which takes place once in every 60,000 or so years. Perhaps I will have something to do with helping Humanity to prepare for the massive upheaval that will take place at that time - or to adjust to the new situation after it has occurred? I don't know! All that I can say is that, hopefully, the human beings of the future will have learnt that they are all connected with each other on a spiritual level, and will start to live in peace and harmony, conserving the resources of the planet, rather than slaughtering each other and destroying their own habitat at the same time.

Then, if all that does come to pass, what has been called 'The New Age' will eventually dawn - and perhaps at last my friends will be able to agree with me when I say:

ALL IS WELL!

~ PART TWO ~

Appendix Section

This Appendix consists of transcripts of talks that I gave to a small group of about 25 people who attended the weekly demonstrations of clairvoyance given at 'Infinity Clairvoyance' in Paignton during 2014. (The group now meets in Torquay). So those to whom I was speaking then were all well aware of the possibility of contacting those 'loved-ones on the other side of life' - it was demonstrated every week. However, few of them knew the spiritual philosophy behind what they were experiencing, so I started the series of talks with the aim of giving them a few of the basic facts behind it all. I made a printed transcript of each talk, and gave it as a handout each night to all who were present. I gave 40 talks over the period of that year, and then my inspirers gave me the idea of collating them into a small book, as a basic primer of information for all who might be interested in the subject. So I condensed the original talks into 19 chapters, each of which is short enough to be read as one unit, but contains enough information to give the reader 'food for thought'.

But then I realised that many *existing* spiritualists - although they might not need any convincing about the reality of 'Life after Death' - have only a very hazy notion of the scientific basis behind Spiritualism. In one of the branches of Spiritualism, the Spiritualist National Union, seven core principles of Spiritualism are preached, but these are bland statements of belief (for instance, 'The Fatherhood of God', 'The Brotherhood of Man', etc.,) but these principles are qualified by the final statement 'with freedom of interpretation', so in order to understand what each of them means in detail those who attend services at the church have to rely on the possibility of the medium for the night touching on that particular subject in his/ her address. So existing spiritualists might also find this appendix of value in providing a simple outline of basic philosophy. (If S.N.U. members don't accept the 'Reincarnation' chapters - I would claim my own right to 'freedom of interpretation').

Finally, in common with many others round the world, I feel that Mankind is ready for a 'New Age' of behaviour and philosophy. There are an enormous number of people of all nationalities, races and philosophies who are tired of 'man's inhumanity to man', and sickened by the violence, intolerance and hatred which is rife everywhere in the world today, often inflamed by the extremists of various religions. Such people may be currently torn between two schools of thought. They can believe scientists, who maintain that everything in life happens in a strictly 'mechanical' way, according to rigid scientific principles, and who reject any possibility of continued existence after the death of the physical body, (but cannot explain human motivation and behaviour). Alternatively, they can believe preachers of various religions, many of whom pay little attention to scientific facts, but attribute all human problems to the fact that those involved do not follow the 'true' religion - and who warn of ultimate death and destruction to such unbelievers.

Such people, torn between the two extremes, may find this Appendix interesting reading, as it puts forward a logical philosophy blending scientific reasoning with the core concepts of all religions, stripped of all the religious dogma that separates them.

However, regardless of the group into which you, the reader, fall I hope that you will find it an interesting and stimulating explanation of a basic philosophy of life.

Chapter 1: What Are You?

Ask yourself 'What am I?' and when you answer it don't think of what anyone else can see. So don't say that you are a man or woman, tall or short, old or young, thin or fat, etc. Everyone else can tell you that. Instead, think of what you mean when you say 'I': what is this 'I?'

Well, there are various possibilities: you may think that the 'I' is your body, or your emotions, or your mind. But let us have a look at each of these possibilities in turn, and see if they are correct.

First, are you your body? Well, that is easy to say - the answer has to be 'No!' Why? Because you can say to your body, 'Do this, or that, or something else' - and it usually will. You can say to your legs, 'Walk!' or your arms 'Wave!' or your head 'Nod!' - and they usually will. (You may have a bit of trouble in later years getting them to do exactly what you want, when you want, but that is a different problem). So the 'I' is something different to your body. If it can tell the body what to do, it has to be different, doesn't it?

Is the 'I' your emotions? Once again, the answer is 'No!' You can control your emotions by an effort of will. Some of us find it very easy to do, others find it more difficult - but everyone can do it. Just do a little exercise the next time that you are feeling sad: think of the happiest day in your life. What it was will differ from one person to another: some will think of the birth of their first child, or the day when they first entered their own home. Others will think of their wedding day (or possibly, in this day and age, of the day they got divorced). But whatever and whenever that day was, think of it and remember all that you can of it. Very soon, you will find that your whole mood has changed - and the 'I' has made it change. So the 'I' must be separate from your emotions - if it can control those emotions, it must be separate, mustn't it?

A Practical Spiritual Primer

But can it be your mind? Well, this is even easier to demonstrate; think of the following in quick succession. Your mother; your father; what you had for breakfast this morning; where you went on your last holiday; what you are going to do tomorrow. In the space of one minute, the 'I' has told the mind to do five different things, and it has obeyed. So the 'I' cannot be the mind either.

Of course, your mind can be very powerful. It can control not only your emotions and your physical body, it can control your health as well, by using the power of visualisation - but we will consider that much later in the book.

So what is the 'I', or - to return to the original question, 'What are you?' Once you can answer that, you can say what every human being is - and that is a massive step forward in your spiritual understanding. Think about it for a few minutes, and try to find one simple everyday word to describe what is the 'I' is.

Possibly the best answer to the question 'What am I?' is the word 'Personality', although as we shall see it is not the complete answer. But let us go with it for the moment.

The next question to ask yourself is, 'What is the difference between a human being and a dead body?' Well, most of you will have seen a dead body, and some of you will have had the harrowing experience of sitting by the bedside of loved ones at the moment of their passing. If so, you will know that, just a few minutes before then, they were still with you, probably - but not always - unconscious, usually having trouble with their breathing, as the lungs lost their ability to supply the body with enough oxygen. Then suddenly - always unexpectedly - there was a hideous silence. And someone eventually said, 'He (or she) has gone'.

And something certainly had gone - what we are temporarily calling 'the personality'. We understand the word 'personality' only because of what we have seen, heard or experienced of the person in the past. We look at the bodies of loved ones and remember what they *have* been. If you looked at the body of someone you didn't know, you would have no idea whatsoever of what their personality had been.

But after the moment of death, not only has the personality disappeared, but also the mind and the emotions at the same time. So somehow, all three are so connected together that they have all left at the same time. Why are they connected? How are they connected?

A1: What Are You?

See if you can find a simple word or phrase to describe a combination of the personality, the mind and the emotions. We will consider why and how they are all interconnected later on.

***

Scientists have discussed the subject for years, and have given this elusive quality the name of 'Consciousness', but have tried to tie it down by relating it to a specific part of the body. Up until recent times, the general consensus of scientific opinion was that 'consciousness' had to be located somewhere within the brain - but exactly where? They never managed to find conclusive proof, but a few years ago something happened which destroyed that theory completely.

Dr Eben Alexander was a professor of Neurosurgery in an American university, when one day he was struck down with a virulent form of bacterial meningitis. He was rushed into intensive care in his own hospital, but soon after apparently 'died'. His body was kept alive on a life-support machine for another week, and his brain was monitored constantly for any signs of activity, which were completely absent, so after the week he was pronounced 'brain-dead', and switching off his life-support machine was considered. However, before this could be done he suddenly woke up, and remembered all sorts of fantastic things which he had done while being 'dead'. So therefore his consciousness had existed, somehow, completely separate from his brain. As a scientific man, he had always dismissed any idea of the continuation of existence after the death of the physical body, but the experiences which he had had completely changed his mind, and he eventually wrote several books of spiritual philosophy, of which the first was entitled 'Proof of Heaven', published in 2012. It is a fascinating book, as was its sequel, 'Map of Heaven' (2014) and is highly recommended to all who are sceptical about the possibility of the continuation of existence after the death of the physical body.

Chapter 2: What is Energy?

Scientists say that the Universe is made up of energy, and Spiritualists say exactly the same thing, although the two sides see the word 'energy' in different ways. But perhaps the scientist's 'energy' is easier to understand.

If we put any item under a high-power microscope, we see that although it looks solid to the naked eye it becomes increasingly like a sponge, with larger holes appearing, as we increase the magnification, until eventually it splits into little islands of matter; these finally become individual circles, which scientists call 'atoms'. No human being has ever seen an atom without using a microscope, because they are far too small to be seen with the naked eye.

But that is not the end of things, because in the middle of each atom is a small core, or nucleus, only a fraction of the size of the atom, and spinning round that nucleus are minute specks of matter which are called electrons, each of which is only one two-hundredth of the size of the nucleus - and so very small indeed.

It takes a lot of energy to keep all those electrons spinning, very rapidly, round the nucleus, and a hundred years ago scientists found out how to split one electron from its parent atom - and in doing so released a huge amount of energy from the atom; the knowledge was eventually used to create an atomic bomb and slaughter a huge number of people in one single blast.

This energy within every single atom is the energy of life itself, and until we can understand that, we have no chance of understanding life. But let us first consider how the atom got its name.

Two and a half thousand years ago there was a famous Greek scientist called Democritus, who had the idea that if you took a piece of gold wire, and cut it in half, and then cut one of the halves in half, and did the same again, and again, and again, sooner or later you would get

A2: What is Energy?

to a situation where what was left could no longer be cut - it was 'α τομος' ('a tomos' in Roman letters) which means 'not cuttable'. Two hundred years ago an English physicist, John Dalton, revived the idea and - combining and cutting short the two words 'a tomos' to one - used the word 'atom' as the start of his work on Atomic Theory, which is still the basis of all modern Chemistry.

There is a fictitious story about a Professor of Physics at an American university who always started off his courses for first year degree students by explaining to them, in a simple way, what energy was all about. At the start of the first lecture he put a large glass jar on the table in front of him, and filled it with golf balls, then asked the students if it was full or not.

Some of them said that it was, but others were more dubious, noting the big spaces in between the golf balls. He then produced a bag of dried peas and poured them over the golf balls. When he had shaken the jar a few times, the peas filtered down and filled those spaces, so he asked the same question. Most students now said that the jar was full.

Next, he produced a bag of very fine dry sand, poured it over the peas, shook the jar until it had filled all the spaces between the peas, and asked the question again. Now all the students agreed that the jar was full.

However, finally he took a large jug of water, poured it over the sand - and filled the jar. He then explained that whether the jar was full or not depended on the students own *level of understanding* of what the word 'full' meant: some of them - on the 'golf-ball' level - thought that it was full from the start, but those on the other levels disagreed. Those on the 'peas' level were equally certain that it was full, but those on the other two lower levels disagreed. All of them on the 'sand' level *knew* that the jar was full - and yet all were wrong. It was only at the final level - the 'water' level - that the jar was undeniably full.

Although the story is fictional, the four levels of understanding give us a very useful tool with which to look at Reality. We shall refer back to them later on, in the context of pure science, but let us for the time being repeat what they are: the Golf ball - coarsest and most superficial, the Peas - finer and deeper, the Sand - even finer and much deeper, and finally the Water - the finest and most profound. We are now going to see the spiritual explanation of how each human being was originally created, and we shall see a remarkable resemblance to those four stages - but in reverse. This is because the first stage of a human being starts with the finest material possible - pure Spirit - and ends with the coarsest - physical flesh and blood.

It ties up almost exactly with what my own inspirers have told me, in their explanation of the initial creation of a human being, so - as I have by now total faith in what they have given me over the last sixty years or so - I will tell you what they said happened.

In this explanation, I will use the following terms:

The Creator:
The creative force of the Universe (not an old man with a long white beard sitting on a golden throne somewhere up in the sky).

Spirit:
The primal energy from which all creation is made.

The blueprint:
The process by which all human beings have been made since the dawn of the human race.

Subtle bodies:
The different main stages in the production of a human being, before the final join to the foetus.

Interfaces:
The intermediate stages between subtle bodies.

The Creator took a large amount of Spirit and fashioned it into a *Spiritual Body* - the **first subtle body.** This is a very high-level of vibrations, and is the permanent body of every human being - the 'I' factor in each one of us. It is often referred to as the Higher Self. (This can possibly be equated to the scientists' 'consciousness' mentioned above).

That process is never done more than once. The following steps form *the blueprint* and are done each time a human being is about to come into incarnation:

A2: What is Energy?

The **second subtle body,** according to the blueprint, had to be at a much lower level of vibration, and a small part of the *Spiritual Body* was used to fashion it. As it was not possible to step the energy down all in one go, an interface was put in as an intermediate stage, before further stepping down created the *Mental Body.* (Electricians will understand that when it is necessary to 'step down' an electrical current, resistors are put into the circuit!)

The same process was repeated to create the **third subtle body** - an even greater 'step down', and another interface was needed before the *Emotional Body* was created.

The **final interface** was the most important one of all, as this was not just an intermediate phase, but also it had a very important role to play. The blueprint said that it had to be an *exact replica* of the eventual human being, containing the spiritual equivalent of every bone, muscle, nerve, gland, cell, etc. which the eventual human being would have.

Now the whole of the spiritual side of the human being - the subtle bodies - was complete, but the difficult part of the task lay ahead. First, a foetus - a physical part of the mother, growing in the womb - had to be chosen. That part wasn't hard to do, as at any one time there are hundreds of millions of women pregnant on Earth. But then the whole of the subtle bodies and their related interfaces had to be inserted into the chosen womb, and every part of the final interface had to be connected up to the physical foetus, and that took a long time - about three months. Commonly called 'the quickening', it is the time when the foetus starts to kick, punch and squirm as each new connection is made.

Then the original human being was born! This process is repeated every time a human being comes into incarnation, The only difference is that before the actual birth, any positive or negative energies that have been accumulated from past incarnations are transferred from the previous *Mental and Emotional Bodies.*

So finally, at the appropriate time, the new baby is born, and is composed - as we all are - of a spiritual body (the Water level) within a mental Body (the Sand level), within an emotional Body (the Peas level, within the final, coarsest physical body (the Golf Balls level). So when you hear it said that each human being has four different bodies, you will now know what that means. (Sometimes people say that there are seven bodies - and that is because there are the three interfaces also).

A Practical Spiritual Primer

We have seen that everything in the Universe is made from energy, at different levels of vibration. Most of the energy is invisible, and only what we consider as 'the real world' can be perceived with our five physical senses, Sight, Hearing, Touch, Smell and Taste.

To understand the idea of different levels of vibration we can take the analogy of water. (An analogy is a simple example that helps us to understand a more complicated idea). If you heat water to a very high temperature it turns into water vapour, which is invisible to the naked eye. Cool it down a little and it becomes steam, which you can see but you can't touch (unless you want to scald yourself). Cool it further and it turns into ordinary water, which we can touch but not hold, and then cool that until it becomes ice, which we can pick up. Water vapour, steam, water and ice are all different forms of water, cooled to different temperatures.

And this is what happens to energy, but instead of being cooled and condensed, it is 'stepped down'. So we saw that when a human being is first formed, the pure energy (spirit) is used to form a spiritual body, or Higher Self. Then this energy is stepped down to a lower vibration and becomes the next subtle body (the mental body), then further still to become the final subtle body (the emotional body). There are minor intermediate stages in the process - what we called interfaces. The last - and most important - interface is the one that connects all of the subtle bodies to the final, physical, body, which will become the new baby.

So every human being is composed of three subtle bodies and a physical body, plus three interfaces (which are sometimes also called bodies). But what happens at the moment of Death? We said that the difference between a living human being and a corpse is the personality, and that personality is what leaves the physical body and its associated interface. Therefore, we can now define 'personality' as being the three subtle bodies, the two interfaces that join them together, and the final interface, which joined the subtle bodies to the physical body. Although it is no longer needed, and breaks away from the physical body on the death of the latter, it still remains attached to the emotional body.

Finally, we saw how the four different levels of understanding, the Golf ball, Peas, Sand and Water levels, all exist within the same space, as all are of different sizes. So all of our subtle bodies and interfaces exist within the physical body, to make us what we are, because they are all at different levels of vibration.

Chapter 3: What is Death?

Before we can start to talk about Death, we first have to decide what we mean when we say the word. Do we mean the end of any form of existence, or do we mean the end of the body's ability to function? The two things are totally different, and yet most people treat them as being exactly the same. So let us see what the difference is.

In an earlier chapter we defined the difference between a human being and a corpse as the presence (or absence) of the *personality* in the physical body. We have seen that the scientific word 'consciousness' is a more accurate word to use, as it implies everything which is not the physical body, but for our purposes the word 'personality' is more common and better understood by most people, so we will still use it. But we have also seen that each human being is composed of three subtle bodies, three interfaces and a physical body - and the only one of these that can be recognised by the physical senses is the last one.

We have also learned that everything in the Universe, including our species, is created out of energy, and scientists tell us that 'energy' cannot be either created or destroyed. It can be changed - and is changed frequently, but it cannot be destroyed. So therefore, when the physical body dies, the remaining bodies and interfaces still exist, somewhere or other. (We will discuss *where* much later in the book).

Now at the moment of death, the personality - everything which is not the physical body - separates from the body. And it is obvious that what was the person is now no more than a body, an empty shell, left behind. The personality - everything else - has left. But as it still exists, it can still be contacted - by anyone who has the ability to tune into the frequency (level of vibration) at which it exists.

We call such people 'mediums', and when mediums sense departed loved ones, they are contacting the personalities of those loved ones, exactly as they were in life - warts and all. The fact that they are no longer in a physical body doesn't mean that they have suddenly achieved wisdom - they are exactly the same as they were before their death.

Before going further, it is worth noting that death happens to everyone, regardless of their race, colour, nationality, politics, religion, or anything else that distinguishes one human being from another. In fact, apart from any obvious physical differences of race or colour, it is impossible to tell whether a dead body is that of a German Jew, a French Catholic, an American Muslim, an English Conservative or a Russian Communist.

***

So what happens to the dying person after the moment of death? Well, a lot will depend on the manner of death, so let us first look at the most common one, when death happens as a result of disease. The first thing to say is that the physical disease is left behind with the physical body, and we continually hear messages in which the loved ones say, 'I am not in any pain any more', 'I can walk properly now' or 'I can do what I like now'. But in a seeming contradiction of this, in most cases the first thing which happens when our loved ones get to 'the other side of life' is that they are taken away for a period of recuperation - what we can think of as a spell in a convalescent home. So why is this?

The answer may seem strange: it all depends how *ill* they were before they died. However, if we think about it, perhaps it is not so strange after all, for there are many kinds of illness, which kill the patient at different speeds. Some, like motor neurone disease or multiple sclerosis, develop very slowly, and so the patient suffers greatly over a long period of time. Others, like meningitis or peritonitis, can kill within days. Then diseases like cancer can develop either very rapidly or very slowly, depending on the particular type of cancer.

As far as the physical body is concerned, the result is always the same, but as far as the mental and emotional bodies are concerned, the effects may be widely different: in some cases they are hardly touched at all, in others they can be totally worn out.

To give a simple example of a case where people die who aren't ill at all: just imagine that they are walking down a street and are struck by a vehicle that has careered off the road. (There were several examples of this sort of accident in the few weeks before I edited this book, in early

A3: What is Death?

2015). They are killed instantly but - not having suffered at all mentally - they are in no need of convalescence at all.

Two personal - and totally different - cases may serve to prove the point: my first wife died of a succession of cancers, which she fought for almost a year. The first two were cured, one by chemotherapy and the second by radiology, but the third one was incurable, and killed her at the age of 63, by which time she was totally - mentally and emotionally - worn out. Although she was fully aware of the reality of survival before she died, she needed a period of convalescence, so it took her six weeks before she was able to come back, through a medium, although I had sensed her for a few days previously.

However, Sybil's mother, who passed in 2012, had a fall at the age of 94 and broke her femur. She had an operation to remedy the problem, but old age and pneumonia meant that she survived it by only a few days. But as she still had all her faculties almost to the end, the day after her passing she was able to appear in the teaching circle of a Canadian medium friend and say 'Tell Sybil that I have arrived and I am all right'.

So the general thing that happens to most people who die of a disease is that they have a period of recuperation, to heal the mental scars that their illness has caused. Incidentally, these include the damage done by the drugs that many will have been given in their last few days to deaden pain. But what happens to those who don't need a period of recuperation?

***

The simple answer is, "They enter directly into the Light." For instance, when someone dies of old age, without any long period of illness, they usually enter into the Light immediately. Why do we say 'into the Light'? Because that is what it is - literally. Many loved ones who come back to contact us from time to time say how bright everything is in their new existence, how vivid the colours are and how everything always seems to be in sunlight, without any sun being apparent. And this is the state into which we all go, eventually.

Now very often, when people die of old age, they start to see the Light before they eventually pass, and many then actually 'see' their loved ones on the other side of life waiting for them. In fact, the greatest service that you can ever do for a loved one who is in the process of leaving their physical life is to tell them, in their final moments, to 'look for the Light'. Then, when they have seen it, ask them to tell you what - or who - they see in the Light, and by focussing their attention you will very often help them to see the loved ones waiting for them, and help them to pass very gently, and without any fear.

But these aren't the only cases of people who pass directly into the Light. Once more, when people haven't suffered for long before passing, they are less likely to need any recuperation - for instance, if someone is killed in an accident, or dies on an operating table. It is interesting to consider the number of near-death experiences that are continually being reported. These are where someone 'dies' - usually in hospital, and then, due to the frantic efforts of nursing staff, is brought back to life again. Many of those who experience this talk about having gone down a dark tunnel into an area of Light, of meeting various people there and then of being told 'You have to go back - it is not your time'. Then, having been resuscitated, they say that they have now lost all fear of dying, as they know where they will be going after death. (It is interesting to note that the phrase 'the Light at the end of the tunnel' has now become part of everyday language).

So the vast majority of people who die have one or other of those two experiences. But what about those who have neither? Who are they, and what happens to them?

N.B. Before we go any further, we have seen that the only thing that dies is the physical body: the rest of the person - the personality - continues to another phase of existence. So in future, we will no longer use the word 'die', and will replace it by the more accurate phrase 'pass over'. At the moment of death, the personality passes over into a new form of existence.

Chapter 4: Rescue

Although most of those who pass over go either into the Light or into convalescence, not all do, for various reasons. First are those who in their earthly life have been so evil that they have put up barriers and enclosed themselves within walls of hatred. Such people have been cruel to others during their life, and have completely shunned any form of love, compassion or kindness, thinking only of selfish gain of power or wealth. In many cases, they have been so lacking in humanity that they have tortured and killed those weaker than themselves, including animals. Into this category falls everyone from the mass murderers of history like Hitler, Stalin and Pol Pot down to infamous serial killers like Dr Shipman, but it also includes many others who are never found out or tried for any crime

Now the dimension into which we all pass after death is a mental one, a dimension of Love in all its forms. But when *these* people pass over, they cannot go into that realm, as their whole mind-set completely rejects it, so they go into a mental Hell of their own making. In this state they stay, in complete isolation, until spiritual beings are able to rescue them and eventually take them into convalescence. (Note that 'Hell' actually exists, but it is not the 'Hell' of classical literature, a physical place as depicted by Dante, but the mental Hell that a person creates for him/herself. In fact, it is not even necessary to pass over to enter this Hell - it is often experienced by people who are still alive, but suffering any one of a number of mental or emotional disorders).

Next are those who are so vehemently against any thought of survival after death that they refuse to accept the possibility of continuing in existence. So when they pass over they go where they expect to go - into nothingness. This is a hazy existence - those who have been there usually describe it as a kind of fog - and they stay there until they, also, are eventually rescued. (In the Catholic Church, this is called 'Purgatory' but others call it 'Limbo!) There was recently a report of a complete atheist who had proved - to his own satisfaction - that there was no sort of existence after death. He had a Near-Death-Experience (NDE) during which he felt nothing but total blackness, and an absence of all sensation. Now most people who have NDEs experience what we have outlined above, although few have such vivid experiences as Dr Eben Alexander (see chapter 1), so what was the difference in this case. Because the man had already decided that he would go into nothingness, that is exactly what happened, so his initial idea turned into a self-fulfilling prophecy. In other words, he made that idea come true!

Finally, there are those who simply refuse to believe that they are dead. Very often, these are people who have been killed suddenly, so quickly that they didn't realise that they were even in any danger, and then they still remain in their own earthly environment and try to carry on as normal. But of course, they can't. No one can see or hear them, other people use their possessions, or live in their house, and they get increasingly frustrated - and often cause many problems - until they, also, are rescued.

A variation on this theme is the people who are so attached to a particular place, either out of love or because they have been killed at that spot in tragic or criminal circumstances, that they are no longer able to leave it.

(Most of the reputed hauntings that are heard of are caused by the souls of those who fall into one or other of the latter two categories).

***

However lost, misguided - or even downright evil - any person has been in life, there is always the certainty of eventually being brought back into the main stream of spiritual development. No one is ever permanently excluded from 'Heaven': tales of being banished to 'Hell' for eternity are only made up by religious leaders of certain faiths in order to keep their followers on the right spiritual pathway. So what happens to those who do not go immediately into the Light? How are they helped?

First, there is a dedicated band of advanced spiritual beings who work tirelessly to bathe lost souls with Love, which slowly chips away the barriers that stop them from being put into convalescence. This process may take several hundreds - or even thousands - of years of our time, but in their dimension, time does not exist, so it isn't a problem.

Then there are a great number of people who have passed over and who are now drawn towards doing spiritual work of some kind or other. The greatest spiritual work which can be done is Service, and what better way of serving others than to bring them into the Light? So these workers add their efforts to those of the spiritual beings to bring lost people into the Light.

From a human perspective, it is quite common in most Christian communities for prayers to be said for the 'souls of the dear departed', and it is reported that so many prayers were said for the soul of the late Pope John 23rd (by Catholics and non-Catholics alike) that his transition from this earthly life into the next dimension was the gentlest possible. And where the 'dear-departed' have entered the self-imposed Hell of separation from the Light, such prayers can help to lighten the fog that surrounds them.

The final way is through human beings who sit in circles for meditation and development. In some of the more advanced circles, 'Rescue' work is done. This consists of contacting lost people, who fall into one of the categories mentioned earlier, and persuading them to go into the Light. The ways of doing this depend on the individual need. In many cases, all that is necessary is to tell them to look for the Light and then to go into it. In others, they have to be convinced that they are actually dead, before they can be shown what to do.

Many mediums have done clearance work, where troublesome spirits have to be removed from homes, and this is also a form of Rescue. In extreme cases, where the spirit becomes abusive or violent, it is necessary to bring in 'the big boys' - usually the Archangel Michael - in order to take it away by force. This process is usually called 'exorcism', and can only be carried out by the most experienced mediums.

Very often, groups of people remain together, and when one of them has been shown how to go into the Light the others will follow, and - depending on the skill and experience of those who sit in the Rescue circle - several hundred can be guided through at the same time.

There is one special type of Rescue work, where one member of the circle is lowered into the stinking Hell into which the most evil human beings have walled themselves, and drags people out so that the rest of the group can work on them in order to send them into convalescence. (This is very dangerous work, and should not ever be attempted by any but the most experienced Light-workers).

Chapter 5: The Other Side of Life

So what can we expect when we ourselves leave this earthly life and go into the next dimension? Let us imagine that we have spent some time in convalescence and have now come into the Light. What are the conditions like, what will we do, how will we dress, where will we live, and so on?

Well, the first and most important thing to know is that the next dimension is not a physical world, therefore we no longer have a physical body, nor do we have any of the conditions associated with our former body. Therefore there is no more illness, disease, pain or suffering, and no problems of mobility or with the progressive loss of senses that are the almost inevitable results of aging. But neither are there the mental or emotional problems that have been associated with those conditions: we don't have any worries about ourselves whatsoever. All of these have been healed during our period of convalescence.

But it is difficult to imagine what it is like to have no physical body - we have never been in that situation before. However, we still have all our subtle bodies, and you will remember that the final interface between the subtle bodies and the physical body was a replica of the physical body. Now, although that interface was no longer needed after the death of the physical body, we still have it - and so we *feel* that we still have a body.

But if there is nothing physical about the next dimension, what is it like? Well, it is a dimension of 'thought', and that has some very unusual consequences. In this earthly life, most actions start off with a thought, although very often there is a long time between the thought and the action. If we want a holiday, it takes a long time to arrange for it to happen: we can dream about being in some sunny foreign resort, enjoying the warmth and the relaxed atmosphere, but bringing it about takes a lot of planning - and saving up.

A5: The Other Side of Life

However, in the next dimension, whatever you think about happens immediately: think about being by the seaside and you are there. Think about going to visit family members on the other side of the world and you do. Think about being with long-departed loved ones, parents, children, relatives, friends - and you are immediately together.

Now this opens up some interesting possibilities: when you ask what you will be doing on the other side of life, the answer is "What do you want to be doing?" We are going to do a little exercise: write down one simple sentence, saying what your idea of Heaven would be; what would you like to do more than anything else? What would really make you happy? Whatever it is, you can do it, or have it. There is only one proviso; you will not be able to harm anyone else in any way: the reason is that all negative thoughts about others, and certainly all desire to hurt others, will have already been removed during your time of convalescence. We will have a look at what you wish for - and the likelihood - and consequences - of getting it, a little later.

***

When I was giving this information as individual weekly talks, I asked my audience to do the same little exercise, and tell me what they would be doing in their individual idea of Heaven. I reminded them that they could have, or do, anything that they wanted in their new dimension, but that what they chose would apply only to them, and to their existence in that dimension. They would not be able to change *anyone else's* life, nor would they be able to directly affect matters in the dimension they had just left - i.e. on Earth.

They wrote down what their ideal occupation would be, and the next week I analysed what they had said, and commented on it. It was interesting to see that, although they could have asked for anything for themselves, (food, drink, possessions, etc.,) not one of those who wrote down a wish actually asked for anything personal - possibly a measure of their own stage of spiritual development by that time.

So here are some of the individual wishes they expressed, and whether or not they would be likely to come true.

Several of them expressed the wish to see members of their family or friends who had already passed away, and that would certainly come true. By just thinking of them, they would be there. One asked to be happy, content, healthy and evolved. The first three will be granted automatically:

she would be doing exactly what she wanted, and without a physical body to give her any health problems. Whether she became evolved or not would depend on the amount of study she did in her Heaven.

One person wanted to visit and learn about other solar systems. No problem. Only think about them, and he would be there. Ask about them, and he would be told.

Two people wanted to help animals. One wanted to help those which had passed - no problem! Another wanted a big animal sanctuary. Yes - if it were in their Heaven. No, if it were on Earth - they could not directly control Earth conditions.

Three people had global ambitions, and regrettably, none of them were likely to come true. One wished to be all things to all life forms, which is a difficult idea to understand, let alone to bring about. One wished to take greed and envy from the powers who think that they rule the world, and the other wanted to bring peace to the Earth. All three were doomed to failure, as they would have no direct way of influencing world leaders at all.

The remainder all wished to help those on Earth in some way, to make a difference in their lives, heal them or give them hope. Whether or not they would be able to do this depended on many things. They might be able to contact people on Earth directly, either psychically - if the people were sensitive - or possibly through dreams, in order to advise them on the most advantageous course of action for them to take. They might be able to add their own healing power to the power of any healers who were attending them, or might be able to contact them via a medium. But they had to remember that they couldn't *change* the life of anyone else. However wrong they thought that that person's pathway was, or however painful their physical condition, that *was* the pathway *they* had chosen, in order to learn the lessons *they* had felt they needed in their current life. So therefore who were those watching - or anyone else, for that matter - to say that those people were wrong.

Finally, I reminded my audience that when they themselves were on the other side of life, they would realise how difficult it was to make any contact at all with loved ones on the Earth plane, and would possibly appreciate what amazing work the mediums who demonstrated for them weekly actually did.

A5: The Other Side of Life

Now, having read the above, have a look at what *you* have written down as your ideas of what *you* will be doing in *your* Heaven, and see how realistic they are.

***

We have said that when we get to the other side of life, we can still enjoy all the pleasures we enjoyed on Earth. But how can we do that, if we have no physical body? And how can we mix with others in the same dimension, if they have no physical body either?

Well, as we have seen, each human being is made up of seven bodies, only one of which is the physical body, and the others - the subtle bodies - still exist after the death of the physical. The final subtle body, the interface with the physical one, is an exact duplicate of the physical and as we will now be in the dimension where subtle bodies can be perceived, we will still have the illusion of having a physical body ourselves, and that others have one also.

Not only that, but the final interface still has the psychic equivalent of all the senses we had when on Earth, but all of these senses are now greatly enhanced. Many of those who come back to contact us note with amazement how beautiful everything in their new existence is - how bright all the colours are, how sweet the smells, how clear the sounds. (Possibly this is because all human illnesses and deficiencies of the senses no longer exist).

So this means that anything that was enjoyed on Earth may be enjoyed even more on the other side of life - the foodies are in their Heaven, as are those who are addicted to drinking (or even more earthy pleasures). But there is one great difference: most of the physical pleasures of human life are bound up with the *effects* that those pleasures have on the body. After a big meal, you feel comfortably (or sometimes uncomfortably) full, after a bout of drinking, you feel one or other of the different stages of drunkenness, etc.

But the problem in the next dimension is that you do not have a physical body, so none of those after-effects *exist*. You can eat as much as you want and never feel full, or drink as much as you want and never get even mildly tipsy. So after a while, what used to be a great pleasure on Earth tends to pall - particularly when you find out that you can induce the same effect just by thinking of it.

So after a while - and time, as we understand it, doesn't exist in the next dimension - we start to look for other pleasures, other interests, something that will not pall after time. And this is where we find that although physical interests pall, mental interests don't: whatever you are interested in, from a practical subject like gardening or craftwork to a mental one like Geography, History or Astronomy, will continually provide new horizons to study. However much you know, there will always be more to learn.

But this is not all: once you have started to learn more, many of you will get the urge to *teach* what you have learnt, and in order to do this you will want to contact those who are on the Earth plane to help them in their own studies. The best way to do this is to find someone who is interested in those subjects, and to try to impress them with what you yourself have found out. Sometimes it will be very easy - if, for instance, they are psychic and you can influence them directly. But if the urge to help them is strong enough, and their interest in the subject is great enough, sooner or later you will find a way through. (This is how all occurrences of so-called 'inspiration' happen).

Some of you will find yourself attached to some high philosophical ideals, women's rights, animal rights, political or religious rights or Ecology, and be attracted to groups on Earth that seek to promote those ideals. Others will help and influence them in their work. Alternatively, some will use their interest and skill in healing more directly, as we have said above, and devote their energies to helping to heal those who have passed over but are not yet in the Light.

The easiest groups of people to contact and influence are, of course, working psychics, so some of you may want to attach yourself to one or more of those. Although it is unlikely that any of us are advanced enough to become a principal guide to someone on Earth, we could possibly become helpers.

So finally, for those who wonder how they are going to be able to fill in their time when on the other side of life, they are a vast number of possibilities, all depending what you feel like doing at the time. But one thing is certain: you will not wish to return to your former earthly life. You may want to come back frequently and see how your earthly relatives and friends are faring, but you will be so happy in your new existence that no thought of changing it for what you had on Earth will ever cross your mind. I personally have heard many thousands of messages from loved ones who have passed over, but never once have I heard any one of them say that he or she would like to be back on Earth.

Chapter 6: The Purpose of Life

We have discussed what happens at, and after, the moment of the death of the physical body, and what happens to us afterwards in the next dimension. Now we start to look at what most concerns us in the here and now.

Throughout history, Mankind has always asked these questions, 'What is it all about?' 'Why are we in this life at all?' and few people have ever been able to come up with convincing answers, if indeed they have been able to offer any answers at all. So let us try to fill the gap.

The simple answer is that we are all here on a mission, to learn and understand *everything* about the human condition. (It is only part of the total answer: the complete answer is that we are here to learn everything about all life forms on the planet, but for the sake of simplicity we will talk only about what affects us directly as human beings).

Many spiritualists talk about Earth as being a 'schoolhouse of learning', and this is in fact a very good analogy, as many aspects of human life can be likened to going to school. When we were young, we all went to school and had to learn a large amount of information, far too much to be learnt in one day. So we went back day after day, year after year, until we had finished our allotted time as pupils, (and hopefully had learnt all that we should have learnt). Then, and only then, we were *allowed* to leave school finally and go on to adult life.

Human life is very much like that. We have an enormous amount to learn, and we can't do it all in one life (school day), so we learn the lessons of that life and then come back again to learn others in another life, and so on. A very simple way to understand what happens is to think of ourselves, before we come into incarnation, as being presented with a gigantic tick-sheet containing all the aspects of human life that we are eventually going to have to learn. And in any one life, we disregard those we have already learnt, and choose which ones we are going to do that time round (we choose the school lessons we are going to cover).

So how many lessons are we faced with? Well, just think of how many human experiences and conditions there are. Hundreds? Thousands? Who can tell? For instance there must be dozens of different ways of dying, and in the course of our time 'at school' we will have to experience every one of them. Not a pleasant prospect, but it will happen. On a more cheerful note, how many pleasurable experiences are there in life? We will have every one of those as well. How many types of relationship with other human beings are there? Once more, we will know by the time we have finished our final earthly journey - we will have had every one.

Once we have understood the basic facts of life we can start to answer some of the questions that are continually being asked about it. The most obvious - and most often asked - of these is, 'Why are everyone's circumstances so different?' The answer is, 'It's all a question of choice'.

***

All of us make choices throughout our life. Some of them are simple and have little importance - what we shall wear, or have for breakfast, or what we shall do today. Others are more dramatic and life changing - where shall we live, who shall we marry, etc. Many choices - apparently unimportant - can turn out to be life changing, such as altering the time of a journey and thereby avoiding being in a crash of the bus/ train/ plane that we would have caught - or, of course, vice- versa.

In the aftermath of the 9/11 atrocity, many stories were told about the simple events which led to individuals being out of the office on that fateful morning - and which saved their life; one man had to drop his daughter off at school that day, another had to get the doughnuts for the morning coffee break, a third had just bought some new shoes, which had caused a blister on his foot, so he called into a chemist's shop to get a plaster. All simple, everyday experiences, which meant that those men avoided being in the wrong place, at the wrong time. Others, of course, had exactly the opposite experience, like the man who had an outside appointment with a client that day, but had forgotten to take the file home the night before, and so had to call into the office to get it on the fateful morning. A simple mistake - which was to prove fatal.

So even simple everyday choices can eventually prove to be life saving - or threatening, as the case may be. From a scientific, rational and logical

A6: The Purpose of Life

point of view, there is no possible explanation for these events and their outcome. They are just dismissed as Chance, and the subject is hurriedly changed. On the other hand, from a religious perspective they are seen as gifts (or punishments, as appropriate) from some beneficial deity, and explained as 'the will of ...' (inserting the appropriate name of the Being worshipped in that particular religion). But from the point of view of spiritual philosophy there *is* an explanation: that the most important choices that we ever make will have been made before we ever came into this life - and those include the timing and manner of passing over.

To return to the question of why everyone's circumstances are so different: it is a trait of human beings to compare themselves - usually unfavourably - with others. Other people are richer, or more beautiful/ handsome than us, or are luckier, or healthier, or have more opportunities, etc. Yet if you think around your own immediate circle of family, friends and acquaintances, you will certainly find many people who are far worse off than you are. But is there a spiritual reason why there are so many differences between the situations of human beings?

Yes indeed, and it is all to do with Mathematics. If you ask a group of people to make a simple choice between five pairs of things, how many are likely to make the same choices as someone else? Have a guess. Just imagine that there are 20 people who are about to come into a new life, and have to choose five different characteristics, man/woman; tall/ short; dark/ fair; town/ country surroundings; large family/ small family. How many people are likely to make the same choices as others? How many of you think three or four?

The real answer is that it is quite likely that none of them would, because there are 32 possible combinations of choices that could be made! (Mathematically, there are two ways of answering the first choice, and that - combined with the two ways of answering the second one, means that there are *four* possible ways of combining the first and the second together! Now multiply that by another two for the third choice, then two for the fourth and another two for the fifth, and you have 32 possibilities!)

Things get even less likely when you have to put things in any order you choose. If there are five particular jobs to do, and you asked 20 people to list them in the order in which they personally would do them, what is the likelihood of any two of them coming up with an identical list? Even more remote, as there are 120 possibilities. (Mathematically, the answer is 5 x 4 x 3 x 2 x 1)!

Incredible as it may seem, if the list contained just 14 jobs to be done, there are more possible combinations than there are people in the whole world.

So what has this to do with spirituality? Well, how many possible kinds of experience can a human being have? At a very conservative estimate, it must run into hundreds, if not thousands. So you see that the mathematical possibility of any two people choosing the same life conditions is so small that it is effectively nil.

***

So if you try to compare yourself with anyone else, you are just wasting your time. It would be like trying to compare the education of two people, one of whom had studied Maths at primary level only, English at GCSE level, Science at A Level and French at University level, while the second had studied Maths at A Level, English at University level, Science at primary level and French at GCSE level, There could be no comparison at all.

To return to our idea of each of us having a gigantic tick-sheet with all the possible experiences we can have as human beings written down, as we go through a succession of lives we are able to tick off more and more of them. We will expand on this theme in later talks.

The moral of all this is that you can never understand, compare yourself with, and certainly should never judge, any other human beings. Even the most apparently evil or repulsive persons may have had - and learnt lessons from - experiences that you have not yet gone through, and so in those ways may be more spiritually advanced than you. A sobering thought! They are having their experiences in the order that *they* have chosen, and learning *their* lessons in *their* way - and you must learn yours in *your* way, and according to *your* principles.

We said that the most important choices we ever make are those made before we come into life. But is there any order in the choices we make? Well, faced with two possibilities, a difficult job or an easy one, almost all of us will go for the easy one: it is a facet of human nature. But when we have to do both, things become slightly more complicated. Which do we do first?

Just take a simple everyday example: you are eating a meal, and on your plate, there is one of your favourite foods amongst the other things.

A6: The Purpose of Life

Do you eat it first, or leave it until last? The choice you make will say something about your general character; if you decide to leave it until last that is called 'delay gratification', and shows that you are slightly more optimistic than pessimistic. The optimist always thinks that the food will still be available at the end, the pessimist isn't going to take the chance of it not being there.

So when we are faced with choices to be made before the start of life, why should we ever choose difficult conditions? There are two reasons: the first is, quite simply, that the difficult conditions exist somewhere or other on our tick-sheet, and so we *have* to do them sooner or later. But the second reason is far more subtle: it is that the only time we ever learn anything in life is when we are having problems!

At first sight, that is a difficult thing to understand, but when you study it more closely things become a bit clearer. Just take one simple example - money. If you are born into a wealthy family, you don't have any money problems: whatever you want, you go and buy. If your only problem is what kind or colour of new car you are going to buy, you are not really going to appreciate the true value of money. However, if you are dreading your next energy bill, or are wondering how to put food on the table for your family, it will certainly concentrate your mind, and make you focus on the meaning and importance of money in our present society.

Another kind of lesson is in the realm of health: some people never have a day's illness during their whole life, while others hardly ever have a day without pain. If we are in the first group, there is never any reason to consider how our healthy body is working - it is just taken for granted that it is. It is only when something goes wrong with it that we start to notice. How many of us ever think of the simple fact that breathing is the main thing that allows us to survive and do anything at all? It is likely that none of us do - unless or until we start to have problems with our lungs. One of the things about aging is that we start to appreciate more what we have - or in many cases, what we *no longer* have. (It is a true saying that we never appreciate anything we *have* got until we have lost it).

So how does that knowledge help us in our daily life? In the first place, when we are going through the good times, having previously been through difficulties, it helps us to appreciate them, and enjoy them more. But when the reverse is happening, and we are going through a really difficult time, it teaches us something about what the most important things in the life of all human beings are. And if we can understand that *that* experience is a lesson, then we can endure the circumstances a little more easily, knowing that - like all lessons - one day it will end and we will be able to move on.

Chapter 7:
The Times in our Lives

We are talking about the good times and the bad times. Everyone has both of these during their life, but in between the two extremes there is a large grey area, when life is neither good nor bad - it is just ordinary.

But whatever the state of your life is at the moment, it is going to change. How do I know? Because Change is built into the Universe. There is not one single moment when everything is exactly the same as it was a short time before. In Astrology, the moment of birth is the most significant point in the chart, for that imprints an individual and unique pattern upon the life of the newborn child - a pattern that will never be repeated before the end of the life of the planet itself.

So your life is *going* to change - that is a certainty. It may change for the better or the worse, but change it will. You may not notice the change until long after it has happened, as most changes happen very slowly, and it is only when they are significantly different to what they were before that we recognise them at all, but one day you will look back and say, 'Things are different now to what they were last ....' - and they will be.

A simple example of this would be that of someone who looks in the mirror every day, and then one day - probably many years later - suddenly realises that he/ she is growing older (and looking old)! It has been happening all the while, but so slowly that it is only noticed when it has reached the level of significant change.

Most people don't know that every cell in the human body, with the exception of brain cells, is replaced every seven years, so therefore you have been physically recycled many times over the years. And with those physical changes come mental, emotional and psychological changes, so each of you is now totally different from what you were as a child, as an adolescent, as a young adult, etc.

On a world level, of course, we are all in a period of intense change, when much of what we thought of as certain, absolute and unchangeable is now being questioned. Massive advances have been made in scientific understanding - most people have now heard the word 'Quantum', although few understand it - religious fanaticism has reached heights - and created atrocities - never seen before, there are more local wars in different parts of the world than there have ever been, there is a world refugee problem of a scale not seen since the end of World War II, etc. On a different note, more people are asking questions about the fundamental issues of life, relationships, institutions and the meaning of life itself - and demanding answers. Strange illnesses have appeared, along with amazing new advances in medical science. In fact, it is not an exaggeration to say that the world today is very different to what it was even as recently as ten years ago.

Psychics all over the world have detected unusual levels of spiritual energy over the last few years, and many have been thrown off balance by the strength of it. My own inspirers tell me that there is a new wave of consciousness coming across the universe, which heralds the start of a new 'Golden Age' for Mankind - and that the current turmoil all over the world is the final clearing-out of the last traces of the old energy. It is an interesting - and hopeful - scenario for the future of the world.

But regardless of your present situation, whether you are in 'the good times' or 'the bad times' at the moment, what can you do about your life, to make sure that you get the best out of it? The answers will vary, depending on the situation, but some general points can be made for everyone. Let us start by looking at those of you who are going through a period of good times, and see if we can make them any better.

The general problem with the good times is that we never really think about them at all - we just sail through them oblivious to what we have (unless, of course, we have had a previous spell of bad times to focus our mind). So what you could do is to set aside five minutes, ideally at the beginning of each day, and ask yourself a few questions.

The most important question we can ever ask ourselves is 'Why?' This is the magic question, for if you ask for some information, and ask 'Why?' and then do the same to the next explanation, and so on, you will eventually get to a stage where there is no further answer possible. (Many parents will resonate with this, if they have a child who is always asking questions, and asking 'Why?' after each answer. But even if you're not a parent, just try it, and you will see). But you are not going to go that far in questioning yourself - just far enough to identify why you are happy with your life,

Take any facet of your life and study it. Let us say you decide that these are good times because you are financially secure. Why? Is it because of something which you have done in the past, or which someone else has done? If the first, think of all the steps you have taken over the years to achieve this state. Think of the ones that came right, and the ones that didn't. Think of the bad times you had, and remember how bad they were. What have you learnt from the whole process? If you had your time again, would you do the same things or are there some things that you would do differently? If part of your financial stability is because of what someone else has done for you, why did they do it? Was it to repay a favour, or a debt, or just because you have always been nice to them in the past?

Very often people don't realise that their own frame of mind has a lot to do with whether or not they are successful, and the frame of mind of all of us starts with what we personally think about ourselves. We shall return to that point in a few moments.

Obviously, the whole process is going to take much longer than just one five-minute session, but stick with it! Make it part of your morning routine, and after a while, you will realise that you have learnt quite a lot about yourself, and in the process, you have also learnt a lot about life. Then, once you have exhausted that topic, choose another reason why you are in the good times, possible health, or relationships, or psycho-spiritual well-being, and do exactly the same.

After a while, the process of looking at yourself becomes a habit, and helps you to appreciate what you have, and enjoy it to the hilt. Just try it and see!

***

But now let us think about the bad times: the basic advice for the bad times is the same as that for the good times - allocate some time for yourself each day to think about the situation, although this time, not at the start of the day but at the end, just before you go to bed - or in fact, when you are in bed just before you go to sleep. The reason for this is that at the end of your little session, you are going to ask for guidance, and that is most likely to come while you are in sleep state.

However, before we go into any details, let us remind ourselves of something we mentioned back in an earlier chapter - about Subtle Bodies. We said that apart from the spiritual body, we have mental and emotional bodies, with their interfaces, and here is where we find out how they all work together.

Before we came into this incarnation, consulting our tick-sheet we decided which lessons we intended to learn, and what experiences we needed in order to give us those lessons. We then had to find people who agreed to give us those lessons, as doing *that* fitted in with their own agenda. So we chose everything about this life, our parents, family, friends, environment, etc., so that once we were born we could start on the job ahead.

Long ago, when I was first given this idea by my inspirers, I asked for an explanation of how it worked, and I was given a simple analogy. I was told that each of us is a playwright, who has written a play which will be the outline of the life he or she will have as a human being. The principal character of course is already chosen - yourself. Now all the other roles in the play have to be filled by other actors and actresses. Therefore, we look around for people to fill those roles.

Now everyone else is also looking for people to fill roles in their own play, and will agree to act in someone else's only if it fits in with their own agenda. Eventually all the roles in our play are filled and we can start on the life ahead. (We will come back to this scenario later on in the book).

When a baby is born, it is like a piece of spiritual blotting paper, it soaks up impressions. Of course, everyone knows how quickly babies learn, but few people are aware of how quickly they can pick up the atmosphere in which they are living - and that includes the attitudes and even thoughts of those who are around them. Not only will they know the thoughts that people have towards them, but also the thoughts those people have towards each other - and in a disharmonious family that can be disastrous. Suffice it to say that by the time a child is about five, it has absorbed all the influences that will affect it for the rest of its life.

Almost inevitably, it will have picked up limiting ideas, thoughts that will hold it back during its life, thoughts like 'Money is tight', or 'You are always in danger of being unhealthy', or 'Relationships are fraught with danger', or 'However happy you are it won't last'. These ideas won't always be at the front of its mind, but they will be there in the subconscious, and affect future attitudes.

So how does that affect the life in practice? Well, very few people understand the power of thought. We create conditions by our own thoughts, and we put out expectations of what we think will happen. These thoughts and expectations affect our emotional body, and then gradually affect the physical body. Sometimes this has an effect on our physical health - doctors talk about psychosomatic illnesses, ailments brought on by the state of mind. (One of the biggest health problems in our modern world is 'stress', and a recently published photo showed a baby in the womb reacting to the stress its mother was feeling). Sometimes thoughts affect our financial situation, or our relationships, or our 'feel-good factor': the Universe - ever obliging - takes the thought we have put out as an order and brings into being exactly what we have envisioned. So we are continually creating our own future. But more importantly, we have already created the conditions that exist in our lives at the moment.

So in your first few sessions where you are looking at yourself, just consider the areas where you want change to come into your life, and put out the request for help to those upstairs. This way, you will have got the process off to a good start.

***

There is a lot to be said about the bad times, and we will be spending some time talking about them. After all, they are more important in the life of most people than any other times, as they affect us more deeply. We hardly ever notice the good times or the grey areas when nothing seems to be happening at all, but when we are in the bad times we are certainly aware of what is happening.

There is a method of dealing with the bad times - and hopefully bringing them to an end - but before we start on it, it is appropriate that we mention the person who brought it in - or rather, who introduced it to a worldwide audience. So we will consider Spiritual Teachers.

There is a hierarchy - a ranking - of spiritual teachers. At the top are the spiritual Masters, the great beings who started some of the major religions of the world. In historical order, they were Gautama (Buddhism), Confucius (Confucianism) and Lao Tsu (Taoism), the Master Jesus, (Christianity) and Mohammed (Islam). In Hinduism, the oldest religion in the world, and its more modern derivative Sikhism, the masters are called 'gurus', the ancient Sanskrit word for 'teacher'. In Judaism, arguably the second oldest religion, it is difficult to choose any one Master, as the religion evolved over several millennia, through the teachings and lives of several prophets.

Further down the hierarchy are the spiritual beings who teach us as guides or helpers. A guide is the being who attaches him/ herself to each of us individually for the whole of our life, and acts as our conscience - something like Jimini Cricket was to Pinocchio. Helpers are those who come in from time to time to help us to develop our individual spiritual gifts.

Then we have the earthly gurus, those very advanced spiritual humans who are the world's spiritual leaders. The most famous of these are the Dalai Lama and the Pope, but there are many others. Then come a variety of other teachers, in descending order of knowledge. And finally, on the bottom two rungs of the ladder, are the ordinary leaders of churches, temples, mosques and synagogues - or any other group of worshippers; they are the priests, elders, imams, rabbis, etc., who are able to understand spiritual reality from only the limited viewpoint of their own individual religion. (In fact, the lowest rung of all contains those teachers who can't really be called spiritual at all, those who are so extremist, bigoted and fundamentalist that they denounce - and even advocate killing - people of any other faith but their own).

One of the most influential of all human spiritual gurus in the 20th century was - and still is to date - Louise L. Hay, who is the High Priestess of Positive Thinking. In 1984 she wrote what is - arguably - the most important spiritual book of the century, 'You can Heal your Life', and proposed a method of neutralising the psychic causes of all sorts of problems which affect us as human beings - financial, health, relationships and spiritual. This is the book I discovered some 20 years ago, when I was at my lowest ebb, emotionally and spiritually. It turned my life round completely, and since that time I have used it extensively (and still do). We will study the method it uses in the next chapter. In the meantime, if you have started to do the evening reflections suggested earlier, and have identified the main reason why you are at present in the bad times, as the final thing before going to sleep put out the thought 'I now release the need for this condition' - and repeat it to yourself several times. (It's better than counting sheep to get you off to sleep).

Chapter 8: Affirmations

Louise Hay's method is basically very simple: it maintains that every problem in life has a psychic cause, usually some harmful idea that has been instilled in the person during childhood. So if it is possible to reverse and neutralise that limiting thought, the condition itself will wither away - just as a tree would if you cut off its roots. And the way of neutralising negative thoughts is by using affirmations.

Affirmations are simple statements that say the *opposite* of what the person thinks. For instance, if you have always been told that you are ugly, then an affirmation might be, 'I am beautiful/handsome'. Alternatively, if you have always been told that you are stupid/thick/useless, an affirmation might be 'I am intelligent/clever/gifted', or something similar.

There are no set formats for affirmations. You can make your own up to cope with any situation, although most people prefer to use standard ones. But if you *do* produce your own, there are certain basic rules you *must* follow. The first - and most important one - is that you should *never* use any negative word - that will just reinforce the condition. If you say something like "I am getting rid of this problem", your subconscious - where the psychic root of the condition is - will immediately pick up on the word 'problem' and will make it worse.

This also applies when you use a double negative. In English, saying 'I am not unhappy' is (almost) the same as saying, 'I am happy'. However, when you use affirmations, the subconscious will first pick up the word 'not', a negative word, and will then pick up 'unhappy' - another one, and will doubly reinforce the idea of unhappiness.

The other thing that you must *never* do is to use an affirmation referring to the future. If you say, 'I will be happy', the subconscious will pick up what you are asking for - a condition in the future, and will put off changing it until the future - and as you know, 'Tomorrow never comes'.

So if you are creating your own affirmation, say that you *already have* what you are wanting.

So let us imagine that you have a problem with finance, and in your meditations so far, you have identified the problem, and have concluded that there is something that you personally can do about it at the moment. (Be honest with yourself: if you are a compulsive shopaholic, drinker, gambler or spendthrift then you probably need professional advice to get you out of those habits). However, here we will assume that none of these things apply - you are just finding things difficult.

Look back on your life and see what imprinted your mind with the idea of scarcity. Were conditions in the family home tough, or was either of your parents over-careful with their spending? Were there family crises where money was very tight for a period of time? Did you have pocket money, and were you taught to budget it, and save up for things you wanted? As an adult, have you had financial setbacks that you could have neither predicted nor avoided? Any of these things could have imprinted the idea of 'scarcity' into your subconscious.

So how can you neutralise that idea? Well, the opposite of 'scarcity' is 'abundance', so start to tell yourself, 'I have abundance'. Just repeat it to yourself, over and over again, until you go to sleep. You will find it hard. After all, if you have been convinced that you have scarcity for many years, it will be strange changing that idea. Then, every time that you go to the bathroom, look yourself straight in the eyes in the mirror and repeat the affirmation a dozen times. (This is when you will realise how deeply ingrained in your subconscious the idea of scarcity is, as the first few times that you do this, saying 'I have Abundance', your eyes will glare back at you and say, 'You b....y-well don't').

But persevere. After all, the eventual prize is ridding yourself of all negative ideas that you have about money, and proving to yourself that you can have enough to get through life without too many problems - and that is worth putting up a bit of a fight for, isn't it?

Don't think that affirmations can be used only at set times of the day. You can say them at any time, when you are walking along, or on a bus, or doing nothing in particular. The more you say them, the easier they will become to say (you will wear down the resistance of your subconscious), and the sooner you will change your present conditions.

A8: Affirmations

For those of you who have a vivid imagination, you can use the power of visualisation, which is even stronger than the power of speech. Imagine yourself standing on the top of a cliff, looking out over a vast ocean. That ocean is the Ocean of Plenty. Close your eyes and say the affirmations, 'I am wide open to receive the wealth of the Universe. I have infinite finances'. Open your arms wide and feel the wealth of the Universe flowing towards you as a gentle breeze. (It might be a good idea to do this only when you are alone and can't be disturbed, else worried family members might be sending for the men in the white coats).

Finally, after every little session, think of what you currently *have*, not what you *haven't*. It is a very simple little exercise, but can certainly help you to keep everything in your life in perspective. The above is only a very simplified introduction to the use of affirmations. For those who wish to study it in more depth, I recommend any of Louise Hay's books. The first of those was 'You can Heal your Life', a classic in its day, and still one of the most important books of spiritual philosophy of recent times. Google her name to get a complete reading list of all her books.

The effect of thought and emotions on physical health is so well-known that the illnesses they cause even have a medical name - 'psychosomatic' illnesses. I have said that the most common problem in our modern age is the problem of stress, and stress can show itself in so many ways that it is probably the Number 1 cause of many psychosomatic illnesses.

What few people know is that every part of the body is associated in some way with a mental attitude or an emotion. Some of them are fairly easy to understand. The eyes are the organs of sight, and if we have problems with the eyes, there is probably something in our life we don't really want to face up to. Similarly, the ears are the organs of hearing, and problems there stem from our refusal to listen to, or believe, what we are being told. The back is the main structure supporting all of the body, and if we have problems there, it indicates that we are feeling the lack of support in our life. The lower back represents financial support, the upper back emotional support.

Then again, the stomach processes our main form of nourishment, food and drink. However, psychically it represents the intake of ideas, or possibly new situations. So problems in that area can often be traced back to the inability to accept new ideas - we even have a saying for it: "I can't stomach that idea'. And the bowels and bladder are the organs of excretion, psychically connected with letting go of the past. So many problems of elimination are caused by an inability to let go of the past.

But possibly the worst emotion of all to harbour is 'resentment', because it sinks deeply into the subconscious and may not even be noticed, unless something comes up which reactivates the memory of a past wrong. In addition, resentment is one of the psychic causes of the most dreaded disease of our modern age - Cancer. (It is not the only one, but it is very often the principal one). Resentment eats its way into our brain and colours our emotions. And when that resentment has lasted for a very long time, it starts to act on the physical body - and eats its way into the appropriate organs. This whole subject is an enormous field of study, and this is where Louise Hay's book, 'You can Heal your Life', is immensely valuable. It lists over 400 different diseases and ailments, gives a possible psychic cause for each one, and then suggests a specific affirmation to help to neutralise the cause, and therefore relieve the ailment itself. It is as valuable a resource as any Family Doctor medical book.

Some twenty years ago, when I was mourning the passing of my beloved first wife from cancer, I was walking through a bookshop one day - I used to haunt bookshops - when 'You can Heal your Life' leapt out of the shelves at me. I was impressed to buy it, and when I found the list of medical complaints at the end of the book, I immediately looked up Cancer, and found - chillingly - the answer to what had killed my wife. All her life she had bitterly resented her upbringing, and particularly her mother, who had continually installed in her that women were inferior to men. From a positive point of view, this had spurred her on to success in her life, and to excel in many fields - even male-dominated ones like teaching and Youth service - but from the negative point of view the deep resentment that she felt had eventually killed her. Just a short time before she passed over she had remembered one of the most searing experiences of her childhood days, which had scarred her forever - and this was some 55 years after the event itself, and the burning resentment it caused.

***

However, there is one sort of medical problem which is not likely to respond to affirmations, and that is the area of physical or mental disability. The reason for this is that such conditions are usually taken on as a specific soul lesson in the life, and therefore cannot be neutralised by

A8: Affirmations

what is basically an act of will. But affirmations can certainly help to calm the emotional problems that often occur in people with such debilitating conditions.

However, one word of warning here: if you decide to use affirmations to try to alleviate a medical condition, don't expect them to work instantaneously. After all, how long has it taken your body to produce the symptoms of the ailment? You are not going to neutralise years of bad psychic conditioning overnight. But there is one thing you can do which can start the process off immediately, and that is to say the following two affirmations:

'I am wonderfully healthy. I radiate good health'.

Once more, visualise yourself standing on your cliff, with your arms wide open, looking out over the ocean, this time the Ocean of Health. Close your eyes, and as you say the affirmations feel a warm breeze coming off the ocean, carrying Health. Breathe in this warm breeze, and feel yourself getting stronger with every breath.

Finally, when you start to do affirmations, choose only one thing at a time. If you have many physical problems, choose the one causing you the most trouble and attack that one first. Give yourself at least three months to master it - as I said, affirmations are not a quick fix.

Chapter 9: Relationships

O f all the bad times in our life, it is usually those in the area of relationships that give us the most trouble. And why is that? Because we come into life to learn lessons, and those lessons can only be learnt through experiences. Since most of our experiences are concerned with relationships with other people, that is the area most fraught with problems.

But, whether we like it or not, most of those problems actually start with ourselves. Due to our early conditioning as children, reinforced by our time at primary and secondary schools, we enter adulthood fully primed to *cause* the difficulties in our reaction with others. How? By expressing - usually subconsciously - what we feel about ourselves, and inviting others to react to that image.

Just imagine that you have a little psychic label on your forehead, which says exactly what you feel about yourself. What is it going to say? Be honest when you answer, for it is the most important question you will *ever* have to answer. A simple place to start is by answering the question, 'Do you like yourself?' It is amazing how many people don't. They don't like how they look, or how they react to situations, or how they feel, or what they can't do - the possibilities are almost endless. Of course, in our society, with its cult of 'the body beautiful', it is very easy to compare yourself with some celebrity, who has access to all the resources and technology of keeping up appearances, and coming to the conclusion that you are not perfect.

But in fact, you are perfect - each one of us is. We are perfect for our *present* situation in life, in the perfect position to gain all the knowledge and experiences that we have decided that we need. Then, when we have learnt our current lesson and have decided that we can move on to other experiences, for which we need to change, we will *change ourselves* in order to be ready for the new situation.

Of course, we will never be perfect in the absolute sense, as if we were, we would have no further need for any more earthly experiences, or any more incarnations. But none of us are yet anywhere near that stage in our spiritual development.

But let us go back to our psychic label: whatever it says, other people will be able to pick up on it, and react to it - according to how that fits in with their own current life agenda. Just imagine, for instance, that your psychic label says, 'I am worthless'. Then others will pick up on that, and will treat you as though you are, in fact, worthless. In addition, if one particular person has the current need to abuse someone, he/she may be attracted to you to start that type of relationship.

Many people go through prolonged periods of abuse during their life, and sometimes they are able to escape from an abusive relationship. But of all those who do, a large proportion immediately get into a further relationship which is just as bad - if not even worse. And why? Because they haven't yet started to value themselves. They haven't changed their psychic label, so the next weak person who comes along picks up on that label and sees an opportunity to pick on someone weaker - and so make him/ herself feel better.

So is there anything that you can do, if you are in an unsatisfactory relationship? Yes indeed, but it has nothing to do with the other person - it has to do with *you*. If you start to feel that you are worthy of better things, then that is the first step in the right direction. So to get yourself ready for the change in yourself, start saying an affirmation to put down the groundwork for changing. Something like 'I am now *worthy* of a happy relationship' might be suitable.

The spiritual science behind this is quite interesting. Only a spiritually weak person will ever ill-treat - or even, get into a relationship with - a weak person. (Here, we exclude helping relationships). No strong person would deliberately enter into such a relationship, as there would be a danger of eventually despising the other person. Equally, no weak person will ever seek a relationship with a strong person; after all, no one will happily seek a fight with someone who is stronger than them, unless, of course, they are masochists. (There is actually one exception to this, which I have dealt with in the chapter on Love, under the heading of 'The Weakling').

So as their victim gets stronger, and starts to change their psychic label, the weak person who is an abuser will start to feel more uncomfortable in the relationship, and will eventually get out of it.

A further interesting development is often that, as the victims' psychic labels change from weak to strong, they will attract stronger people into their life, with a possibility of far more successful relationships. Therefore, if you want to get out of an unhappy relationship, start the process off by doing the affirmation; this will prepare you to use the Master affirmation, which is capable of changing anyone's life.

***

What I call the Master Affirmation was introduced by Louise Hay in her first book. It is the most powerful affirmation that you can say, and is 'I love and approve of myself'. It is the most powerful for two reasons: first, when you say that you *love* yourself, you are telling your subconscious mind that you love yourself as you are, without any reservations, no ifs or buts, no holding back at all. You are accepting that you are exactly right for your present situation. In fact, you are *perfect* for your situation, have the right skills and talents, have the right disposition, the right frame of mind, etc.

The second part of the affirmation, saying that you *approve of* yourself, means that you are happy with the way that you act in your life, the way that you react with others, the way that you behave in all situations, the way that you think, etc.

Now this really focuses the mind, doesn't it? Is there any reader who can, with hand on heart, honestly say all that? There are very many people who can't even bring themselves to say the words individually, never mind as an affirmation. Yet if you can - or shall we be positive, and say *when* you can - that will change the whole of your life for the better.

I once had a client who literally couldn't say the words - she had a complete mental block, and all that I could do was just leave it to her to work on, hoping that somehow she would find a way to make a breakthrough. Shortly after she phoned me to say, 'I think I have done it'. I congratulated her, and said 'You can now say the whole affirmation, then?' 'No'. she said, 'But I can say 'I like myself a little bit more than I did yesterday'.' She continued working on it, and a few weeks later she was able to say the full affirmation and start changing her life.

The spiritual science in this is quite interesting. Everything in the Universe exists as a possibility (quantum physicists are now accepting this as a fact). Furthermore, you can think of all possibilities as being on a ladder, with the most likely at the top, and the most unlikely at the bottom. Now every time that you state something as a fact, whether it is or not, you are pushing that possibility up the ladder, and sooner or later, if you try hard enough, you can push that possibility to the top. (But be aware that it might take a few years of concentrated thought before you make it give you a Lottery win).

So when you state that you love and approve of yourself, you are definitely increasing the possibility that you eventually *will* - it is a form of self-hypnosis.

But what has all this got to do with relationships? In a word, *everything!* To start with, if you don't really love yourself, why on earth would anyone else want to love you? Remember the psychic label on your forehead? If your label says 'I want you to love me but I don't really think that I am worth it', then possibly-suitable companions are going to be put off immediately, aren't they?

The most common question asked by women who are desperate to have a loving relationship is, 'When am I going to meet Mr. Right?' And the best possible answer to them is, 'When you are *Mrs*. Right'.

(That isn't really a sexist remark. It is just that women are more likely to *ask* the question than men: men might think and worry about it, but won't actually *say* it. It might hurt their macho image).

As soon as you start to say the affirmation, you start working on yourself, and you start to change. You yourself may not feel, or see, anything different for quite a time, but others who are close to you certainly will. What's more, the more that you do it the easier it is to do: you start to 'go with the flow'.

After a time, people will start to react differently to you: after all, you are changing your psychic label to something different, and they will have to adjust to that difference. If you want somebody to change their attitude towards you, don't try to dream up an affirmation such as 'X has changed his/ her attitude towards me'. It won't work. You can't change anyone else's mind for them. However, if you say something like 'I am in a wonderful relationship, I have a marvellous boss/ husband/ son/ colleague', etc. then you could well find that things will change in ways that you couldn't have even hoped for. You are not changing the other person concerned, you are changing yourself and what you feel that the relationship is - and they are reacting to that.

So start using the Master Affirmation today, and see how soon it can change the conditions in your life.

Chapter 10: Case Histories

We have been talking about Louise Hay's Master Affirmation, and have said how powerful it is. I will tell you two stories which illustrate this. The first is just part of the whole story of one woman's life, and it refers back to what I mentioned earlier, about the psychic labels on the foreheads of each of us.

Ann had great problems when I first met her; she had had an appalling life, in which it seemed that everything that could possibly go wrong had actually happened; she suffered in childhood the death of one of her parents, had a severe nervous breakdown, leading to a time in a psychiatric hospital, where she was raped on two separate occasions, had a disastrous marriage, had children who got deeply into drugs, lived in desperate poverty, had no work qualifications, etc. The catalogue of disasters seemed endless - and hopeless. When I first met her, I had the psychic vision of being in a car without lights, with no brakes and faulty steering, careering down an unlit, hilly, narrow street on a dark night. It was the most chilling psychic analysis of someone's life that I had ever experienced.

I worked with her for quite a time, and eventually - after much resistance - got her onto using the Master affirmation, and the conditions in her life gradually started to clear up. Then one day, after several months of work, when she appeared to be making real progress, she asked me an interesting question. She said, 'Why am I losing some of my friends?' I couldn't give an immediate answer, so I asked her to give me an example. 'Well', she said, 'There is Joan'. I asked why she thought she was losing her friendship, and she replied, 'At one time she always used to be calling round to see me: she would ask if I could pick her child up from school, or run an errand for her, or do odd little things like that, but I haven't seen her for at least a fortnight now'.

A Practical Spiritual Primer

I explained the idea of psychic labels, and told her that at first her label had said 'I am weak and helpless: Use me'. And Joan, who was obviously a weak person herself, had seized on the opportunity to dominate someone weaker, and had used her. Then, as she became stronger, her label changed, and her friend recognised it and stopped trying to use her. And since that was the only reason for the friendship, she stopped visiting as well.

Ann thought about it for a few minutes, and admitted that it could be a possible explanation. But the matter was clinched when I said that as her label had now changed to something far better, something like 'I am a strong person, and well worth knowing', she would probably start to attract far more beneficial people into her life - and she said that she had just met a lovely spiritual lady who looked as though she could become a close friend.

That is one example of how using affirmations - and particularly the Master affirmation, helped to change a young woman's life. Here is another one:

I met Little Sue when she was thirty-two. She was another woman who had had a difficult start to life. Born into a large and very poor family, she was the runt of the litter, the last child born and physically the smallest and the weakest. Her mother passed over when she was still fairly young, and she was brought up by a father who was himself not very capable of looking after his family. She also had one very difficult physical disability - she had exceptionally large breasts which, on her tiny frame, made her look freakish and caused her a great number of problems - physical and psychological - all through her life.

But - totally different to the last case - the hardships she suffered only made her tougher, and more determined to succeed in her life. And she did. When I met her, she was holding down a steady, although not particularly well paid, job and was living independently in her own rented flat.

However, her big problem in life was her inability to have lasting relationships, and when I met her she had already had seven failed live-in relationships; she had run away from home at the age of sixteen to start the first one, and was currently on her eighth, which was obviously another one doomed to failure.

A10: Case Histories

She had no problems whatsoever with the idea of affirmations, and took to the Master affirmation like a duck to water. She worked so hard on herself that her psychic label soon changed to something more positive, and very soon afterwards her current lover decided to move out of her life. (Another example of what I have spoken about above, in Ann's case. Her psychic label had changed, and the lover could no longer stand it).

Little Sue was a very attractive young lady, and should have had a large number of friends, but she hadn't, which was very strange. However, one day I found the answer, when I asked her if there was any aspect of her life she would like to improve. She said, 'I would like to have a better social life. I have no close friends, as my last boyfriend was jealous, and wouldn't allow me to socialise'. So I suggested that she should create and use an affirmation to remedy this - something along the lines of 'I have plenty of friends and a wonderful social life'.

I didn't see her for another few weeks, as I was away, but when I came back, I phoned her up and asked her how her life was. She replied 'Dreadful!' - and I was horrified and asked her why. She replied, 'Because there aren't enough days in the week for me to take up all the invitations out that I am receiving'. Apparently, through an acquaintance she had joined a social club, and had become an instant hit with the members (of both sexes), and all her concerns about her social life had been totally demolished.

She became close friends with one member, Jerry, a man much older than herself, who was almost like a father figure to her - possibly supplying what she had always wanted in a father, but had never had. Jerry was able to give her a very stable relationship, and several years later she married him. There are other stories to be told about her spiritual progress, but I will leave these until a more suitable time later in the book.

Chapter 11: Summary

In the last few chapters, we have been talking about what we can do to improve our lives, and to overcome some of the problems that we experience. So now, before we go on to a completely different subject, let us remind ourselves of the basic philosophy which lies behind all of life.

We come to this planet with the mission of learning everything about all the life forms on it, and we have now come to the last phase of that exploration - finding out all about life as human beings. So in this phase we will have every possible experience that any human being can ever have, from extremes of happiness and pleasure to extremes of sorrow and despair.

Sooner or later, all of us will have experienced everything, and then we will move on into another dimension and leave this planet behind. And it will be only then that we will be able to compare all our experiences with those of other human beings, and find out that we have *all* done - and learnt - the same lessons (although obviously in a different order).

But while we are travelling our *own* individual pathways, we have complete freedom about the order in which we choose our experiences: we talked about a giant tick-sheet, with everything we have to do written down on it, and each particular life brings us the conditions we chose, in order to give us the experiences which were necessary for our current set of lessons. So we are responsible for our own life. We chose it in the first place, and the sooner that we accept the fact, the sooner that we can do something about it. But how?

When we chose this life, we chose not only the experiences we would have, but also the gifts and talents that would help us along the way. It is like a craftsman going out to do a job of work: he always makes sure that he has all the tools he will need to cover every eventuality - and usually ends up by taking far more than he actually uses. We have all the gifts and talents that we need to help us to do our job in this life - if we only use them.

But unfortunately, it is part of human nature to refuse to accept responsibility for our own situation. When things aren't going right, we always try to find someone to blame for the problems: it might be our parents, or other members of our family, or our employers, or neighbours, or colleagues, or the local authority, or the Government, or anyone else who comes to mind. And in the final analysis we can always blame 'God' (if we believe in such a being), or Fate/Destiny (if we don't).

There is a well-known saying that 'There are no problems in life, only opportunities'. And most of us don't realise how true this is. If we accept that there is a problem, but think that it is caused by someone or something outside ourselves, then we tend not to do anything about it - and so just suffer (although not always in silence). However, if we can say, 'I accept that I originally chose this situation as an opportunity to learn, so what am I going to do about it' then that pushes us into finding a solution.

Most people don't realise that everything - and everyone - has a sell-by date - and that includes problems. When we were at school, and were learning our tables, we started with the 2-times table; but when we had learnt that, we didn't stay on it forever - we moved on to our 3-times table, and so on.

And it is exactly the same thing with our problems in life: we have chosen them, and we can sort them out. Then, when we have done so, they will disappear. They might well be replaced by others, but leave thinking about that until the time that it happens: there is a very wise old saying, 'Never trouble Trouble until Trouble troubles you'. (Alternatively, if you are of a more religious frame of mind, there is a Biblical saying 'Sufficient unto the day is the evil thereof').

As an aside here, there are many problems associated with old age, but one of its great advantages is that it usually gives an individual time to think. (Some old and lonely people might say too much time, but that would depend on their own particular circumstances). And when we look back, we can remember past events in our life, and see that in every case, where there were problems, those problems were eventually resolved.

Sometimes they were resolved by events beyond our control, in which case the memories don't have much effect on us. But when they are resolved by something that we ourselves did, then we get a sense of pride at how we managed to sort out the situation and move on in our life. But you don't need to have reached old age in order for this to happen. One of the greatest bonds you can have in human relationships is that of looking back at past difficult situations that have been resolved by the joint action of *both* people, and realising the value of working *together*.

This reinforces what we were saying in an earlier chapter, when we were discussing the idea of change being part of every life. There is a famous saying, 'This, too, shall pass away', which you may have heard. It has been (mistakenly) thought as having a Biblical origin, but although the general idea appears in many religious texts, the specific words do not. In fact it was the title of a poem written by an American, Lanta Wilson Smith, the daughter of a Methodist minister. She wrote a large number of hymns and inspirational poems, and this particular poem is well worth looking up on Google.

All of us have had a wide range of experiences over many lifetimes, and an interesting way that this shows is how we react to the various conditions *we* see happening in other people's lives. If you find yourself particularly moved by a story of hardship, although it doesn't concern you directly, there is a strong possibility that in a past life you suffered in the same way as those others are suffering now, and that you still have that memory in your subconscious. Some people are so strongly affected that they dedicate their whole life to a cause, and many of the great crusades in social history, (the anti-slavery movement, the movement for the emancipation of women, the Trades Union movement, etc.) owe their roots to campaigners who have themselves suffered injustice in its various forms.

This now brings us on to the topic of Reincarnation, which we consider in the next chapter.

Chapter 12: Reincarnation

Most people have heard of the word 'Reincarnation', but very few know much about it, so here is that basic information.

Reincarnation is the belief that all human beings have many lives, and that we are taught lessons in each life until eventually we are allowed to progress beyond this earthly planet and go to other spiritual dimensions. At least one-fifth of the world's population have this belief: it is one of the principles behind the oldest formal religion in the world, Hinduism, which has a 5,000-year history, and behind Buddhism. Buddhists describe the system as 'The Wheel of Rebirth'. It is also mentioned in other religions, and a few verses in the biblical New Testament (Matthew 17, verses 10 - 13) seem to indicate that the Master Jesus also believed in it.

It is difficult to understand the idea of Divine Justice if one is convinced that there is only this one life in which we are living. There are so many differences in the conditions of human beings, between extreme wealth and extreme poverty, extreme health and extreme sickness, vast surpluses of food and extreme starvation, etc. And terms like 'the Good' and 'the Bad' become meaningless when it is seen that 'the Good' are often punished in life, while 'the Bad' are rewarded.

However, if we try to find answers to the questions which life raises, and we are not able to accept Reincarnation, we are already doomed to disappointment. Perhaps we are looking in the wrong place for those answers. In this context, I am reminded of a story told by an Aboriginal friend in Australia, many years ago.

Dino was a tribal elder of the Nyoongar tribe in Western Australia, and wanted to go out to a meeting in the bush with a friend. Neither of them had a car, so they borrowed one from a friend who had a garage. Dino had never driven this kind of car before, but he was an experienced driver, so had no difficulty in handling it. However, when they were returning late at night. the car suddenly broke down, and Dino and his friend got out to see if they could sort out the problem.

They opened the bonnet, but found to their amazement that there was not an engine - in fact, nothing even resembling part of an engine. So after much scratching of heads, they walked back to the city, arrived in the middle of the night, and roused their friend, who drove them back to the car. He opened the boot, fiddled with something for a few moments, and re-started the car. The vehicle was a Volkswagen Beetle, which had its engine in the boot, and they had been looking in the wrong place for it!

It is the same when trying to make sense of this life without knowing about Reincarnation. We are like a tribesman in the Amazon jungle, who sees a car for the first time, watches the driver put something, which looks like water, in the back, and then drives off. Without knowing that there is an engine (or even knowing what an engine is,) he has no way of understanding what he has seen. And for human beings, Reincarnation is the engine that explains what happens - and why it happens.

About 15 years ago, I was asked to give a talk on Reincarnation at an Afternoon Guild in a Spiritualist church. I had given a talk there before, and I said to my wife, 'The last time I gave a talk there, half of them were asleep before I had finished; but then, most of them are fairly old - some must be nearly seventy'! (These days, someone who is not yet seventy seems to me to be almost like a 'Spring chicken': how perceptions change as we grow older!)

So I asked my inspirers for something to hold the interest of the congregation, so that they stayed awake for the hour, and they gave me this parable to explain Reincarnation.

***

Authors Note: This parable - and the rest of the chapter - was quoted in the first part of the book. Although it was appropriate to insert it into this course of talks, which study the whole subject of Reincarnation in far more detail than that in the first part of the book, it is not necessary to read it again.

Once upon a time, there was a land in very mountainous area. The people there lived a miserable existence, having to work hard to scratch a living out of the difficult, stony soil. The country was totally ringed by mountains, and the people were cut off from contact with any others anywhere - so they thought that their own land was all that existed in the whole world. No one knew how their ancestors had originally reached this desolate country, but there were ancient legends that told of a journey from a far distant 'land of milk and honey', which the ancestors had originally inhabited. Some great catastrophe had taken place, which meant that the people had been forced to leave, and ever since that time their descendants had lived out their pitiable existence in this poor mountainous terrain.

Then one day there was great excitement in the country, when mysterious posters appeared all over the place inviting the people to take part in a journey back to the land of their original ancestors, which they were told was called 'Paradise'. They were warned that it would be a long, hard journey, but when they arrived, they would find themselves in a state of happiness such as they had never dreamed of before, in a place where life would be perfect in every respect. All they needed to do was to enrol to go on this journey, and the rest would be explained to them in due course. Naturally, everyone wanted to go, so they all enrolled.

When they had enrolled, they were told of the conditions that would apply throughout their journey - and these seemed to be very strange. The first was that the journey would take a very long time, and they would be travelling for many months. At the start of each day, they would be shown a map of the overall area, and would be invited to choose the way they thought would be the best one to take. They would have advisors to help them, and to tell them the general direction of the 'Promised Land' - but the advisors would not have the power to tell them which way was best - they would have to make that decision for themselves. However, the advisors *would be* allowed to tell them what sort of equipment and clothing they would need, according to the different routes each one chose. They would then be issued with whatever clothing and equipment they were told that they needed, and food and drink for the day, and everything would be put in the rucksack with which they would also be supplied. Then, when they had studied the map and decided on their route, they would be told to memorise their chosen route well, as once they started the map would be taken away from them.

The second condition was that every night they would be picked up from wherever they had reached and taken to a hostel, where they would meet their advisors once more - but the next morning they would have to start from the same place they had reached the previous night. When they met their advisers at night, they would be shown the map and would see what they had wanted to do - and what had in fact happened. They would then be able to discuss what progress they had made, where they had gone wrong and strayed from their planned route, which parts of the day's journey had gone really well and - most important of all - what they intended to do the next day. They would have to choose their route again - remembering that they had to start from where they had left off - and would have to memorise the map once more, as it would be taken away before they started the next day's journey.

Everyone was still willing to make the journey, despite the strange conditions, so on the appointed morning they all set off. Some walked fast and with purpose, intending to make the best progress possible during their first day, while others dawdled and dallied, reasoning that if they had a journey of several months before them, they didn't need to go very far on each day. Most kept to the main road which led away from their starting point, but one or two took some of the minor side roads, which they had previously calculated would be short cuts and would save time. All went well for the main party until they came to the first major fork in the road: some remembered which way they had planned to go, but many had forgotten, and so the parties on the road split up, going their own separate ways. This process continued at every fork in each road, until there were travellers scattered over a wide area.

At the end of that first day's journey the travellers were picked up, tired and weary, and taken to their hostel for the night, to be fed and watered and to have their planned meeting with their personal advisors. Some had kept to the main road all day, and had achieved what they had hoped, while others had pushed themselves hard and were in fact far beyond their original planned destination for the day. But whatever had happened, all were faced with the necessity of planning for the next day.

When they met their advisors, they were shown the map again, and the place they had reached was indicated - and many realised with horror how far they had strayed from their planned route. The general road led upwards and round the mountains, but many had taken side roads which led them in a downwards direction, and so they now had to decide how to get back to where they would have been had they followed their original plan. They could, of course, just retrace their steps and go back to the start, but that would mean accepting that the first day's journey had been totally wasted - and none of them wanted to do that. So in most cases they chose a rougher path to get back to the original road - or even chose to abandon all paths and just scale up the hill through the tangled undergrowth in order to get back on course as quickly as possible.

They soon got into the daily routine of planning, travelling and then resting each night, while surveying the progress they had made. They always travelled in the company of others, but usually it was with people they didn't know. Sometimes, however, they met people with whom they had travelled before, and their reactions to them depended on what they remembered of the previous meeting. If they had had a pleasant journey together, or if the others had helped them in some way, they welcomed them with pleasure, but if the others had harmed them in any way, then their reaction was hostile from the beginning - although they could do nothing to stop those people from travelling on the same road as them. In fact, they usually found that when they met such people, *they* would be just as hostile in return. Occasionally they met a group of several people with whom they felt totally comfortable from the start - and only realised much later that they had all travelled together on a good day in the past.

More mystifying were the times they met someone and took an instant dislike to the person from the start - and couldn't find out why - until at the end of the day they asked their advisor, who explained that they had had a bad experience with the person on one stage of the journey, but it was so long ago that they had completely forgotten it.

The travellers had realised from the very first day that there were little stalls from time to time along the road, and these stalls all proclaimed that they knew the best way to go to the destination. For a small fee such stalls would even give out what they claimed were accurate maps of the area. However, having bought such maps on one or two occasions in the past, and having found out that the maps were only partly correct, giving a very limited view of a portion of the overall map, our travellers realised that the best way was to rely on their own memory and follow the route they had chosen personally before the start of each day.

Then one day, when they were fairly advanced on their journey, they found out a remarkable fact. Before the start of each day they had always been given all the tools and equipment they would be likely to need during that day's journey, and these had been put in the rucksack each carried on his/ her back. One day when examining the rucksack more closely than he had done previously, one man found that it had, built in, a tiny two-way radio, which was tuned into the frequency of the hostel where they all met their advisors every night - and he told the others in the party. From that time onwards, things became considerably easier, as when they were lost they could always tune in and get advice from their own personal adviser.

Another thing they had realised by now was that they could take short cuts from time to time, without running the risks of losing themselves, which they had experienced in the early stages. When the road snaked backwards and forwards in a very mountainous stretch, they realised that by doing a vertical climb to the road above on one day, they could save themselves many days travelling, as the road would lead round to that very spot eventually. Granted, it would mean that they would have an incredibly difficult day's climb, but they would have all the equipment necessary to do it, and would be able to tune in to their adviser for help - so many decided to do exactly that, and voluntarily accepted one difficult day's journey in order to save many other days of time. In fact, the nearer that they got to their eventual goal, and the more they started to feel the 'buzz of excitement' which that knowledge brought, the more they were likely to go for the short cuts and do far more than they would normally have planned for one day.

There was another strange thing they realised after a long time on the journey: they started occasionally to meet people who appeared to have a great deal of knowledge about the whole journey, as if they themselves had already made it to the finish. Such people never told anyone what they *should* do, but were always available to listen to ideas and to stimulate the individuals to take responsibility for their own decisions.

The end of the story, of course, is that everyone eventually finished their own personal journeys - and found that all the legends were true, and that the land to which they came was the Paradise which they had expected: in fact it was far better than anything they could have ever wished for - and looking back over the many months of travelling they realised that it had all been worthwhile.

***

I was given that little story as a parable of our own journey back to the 'Paradise' from which we originally came. We travel through a series of lives, each of which represents one day's journey, and at the end of each

A12: Reincarnation

life we are taken back to the 'hostel' where we are allowed to rest and take refreshments. We then review, with our own Higher Self (our personal spiritual advisor), what we have achieved during that last life, the triumphs we have had and the difficulties we have encountered. We see how much of our original plan we have fulfilled, and we decide what we need to do in order to get back on track or to make even more rapid progress during the next life, as the case may be.

When we first come into life, we have a master plan, which we have conceived during our rest period, but as we go through the life we are often distracted from what would be our best way, and so we make detours or run into blind alleys, from which we have to extricate ourselves. However, nothing is ever wasted, as we learn from the 'mistakes' we have made, and in learning we complete some of the lessons for which we came into life in the first place. Finally, we realise that there are never any real 'mistakes' in life - there are just 'learning curves'.

The people in our life with whom we feel an instant rapport are those with whom we have travelled in previous lives, and of whom we have pleasant memories, whereas those whom we meet and from whom we feel an instant aversion are those with whom we have had difficult relations in past lives. It is interesting that the reason why they have been brought into this present life to meet us again is to see if we can resolve those past problems, so that we can wipe the slate clean and get rid of things that are holding up our own spiritual progress. (This, of course, works both ways, as *we* have been brought into *their* life with the same intention).

The stalls which we see along the way are the different religions, philosophies and -isms which we encounter in life, all of which claim to provide the only true way to get to the Promised Land. However, each of these mind-sets provides only a limited view of the Truth, the reality of which is far greater than any one of them could ever indicate. That Truth, in all its complexity, can be seen only when we reach the end of our life, and are shown the overall map again by our Higher Self.

Finding that all travellers carry a personal two-way radio, which came only at a late stage in the journey, is the realisation that each of us has a direct connection with our own Higher Self, and if or when we decide to start to use that connection we find that things become a lot easier in our own journey through life.

A Practical Spiritual Primer

When the travellers got towards the end of their journeys, they started to feel the buzz of excitement which that brought, and realised that they could cut the journey by several days if they voluntarily took on a particularly difficult climb. So it is with us: when we become spiritually developed enough, we are likely to take on greater burdens during our life in order to make faster spiritual progress. This may be seen in the fact that many people who have enormous mental, physical or emotional problems in this life are in fact some of the loveliest and most advanced souls whom one could ever wish to meet. However, in the story all the travellers had always arranged to take all the tools and equipment needed for the next day's journey with them - and so it is in our earthly life: we always possess all the gifts and talents which are necessary to help us to get through our lessons - although many of us refuse to accept the fact on a conscious level. There is an old saying that 'No-one is ever given a load which is too heavy to bear' - and if we only accepted the truth of that and used the gifts which we have, we would find the inner strength to face many of the challenges of life which at times might seem insurmountable.

Finally, the strange travellers who appeared to have done the journey before are those enlightened souls (or Ascended Masters) who have in fact finished their cycle of earthly journeys and who have voluntarily either stayed behind or have come back in order to help humanity to progress onto the next stage of its spiritual journey. We are at the moment at the end of a cycle of evolution when the human race is on the verge of taking a massive leap forward in consciousness, and there are many highly evolved souls who have volunteered to come into incarnation at the moment with the express purpose of helping us to make that next quantum leap.

One of the heartening facts about the doctrine of Reincarnation is that it means we don't need to do everything in one life. In many religions and mind-sets, you have one chance, and one chance only, and if you 'blow it', then you are condemned to eternal damnation. Once you realise that you have many lifetimes in which to reach the state of perfection the pressure is off. However, the doctrine of 'Karma' still applies, and sooner or later we must sort out all the problems we have caused in all our lives - although we don't need to do it all in one lifetime.

However, a belief in Reincarnation has other, more immediate results. One of the precepts of many religions is that of doing to others what we would wish they should do to us. If this idea just remains a platitude, to be trotted out and quoted when it suits us, or when we are trying to impress someone with our own spirituality, then it does not do much good. However, if we realise that it is a real fact of life, (in fact, that whatever we do to others *will* be done to us,) then we can start to behave towards others in a different way, and treat them as we ourselves want to be treated in our own future - and this starts to have dramatic results in a short time. The Law of Spiritual Interest* kicks in, and we quickly begin to reap the benefits of what we are doing - once again, biblically, 'We reap what we have sown', or - to put it into the modern idiom - 'What goes around comes around'.

* *(I talk more about the Law of Spiritual Interest in an earlier chapter).*

Another result of the doctrine of Reincarnation is that fundamentalism in any religious mind-set is seen for what it really is - ridiculous. If one can be a Muslim in one life, a Christian in another, then a Jew, Hindu or Buddhist in the next, the absolutism of each religion is obviously totally inappropriate. However, each religion has much to contribute to our overall understanding of the essence of what 'God' (or whatever name we care to use) actually is - so seen from that perspective each religion has an important part to play in the spiritual evolution of the human race. Each one sees Reality from one viewpoint, and by looking from several viewpoints successively, we have a greater opportunity of seeing more of the whole picture.

I am reminded of the old story of how a wise ruler in India once called together six blind beggars and said that he would put them in front of an object and ask them to identify it. Whichever one then identified it correctly would be given riches untold. The first beggar touched the object and announced confidently that it was a spear. The second was equally confident that it was a rope. 'Not so', said the third, 'It is a large leaf'. Each of the other three had his own interpretation; one saying that it was a wall, another a tree trunk and the last one a snake.

Each one was wrong - and yet in a way each of them was almost right, as the object he touched was similar to what he had said. It was an elephant! Each beggar had touched a different part of its body - a tusk, its tail, an ear, a side, a leg and its trunk - and so had made his identification.

A Practical Spiritual Primer

The whole story could only be found by putting together all the different views - and no one had done that.

I think that it is symptomatic of our human condition that we are all searching and want to find *the* answer to the meaning of life. The problem is that there is not just one answer - there are as many answers as there are questions, and each of us has a different way of interpreting any one answer which is ever given. In fact, as there are over seven billion of us on the planet, there are those many views as to what the answers really mean.

I once heard a story about four men who wished to climb a great pyramid. They had been advised that the best way to climb it was by starting from one corner and going up the ridge of the pyramid, rather than by starting in the centre of one of its sides and going up its face. The only problem was - which corner to start from? They walked round to every corner in turn, and saw a crowd of people at each one, all extolling the value of starting from there and following their particular route. Eventually they each decided on the corner they thought best - and by chance each one chose a different corner.

Once they had chosen their corner, each one was congratulated by the noisy crowd at that point, and was cheered as he started to climb. However, as he got higher and higher the noise of the crowd faded away, and he could now concentrate on what he was doing. He saw others climbing by the same route, but found that they were not very talkative - they were all too intent on where they were going. The higher he got the more difficult the climb seemed to become, but he persevered and finally reached his goal on the summit - to find that all his friends arrived there at about the same time. So the noise and fuss at the start had all been useless, as it didn't matter which way any one of them had taken, they all reached the same destination eventually.

Doesn't this little story contain a lesson for each one of us? The lesson is that eventually we all have to make our own mind up, and decide which way to take, and we can't choose the path for other people, any more than they can choose the path we should take. Whatever we do is right for us, but may well be totally wrong for another - and vice-versa. The only thing we can do is to follow our intuition and do whatever we feel is the right thing - and let others follow their own intuition, without judgement on whether what they are doing is right or wrong. In fact, there is a verse somewhere in the Bible that says, 'Judge not, so that you are not judged'. If only we could all follow that precept what a different world it would be.

The other thing that one learns from this little story is that all the people who were making the most noise were those who were at the foot of the pyramid. Once the four men had started the ascent there was no one to tell them whether they were doing right or not. Isn't this indicative of much of human life? The ones who do the most shouting are usually not the most advanced on their own journey - if they were, they would be far too concerned with their *own* spiritual progression to worry about what others were doing about theirs. This ties in with what someone once told me about true gurus: the way in which you can always distinguish them from less spiritual teachers is that they will never *tell* you what you *should* be doing - they will always *ask* you what you think you *could* be doing.

Chapter 13: Reincarnation - Stages

We have seen that - as in the parable - we are all on a journey, the journey back to the Promised Land. Each of us is an individual, and we all choose our separate paths using our own free will. We all have the same lessons to learn overall, but the order in which we do them is our choice. This is why it is impossible ever to compare yourself with anyone else: although you may be ahead of them in some areas (you have learnt those lessons), you are almost certainly behind them in others.

But regardless of that fact, all human beings go through the same stages in their succession of lives, and there is a pattern to those stages. There are four stages, and they correspond roughly to parts of the parable.

First Stage:
We have just started our journey, and everything is possible. We can hurry along or dally, take the main road or any one of the innumerable side roads. We have complete freedom of choice.

When we first come into incarnation, we are faced with totally new conditions, new sensations, new abilities. We can do anything that we like, so we choose to do things for our own pleasure. There are no constraints, nothing is holding us back, it doesn't matter about anyone or anything else - we have no moral or ethical background at all.

Second Stage:
We return to the hostel, and find out how far we have strayed from the ideal path, which would have taken us to the destination most quickly.

A13: Reincarnation - Stages

After several hundred lives of self-indulgence and brushing aside everyone who stands in our way, we gradually come up against the unchangeable Law of the Universe: the Law of Cause and Effect. Whatever we have done which has affected others in a negative way has created a negative energy, which has closed round us like a fog, becoming denser and denser, until it reaches a point where some of it *has* to be neutralised. So in our next few hundred lives we suffer a series of setbacks and problems, as we have experiences which will teach us the lessons we need to learn. And each of those experiences, in which we receive the same treatment we have inflicted on others, will neutralise another bit of the negative energy that has built up round us.

Third Stage:
We start to pay attention to the stallholders whom we pass along the way, and hear their interpretation of the best way to go forward, and buy some of the maps they sell.

For the next few hundred lives we are starting to believe that there must be some reason why the whole of the human condition is as it is, and wonder what the overall purpose - if there is one - is. We become attracted to one or more of the stalls which we pass, which represent the many religions, political movements, cults, and -isms there are in being, with various degrees of intensity. All of them proclaim that only *they* know the Truth, so *theirs* is the only way to find it. Sometimes we argue with other fellow travellers, saying 'My religion/ party/ -ism says this, so yours must be wrong'. In fact, sometimes feelings grow so high that we come to blows over the issues - not realising that by hurting anyone else, for any purpose, we are in fact hurting ourselves by attracting more negative energy.

Fourth Stage:
We find the mobile phone at the bottom of the rucksack, and realise that we have our own personal direct line to the source of all wisdom and Truth.

For our last few hundred lives, we have the advantage of knowing that we do have a direct connection to Truth, via our own Higher Self, and through our own personal guide. We now realise that we have to face the task of neutralising all the remaining negative energies, which we are still carrying after so many hundreds of lives, and so in each life we take on progressively more and more difficult situations. But in doing this, we realise that we always have enough help to get us through every situation. This is the reason why some of the loveliest and most spiritual people on the planet seem to be beset with problems of all kinds, so that some religious people say 'Why does God allow these things to happen?'

All of us are somewhere near this last stage, along with many devout members of other religions, or honest and sincere members of political or philosophical affiliations. You can always tell who they are: if ever the talk comes round to 'What is life about?' they will state their case, but accept that your ideas are just as valid - for you - as theirs are for them. But however much we know, we will never know everything - we will have to wait until the end of our personal journey to get to that point.

***

The parable explains our own journey as human beings, and each day represents one life. The journey lasts several months, and our own journey will last for very many lives. Before the beginning of each day, we plan what we are going to do, and choose the road we will take. But that road, and our plan, is dependent on where we have already got to in our journey, because each morning we will be taken back to the point we have already reached the night before.

That means that when we come into each incarnation, we have all the knowledge we have accumulated in previous lives built into our subconscious. Often children - and particularly *sensitive* children - will remember something of their past lives; however, in the process of growing up and having new experiences most of us forget our previous lives completely - we don't remember the map we have memorised before we set out.

The most important thing to understand about this is that in the parable, before each day's journey, we can see where we have reached on the map, and we plan what we mean to attain the next day. So before we start our human life, we have *already* decided what lessons we want to learn in this incarnation, and have chosen the environment that will give us the experiences to bring about those lessons. So as we have already chosen this life, we cannot blame anyone else for the conditions that we are undergoing.

Nor, in most cases, do we remember the people in the group in which we travel. However, we find ourselves instinctively drawn to some people, while we keep our distance from others. Usually this is not a strong enough feeling to be noticed, but occasionally we have dramatic flashbacks in which we re-live an event in a previous life, with or without the people who were with us at that time.

There is a saying that 'Birds of a feather flock together', and we often see this happening in our own life. When in the company of those of like mind, we feel completely at ease, and when this is really pronounced, it is almost certain that we have been together before as a group, not necessarily in the same relationships but in others equally harmonious.

But when we try to distance ourselves from others in our life, we are re-living unhappy connections we have had with them in a past life. Strange to relate, the reason we have been brought together in this life is to try to put right what went wrong in that life. (It is another example of 'There are no problems in life, only opportunities').

The stalls we pass along the way are the different religions, politics and -isms with which we are faced as we go through life. All of them maintain that they have *the* answer to the mysteries of life, but none of them know the whole Truth. In fact, what is Truth to some of them is in fact the exact opposite, as we can see at the moment in some of the horrendous stories coming out of the Middle East. So the best thing to do is to not accept what others tell you is the *right* way to take, but instead rely on your own Higher Self to guide you.

Then we have the mysterious people who come into our life and seem to have an inner serenity and wisdom, which can only come from having travelled the path many times before. In human terms, these are the Ascended Masters, and when we are ready to hear their wisdom, we will find that they appear in our life. In spiritual terms, 'When the pupil is ready the Master will appear'.

When we are fairly advanced on our journey, we find our spiritual mobile phone at the bottom of the rucksack. In human terms, this means we realise that we have the power of contacting our own Higher Self to ask for help in difficult situations. So many people do not realise this - after all if you do not even know that you have a Higher Self, you are never likely to try to ask for assistance, are you? But once we know that we have that support, then life becomes far easier - or at least, if not easier,

A Practical Spiritual Primer

we realise why things are coming into our life in the way that they are, and we can get specialist advice.

Towards the end of the journey, the road became steeper, and started to snake backwards and forwards as the party went higher up the mountain. And so it is in our human life. As human beings, we often leave the tough tasks that we have to do towards the end of a series of jobs, and so it is in our succession of lives. In fact, as we near the end of the journey we start to 'feel the buzz', and are empowered to take on the most difficult tasks of all, those concerned with physical and mental illness. But we will consider those things later on in these talks.

Finally, of course, we all arrive at the promised land, the Paradise which we are all subconsciously seeking, and we find that it is not only as good as we expected, but in fact far better than we could have ever imagined. And it is only then that we can leave this earthly series of lives, the 'Wheel of Re-birth', behind and begin our personal journey through the spiritual dimensions

Chapter 14: Reincarnation - Threads

We have said that there is a pattern to our overall series of lives, but there is also a reason why we choose any one particular life, and the lessons it brings. Each time that we incarnate, we follow one of three threads (successions) of lives. The three threads are the three Cs, Continuation, Compensation and Consequence. Let us first talk about Continuation.

All of us have an interest in something, and often this develops into a pastime or hobby. Indoor hobbies can range from reading or watching TV to modelling, painting, or collecting items, outdoor ones from gardening or sport to ecological activities such as conservation. Many people have an interest in DIY activities or one of the wide range of craft activities such as woodwork, knitting or candle making.

Sometimes our interest in one thing becomes so extreme that it takes over our life, and becomes an obsession or mania. Most of us know someone who is either a shopaholic or a workaholic, and in the wider sense an interest in religion can develop into bigotry and fanaticism - even to the extent of people slaughtering other human beings who are not in total agreement with their own extreme religious views - as we can see in the present events in several parts of the world.

But occasionally we find someone who is born with an apparently in-bred instinct and ability for doing something, and we call young people with outstanding talents 'child prodigies'. Very often these talents are connected with either Music or Mathematics (it is strange how the two seem to go together). From time to time we hear of children going to University at a ridiculously early age (the other day I heard of a child being accepted to study Mathematics at the age of nine), and Mozart composed his first symphony when he was eight.

In my own life, I currently know two such people. One is a genius in electronics - he built his first computer when he was seven - and the other (at the age of 13) is already giving piano recitals in concert halls, and has recently learnt to play the violin in three weeks. In addition, a school friend of one of my sons always - from a very early age - had an interest in reptiles, and is today the world's greatest expert on snakes.

So what is the reason for such amazing cases? Well, Death is a portal into the next life - in our parable it was when we were picked up and taken back to the hostel where we reviewed our day's journey with our own personal advisor. And when we have passed through that portal, we review with our own Higher Self all that we have done in our life, what our successes have been, where we have failed, and what we need to put right in a future life - the lessons we will have to learn.

Now part of that review is noting if we have found any particular interest pleasant, stimulating or fulfilling in the life, and when we are planning our next life, we could well decide to continue with that interest, provided that it won't interfere with the main lessons we want to learn. If this happens over a number of lives, the urge to continue the interest increases and shows itself progressively earlier, until eventually we might incarnate as a child prodigy.

But, if we don't remember our past lives, how do we remember what we found interesting previously? Well, although we don't *consciously* remember, the memory of all our past lives is still kept by our Higher Self, and those whose have studied spiritual philosophy will have come across the term 'the Akashic record' to define this overall memory.

Psychologists do not accept this philosophy, or the term 'Akashic record', but they do consider that there is a part of us called our 'subconscious', which is a store of information which we have never consciously learnt, which is something similar.

Our subconscious mind *can* be accessed by us. The usual way is by hypnosis, but by concentration we can sometimes do it ourselves. If you feel particularly drawn to a place, or a certain period of history, sit quietly and concentrate on that place or period, and you could well start to get impressions about events there, or then, when you personally were involved.

A14: Reincarnation - Threads

Some of the most convincing evidence for reincarnation has come from hypnosis, in which subjects are regressed (taken back) to past lives. One of the greatest psychiatrists of the last century was Dr Ian Stevenson, who wrote arguably the best book on the subject - 'Twenty cases suggestive of reincarnation'. He passed over in 2007, but his books are still available - although very expensive - and it is worth looking him up in Wikipedia.

Nevertheless, a continuation of interest over a number of lives can eventually bring problems, so now we will consider the second thread - Compensation.

***

One of the aims of the whole series of incarnations of every human being is to produce someone who is a completely rounded individual, totally balanced; but over-developing one characteristic in a series of lives leads to an imbalance, and so has to be corrected.

It is very interesting, in this context, to note that in astrological charts there are two points of great importance. Technically they are the Nodes of the Moon, but they have more common (and interesting) names - the Dragon's Head and the Dragon's Tail. The Dragon's Tail shows where individuals have reached in their overall spiritual journey to date, while the Dragon's Head shows what they aim to achieve in this incarnation. The important thing about these two points is that they are diametrically *opposite* to each other, to keep the whole personality balanced.

A very simple example, to illustrate the idea of balance, is the example of gender. When all of us have come to the end of our circle of lives, we will find that we have had an equal number of lives as men as we have as women, so that we have had all the experiences each sex can have. Therefore our lives alternate roughly between being men and being women - not in strict rotation but approximately. However, if we decide to develop the characteristics of either sex in a series of lives (Continuation) then at some time or other we have to reverse the trend to compensate for it - and that can have serious consequences as it can lead to individuals who are masculine mentally, but feminine physically, or vice-versa.

One of the saddest cases of which I had personal knowledge was that of Beattie. Over many lives as a woman she had obviously developed extreme feminine characteristics, so that eventually her

A Practical Spiritual Primer

Higher Self had decided that she had become too imbalanced, and needed to be a man in this life. So she incarnated as Bob. Bob was a definite man - no query about that: he was a six-footer, with a male physique, very strongly male features and size 13 shoes. But the problem was that he still had a female psychology. He hated everything about his manliness, but most of all he hated his own male genitals - and it became an obsession to have them removed.

At about this time a law was passed to enable sex-change operations to take place in this country, and because of his extremely fragile mental condition - and the possibility of him self-harming - he was accepted for one of the early NHS operations, and started a preliminary course of treatment with female hormones. However, soon afterwards he had to change his address, and I lost touch with him.

I heard later that he had had the treatment, and then the operation, which had been - physically - a complete success, but had brought about some hideous psychological problems. He was now Beattie, a 6-ft woman, with a small bust but very broad shoulders, who had the features of a man and still had a deep voice. And she had found that it is very difficult to find women's size 13 shoes. She had suffered so much humiliation when using women's public toilets that she learned never to use them at all. Worst of all, most people whom she met regarded her as a freak, and tended to avoid her. And I have to admit that, when I met her by chance about two years after her operation, I found it very difficult to relate to her, even though I knew her history.

Now that was a very extreme example of the problems of Compensation, but there is a less traumatic example a lot nearer home - me! Over many lives, I have developed mental skills, to the extent that in this life I have always prized 'intelligence' over everything else, and have became totally obsessed by it. Most of the pleasures of my life (but not all) have been mental, involved with studying, gaining knowledge, learning languages, doing puzzles of all sorts, researching various topics on the internet, and the like. And the associated skill involved with that is teaching whatever I have learnt, which still gives me great pleasure.

But all this has come at a price, as my dear long-suffering wife will confirm. I have become totally unbalanced, as my whole life is orientated towards mental skills, with nothing to show practicality - and even less to show common sense. My astrological chart shows this - it is all Air signs (mental activity), and there is hardly anything in there to give me any practical ability at all. I recently tried to trim the top of a tall hedge, and fell off the stepladder *backwards*. Then I tried to put a screw into a piece of wood - and pushed the screwdriver through my finger. And as for common sense - forget it! Probably every reader has more common sense in their little finger than I have in my whole body. Finally, I have never been able to relate to emotions, and as in old age I have become more sensitive, psychically, I am having great difficulty in controlling the emotions that come with it.

So in short, I am a walking disaster. I think that in my next life - as a classic case of Compensation - I will reincarnate as a village idiot, who knows nothing but can do everything!

Chapter 15: Karma

Before we talk of the last - and most controversial - thread of Reincarnation, we have to remember that the object of us being on Earth is to learn everything about every life form on the planet. As far as we are concerned at the moment, studying the implications for human beings, we are here to learn everything about what it means to be human, and so - before the end of our personal journey - we will have every experience that a human being can possibly have. And by the end of that journey we will have become a completely balanced person.

We can liken our journey to walking down a road: in the middle of the road, there is a white line - the ideal. If we walk to the left or right of that line, we have an invisible piece of elastic tied to us which pulls us back onto the line - what we can call 'the straight and narrow'. And the further we move away from the line, the stronger the pull.

A very good analogy is a pendulum: the further it goes in one direction, the higher it rises, and the greater the force pulling it down and back becomes - until eventually that force is so great that it overcomes the force pushing it up, and the pendulum starts to move down again, and in the opposite direction.

The only difference between our journey and the pendulum is that the latter is one continuous swing, whereas our life consists of a great number of small incidents, each of which has its own energy.

But what is the force pulling us back towards balance, the elastic pulling us back to our white line? It is usually given the name 'Karma', which is a word in ancient Sanskrit, the holy language of Hinduism (the oldest religion in the world). 'Karma' actually means 'action, word or deed', but over the centuries it has come to mean 'Fate, Kismet, Destiny' or 'what we have stored up for ourselves'. We call it 'the Law of Karma', but it is actually not a separate law, only a special example of the main law of creation, the Law of Cause and Effect - every cause has an effect, and every effect has had a previous cause.

Karma is very often called 'the Law of Retribution and Reward', but this - although true - is a very crude way of describing it. It gives visions of judgement, of some stern being handing out punishments (and occasionally, goodies), for what we have done in the past. In Christianity, the Bible has had a lot to do with promoting this idea, with talk of 'Hellfire', 'sorting out the sheep from the goats, the wheat from the tares', etc. In fact, Karma can better be described as the way in which the Universe helps us to get back on track when we have strayed from the ideal pathway. There is no sense of condemnation or punishment at all - it is just a natural force. If you touch something very hot, you will be burnt. If you jump into water, you will get wet. If you sunbathe for too long, you will get sunburnt. You could, if you wished, say that getting burnt or wet or sunburnt is a punishment for having done something silly, but it would be a very strange way to look at things. (It would be even stranger to say that the heat, or water, or sun had 'punished' you).

Yet we have sayings in English that describe the situation exactly: 'As you give so shall you receive'. 'What goes around, comes around'. No sense there of punishment, just a statement of natural law - which is what folk wisdom is.

Once again, when we use the word 'Karma', we usually think in terms of experiencing something nasty, but it is equally true that we can have something good happen to us. When we are walking down the middle of the road and stray off the middle line, either to the right or the left, we are pulled back in the opposite direction. So there is 'good Karma' as well as 'bad Karma'. We will receive what we have given out to others, whether it is 'good' or 'bad'. Once more, if it is good, there is no question of reward, it is just the natural consequence of what we have done in the past. If, in physical terms, we have done something strenuous and are all hot and sweaty, after having had a bath or a shower we feel nice and refreshed - not rewarded.

So the thread of Consequence is all to do with the workings of the Law of Karma, and when we realise that the old saying 'Do unto others what you would wish that they do unto you' really means 'Do unto others what *will be done* unto you', then we can really make some progress in our spiritual journey.

A Practical Spiritual Primer

Now we are ready to look at our own life and see how this thread has worked out in practice.

Who is responsible for the problems we have in life. Well, in a word, *we* are. For two reasons: the first is that we all choose what lessons we want to learn, before the start of each incarnation. We have mentioned before that we have the equivalent of a giant tick-sheet, which contains boxes for every kind of human experience and lesson, and before each life, we choose the ones we want to have. So whatever happens to us in this life does so because we have *chosen* it beforehand.

That is the reason for all the problems of health and fitness that we suffer, although as we have explained previously, many of the problems of health are psychosomatic, and brought on by our own emotional and mental states. But what about the problems caused by other people?

This is where it gets really controversial, because if you have been deeply hurt by someone, and are still in an emotional state of mind, there is no possibility of you understanding the philosophy behind it - and it is even less possible when someone you love deeply has been hurt. But let us assume that you don't fall into either of these categories, and consider what has happened.

We have already explained that the first few hundred lives of our long journey on Earth were spent in total self-indulgence, doing what we wanted, regardless of whether or not we were hurting others, and in doing so we were creating - or more correctly attracting - negative energy, which sooner or later had to be neutralised by us. The fact that those early lives took place tens of thousands of years ago doesn't make any difference to the need for them to be neutralised - energy doesn't decay. (There is a very good reason why the worst parts of human nature happen in the early lives, but we won't come onto that until much later in the book). And the fact that now, in our present state of knowledge, we would never dream of murdering, raping, robbing, deceiving, abusing or beating up anyone else doesn't mean that we have never done so in the past - in fact it is almost certain that we have!

So over a succession of lives since then we have been slowly getting rid of this negative energy, and learning lessons in the process. Now we have come to the stage where we have a basic understanding of what life is all about. But that doesn't mean that we have cleared everything harmful from our past - far from it. We still have quite a lot to do. But it

A15: Karma

does mean that we are more anxious to clear off the remainder of those past actions as quickly as possible.

This explains why some people, who apparently live almost saintly lives, have so many troubles of all sorts, health, relationships, finances, emotions, etc. In fact, from time to time we hear horrendous stories of pillars of the local community, teachers, clergymen, good Samaritans, social workers and others, who are savagely beaten to death, or have their life terminated in other grisly ways. And when that happens, people ask 'How could such a thing happen to such a lovely person?' (Or, if they happen to be religious, 'Why did God allow this to happen?')

The one big problem that people have with understanding why things happen is that they can't see beyond this present life. They don't understand that although a person may be a saint in this life, that doesn't mean that he/ she has been the same in previous lives - if in fact they can even accept that there have *been* previous lives. Some years ago, when Sybil and I organised clairvoyant demonstrations in Torquay, we had a medium who was a pillar of respectability at a local Spiritualist church, and I happened to mention the subject of Reincarnation when talking to her after the demonstration. 'Oh, I don't believe in that', she said, 'I can't imagine how I could have *ever* done anything bad in a previous life'. I don't know what amazed me more, her ignorance or her arrogance!

So does this knowledge help us at all in our daily life? Well, that depends to what extent we can understand, and accept, it. If we can see that everything that happens to us happens for our spiritual benefit, then we are more likely to be able to recover quickly after being hurt by someone else. We are more likely to be able to say - after the initial hurt and shock have passed - 'What did I learn from that experience?' And once we have analysed it, we are more likely to be able to move on in our life. But that does not mean that we will be able to condone, or forgive, the actions of the other person involved!

***

One of the deeply disturbing facets of modern life is the number of times that we hear of cases of horrendous abuse of children, ranging from neglect and deprivation to physical abuse, torture and - in extreme cases - murder. So what can we make of all this? Is it a modern phenomenon, or has it always existed, but it is only in modern times that we have become aware of it?

A Practical Spiritual Primer

Well, child abuse has always existed: it is in human nature to compare oneself with others, and create a 'social pecking order' into which each of us fits. It is almost as though we need some sort of structure in our life to tell us what we are, and who we are. This is shown in many different ways in society, from the idea of the class system down to levels of Government, and Local Government.

And in the life of ordinary people, the smallest and the weakest are the children, so they are the ones who are most likely to be exploited, in many different ways. In the Western world, we have long gone past the time when children were used as a labour force: for instance, once children as young as 10 were employed in coalmines - and it took a lot of Parliamentary time and debate before *that* was finally stamped out. But still today, all over the world, children are used as a labour force. We in the West may deplore that, and talk about 'children's rights' - but then, we can't understand the depths of abject poverty in which people live in some countries, where even the meagre earnings of a child labourer can make the difference between life and death to a family.

But in our 'enlightened' community, where the exploitation of children as a labour force is virtually non-existent, we can focus on other ways of exploitation, which come under the general heading of child abuse - and the two ways which arouse most emotions are physical and sexual abuse. As far as the latter is concerned, we are only just waking up to the reality that it not only exists, but it exists very widely - and has always existed - in all levels of society, up to the very highest. Celebrity cases over the last few years have taken the lid off a can of worms, and as more and more investigations go on, most of us are horrified at the network of people involved - not only as perpetrators, but as those helping to shield them.

This network extends to the upper echelons of society, of Government and the Entertainments business and even of the different churches - and indeed some of the saddest cases of all are those concerning care homes, including religious care homes, where children for decades have been routinely preyed on by the very people whose job it was to look after them.

In addition, there have recently been many dreadful cases of young girls being preyed on, and exploited sexually, by gangs of men - and still new incidents are coming to light almost monthly.

A15: Karma

So how can we explain this in terms of Reincarnation? Is it at all possible, or is it an example on which the whole idea will founder? Well, there is an explanation - a very simple explanation - but one that most people will find totally abhorrent. Let us go back to the start, and see if we can understand it logically:

A child is abused by one or more adults - and it doesn't matter in what way, physically, sexually, emotionally - there is no distinction: abuse is abuse. Instead of looking at the matter from the position of the child - which is where most people would start - let us consider it from the position of the adults concerned. Where it is a really horrific case - such as the torture and eventual murder of the child - many people would say of the adults, 'They ought to have the same thing done to them'. And the simple answer is, 'It will be'! The adults have coated themselves with negative energy, which can be neutralised *only* by experiencing the reverse of what they have done - i.e. by having the same thing done to them.

But how can that happen? Adults can't be abused in the same way as children, and as the only way to neutralise the energy is by them experiencing the *same* action in the *same* sort of environment, the only way that it can happen is when *they themselves* are children, in future lives.

It is often forgotten - if, in fact, it has ever been known - that children are only children in human terms: in spiritual terms, a child is a mature *adult* being, and as an adult being has already *chosen* the lessons it wants to learn before ever coming into incarnation; so in order to learn those lessons, it has already chosen the experiences it will have. And having those experiences will neutralise some negative energy from the past and allow it to move on in its spiritual journey.

It is an interesting fact that when children have been abused in any way - and particularly sexually - they will often feel that it was 'their fault' that it all happened. Perhaps, with the spiritual clarity which most children have before it is indoctrinated out of them by adults, such children are more in tune with the spiritual reality than we adults are, and can sense what has happened in previous lives.

Finally, if you have, or anyone near you has, been personally affected by any form of abuse, it is very unlikely that you will be able to understand any of this, let alone accept it - because you are too emotionally involved in the issue. But it forms an important part of the whole doctrine of Reincarnation, and shows that all of us - even children - are subject to the basic Spiritual Law.

Chapter 16: More on Reincarnation

Many years ago, there was a famous English person who was rash enough to make a silly public announcement about handicapped people: he said that they were suffering their handicaps as a punishment for what they had done in a previous life. This caused immediate public uproar, as a result of which he eventually lost his job - he was the coach of the England football team. Well, he might have known something about football, but he certainly didn't know much about Reincarnation - nor did his mentor, who was apparently a Spiritualist healer and had taught him about it. One must query how much she herself knew about the subject, if she thought that Reincarnation was only about Karma, Reward and Punishment, and getting what you deserve. The moral of the story is, 'Never make a public statement about a subject you don't thoroughly understand yourself'.

So what can we say about the subject of Handicaps. Well, first of all, the Law of Karma applies when someone has hurt another person in any way, and ensures that they have exactly the same thing done to them. So if someone had caused great suffering to a handicapped person by ridiculing them, it would be inevitable that in some future life they themselves, while handicapped, would be ridiculed in the same way. But that would not be the primary reason for them to have the handicap in the first place!

This is where we must go back to our first principles of Reincarnation, and state that we are on Earth as human beings with the intention of experiencing *everything* about the human condition. So therefore, before we end our wheel of Rebirth, we will have enjoyed - or endured - every possible condition known to Mankind, including every possible medical condition. We have previously mentioned our gigantic tick-sheet: we will not have finished our Earthly journeys before we have every box ticked off.

It is obvious, therefore, that questions of illness or incapacity can have little to do with the operation of Karma and the thread of Consequence - although on a personal note they might be the result of us abusing or neglecting our own bodies in early life, and regretting the consequences in old age.

So what can we say about handicaps? Well, first of all they are some of the most difficult conditions human beings have to endure, and since it is in human nature to put off doing difficult things as long as possible, very often in a series of lives they are left towards the end, as part of the final clearing-up process. Referring back to our Reincarnation parable, as the travellers came towards the end of their spiritual journey, they started to sense that the Promised Land wasn't very far away, and feel a buzz of excitement. This made them redouble their efforts to get there more quickly, sometimes by choosing particularly difficult climbs in order to cut short the remaining journey. And that is exactly what happens in our human life. But it also means that by the time that people undergo the final, extremely difficult conditions created by handicaps, they are very spiritually advanced. There is a saying that 'No-one's cross is too heavy to carry' - and this is certainly true of handicapped people, who are some of the most spiritually advanced beings on the planet. It is very rare to find an evil handicapped person - most of them are so positive and determined to make the most of their life that we can only marvel at their dedication.

This is shown most impressively at the Paralympic Games or in the more recently inaugurated Invictus Games for war-handicapped military personnel. But apart from such public figures, ordinary people with handicaps often show amazing mental and emotional resilience when carrying on their everyday life.

But what of those who are not able to look after themselves, those with mental handicaps or - probably worst of all - with both mental and physical handicaps, who have to be looked after 24 hours a day? Once again, those who know them best, and are involved in their care, often report how amazingly spiritual they can be, and what kind and gentle traits they can show, despite their conditions.

Finally, although those with handicaps can be some of the most spiritually advanced human beings on the planet, not far behind them are those who take on the duty of raising and looking after them in this life, and effectively sacrifice their whole life in providing care and protection for their children. My wife and I know of two such people, who late in life adopted a Down's Syndrome boy and who for the last 35 years have moulded their whole life around providing a protective and enlightened environment for him to grow up in. We can only marvel at their dedication.

So when you see anyone who is handicapped, physically, mentally or both, know that he or she is a truly advanced soul, and could well end his/her round of Earthly lives long before you or I ever will.

***

Earlier, we spoke of the possibility of remembering past lives we have had, and I mentioned the word, 'Flashback'. Let me expand a little on the subject now.

A flashback is a spontaneous vision of an experience in a previous life. It is spontaneous because it is totally out of the control of the person concerned, and can happen at any time. We have all had something similar happen to us in our everyday life. We see a person who reminds us of someone we once knew, or we hear a piece of music, or see a picture, or even smell a perfume, which immediately takes us back in time and reminds us of something - or someone - in our past. This happens to everyone at some time or other in their life, and it is particularly noticeable as we grow older.

There is little difference between that and a flashback, except that the latter is more often brought on by a scene or picture - but the great difference is that with a flashback the memory is of nothing we have experienced in this life, but something from one or other of our past lives.

***

Authors note: Some of the examples of flashbacks have already been mentioned in the earlier part of the book.

I had my first dramatic flashback about forty years ago in France. I was camping with my wife and family in the South of France - a country I love - near the ancient walled town of Carcassonne, which we had never visited. It is a very famous town, visited by hordes of tourists every year, and visitors' cars are not allowed into the town, but have to use the huge public car park outside the walls.

A Practical Spiritual Primer

I parked the car and then turned round to get my first glimpse of the battlements - and I froze. I was terrified, and couldn't move for at least two minutes. I was re-living the last time I saw those same battlements, little changed, some 700 years previously. At that time I was a soldier, part of a besieging force attacking the town, and I was climbing a long ladder, from the dry moat below. Then suddenly, hideously, I was hit by some scaldingly hot liquid poured down on me by the defenders on the battlements, and I fell off the ladder - into oblivion.

My poor wife and family were terrified, as they didn't know what was happening to me, but when I eventually did come to my senses and was able to move, I explained what I had seen. I don't think that they could understand it, although they had seen how badly it had affected me, so I think that they (charitably) thought that I had suffered a touch of sunstroke which had 'sent me a bit peculiar' for a while.

Since then I have had many flashbacks, but strange to relate most of them have been brought on by concentrating on faces. Previously I mentioned that we often meet someone new, and either love them or hate them from the first moment, and this has happened to me on several occasions. But when the feeling is exceptionally strong, I usually try to find out why, and meditate on the relationship. By doing this I have traced several relationships in my present life back to different periods of history, one to Atlantis, two to Ancient Egypt, one to Ancient Greece, one to 14th century Eastern Europe, three to France, one to early 20th century England, and several to pre-European Australia.

As a matter of interest, just as there are threads of Reincarnation evident in the lives of all of us, there are also threads of time and place. One of these is Atlantis, Ancient Egypt, Ancient Greece, Rome, mediaeval France, the French revolution and modern times. I can relate to every one of the countries and times in this thread, as I have had a fascination for each of them all my life, studied Classics at Grammar School, lived in France, studied French history and became a French interpreter, and have read as much as I could find on Atlantis and Ancient Egypt.

My flashback to the 14th century Europe was particularly interesting: about ten years ago I met a lady who had recently been widowed, who has since become a close friend of my wife and me. Both she and my wife love travelling, although I prefer to stay at home, so they have become travelling companions also. But the amazing thing about my relationship

A16: More on Reincarnation

with her is that from the start I felt an urge to help her in every possible way except financially (of which she has no need). This became so pronounced that after the first year of our acquaintance I realised that there was a Karmic connection between us. (A Karmic connection is a link brought forward from a past life together). So I meditated on it and I saw a scene in some area of what I knew was Eastern Europe - probably what is Poland in modern times.

I saw a river at the bottom of a steep-sided gorge, heavily forested, and I felt that I was drowning in that river when I was rescued by my close friend, who at that time was a man, as I was. The picture lasted for only a few moments, but it cleared up the mystery.

**

Apart from the first one in Carcassonne, most of the rest of my flashbacks have happened in the last twelve years, for an interesting reason. I said earlier that the whole of my own astrological make-up is totally unbalanced, being heavily weighted towards Air signs (mental interests). I have only one Earth sign (practical ability), and also very little Water sign influence (emotional and psychic sensitivity). So throughout most of my spiritual life I have been more interested in philosophy than in practical mediumship, and never thought of myself as having much in the way of psychic ability whatsoever. But all that changed when I went to Australia in 2004. I stayed in the country for almost 10 months, and during that time, I met some very spiritual people, many of whom were Aboriginal elders.

I grew very close to several of these, and the more that I learnt about Aboriginal culture and traditions the more that I came to respect them. Much of the traditional lifestyle has now been swamped by European and American influences, apart from in the extreme North of the continent, and today many Australians look down with contempt on 'Abos', whom they regard as almost a sub-species of humanity. And indeed, in most Australian cities, there *is* an underclass of Aboriginals who, deprived of their history and culture, and unable to fit in with modern living, have taken refuge in drink and drugs.

Strangely enough, some of the problems of the Aboriginal people have been caused by well-intentioned 'do-gooders' over the years. At one time early in the 20th century, such misguided individuals came to the conclusion that the 'savages' - as they considered them - could be redeemed by taking away children from the parents and 'educating' them to be 'good, responsible Christians', and a hideous social experiment was inaugurated. Over the one-hundred-and-fifty years or so since the first European colonisation, many Aboriginals had become partners of white people, so that now there were a large number of children of mixed race in Aboriginal communities. So a law was passed in 1931 to forcibly remove these children from their environments, put them into institutions (usually run by religious bodies) and allow them back only when, as young adults they had been 'reformed'!

This disastrous experiment was ended only in 1967, and during my time in Australia I met one of the Aboriginals who had herself been the victim of enforced separation from her family!

However, even that attitude is better than what has happened in the past history of the relations between white men and Aboriginals. There are always difficulties when two populations with different cultures meet, as is obvious today all over the world, when extremist religious philosophy clashes with more liberal Western culture; and the history of post-1788 Australia - 1788 was the year of the first English penal colony in Botany Bay - was no exception. There were increasing clashes between Aboriginals and the new settlers, which sometimes broke out into open warfare locally, and led to Aboriginals being hunted down and killed like wild animals. This was particularly evident in Tasmania, where a large Aboriginal population (estimated as between 5,000 and 10,000 in 1803) was almost exterminated by persecution and European diseases, until the last few remnants - about 300 - were finally expelled from the island in 1833. They were re-located to Flinders Island, where the last survivor of the whole nation died in 1876.

Author's note: Anyone who is interested in learning more about this period of Australian history, and the 'Lost Generation', is referred to the 1996 book 'Follow the Rabbit-Proof Fence', which is the true story of three little girls who ran away from an institution and tried to get back to their home, more than 1,000 miles away!

Chapter 17: Tribal Initiation

However, those whom I met were all in the higher levels of Aboriginal society, and they taught me a great deal about the basic abilities of human beings. One amazing instance was when my friend Dino was at the birthday party of a family member when a young Aboriginal - crazed by drugs - gate-crashed the party, picked up a cauldron of kangaroo stew, which had been boiling on the campfire all day, and threw it all over him. He put up his arm, and managed to shield his face, but was severely scalded on his head, arm and body.

Rushed into hospital, the diagnosis was not good: third degree burns, which would certainly need skin grafting and months of painful treatment. Dino was not happy at this thought, and voluntarily discharged himself from hospital, opting for traditional Aboriginal treatment.

Ten days later I happened to be visiting the home of a mutual friend, and was staggered to see Dino there. And what was more, his wounds had healed completely - which was logically completely impossible. He showed me his arm, which had been the most severely hurt, and all that was apparent was a big scar from elbow to wrist, pink against his smooth brown skin. I asked for details of his treatment, but all that I was told was that it had been traditional Aboriginal medicine - and that was that.

During that stay in Australia, I saw and learnt many things about Aboriginal culture, things that were totally unknown - and impossible - to my Western mind, and when I came back home I brought with me a deep respect for their whole traditional culture and lore.

However, the two things that happened to me, which were to change the rest of my life - although I didn't realise it at the time - were the two initiations that I had into the local Aboriginal tribe - the Nyoongars. I had introduced some spiritual products which I was then helping to market to senior members of the tribe, and had presented a complete set of the products to the senior Aboriginal lady in Australia, and another one to a top elder at a national level, so I suppose that the first initiation was their way of saying 'Thank you'.

This initiation was carried out by a white lady, who had worked with Aboriginals for so long that she had been accepted into the tribe as an elder, and allowed to carry out initiations. The process was very long and complicated, lasting about two hours, and it started off by having my feet 'ochred' (pronounced 'Oh-kerd'). Ochre is a kind of earth, ground up into very fine powder. There are three levels of initiation, each using a different colour of earth. The first two are red and yellow, and the final one is black. I think that my first time was with red ochre, although after so long I can't be sure.

The whole process started with having the feet massaged in kangaroo oil for several minutes - a very relaxing sensation - and then having the ochre applied to one foot and massaged in. I assume that the oil opened the pores, and allowed the ochre to be completely assimilated, as there was no residue left on the skin afterwards. The same thing was then done to the other foot. By this time about half an hour had passed, and then I was told to close my eyes and relax completely.

After a short while I was asked how I felt, and asked if I could see anything (a strange thing to ask of someone who had his eyes closed). But even stranger, I *could* see things. I had the impression of being in the open air in front of a campfire (I later learnt that the campfire was a very important part of Aboriginal culture) and there were a number of people standing round it, all looking at me. I was then told to concentrate on one of them, and to describe him or her. I focussed on the person in the middle, and as my vision became clearer, I saw that she was a lady - but what a lady. She was only very small, but extremely well-built - in fact, she was probably as round as she was tall. She had a broad smile on her face, and it felt almost as though she was physically wrapping me in her arms. But the most amazing thing about her was the enormous sense of power that she radiated.

I was then questioned about what I was seeing, and I found myself giving answers I couldn't possibly have known - at least, not logically. Not only was I able to describe the people who were there, but I knew that they were all members of my immediate family. The lady in the centre, for instance, was my grandmother, and the matriarch of the whole tribe.

A17: Tribal Initiation

As time went on the questions became more and more detailed, and I found to my amazement that I was starting to answer them fluently, without hesitation. I gave my age, my own name, the names of other members of the tribe, the name of the tribe, its location in Australia, and many other things I could not possibly have known in my conscious mind. In fact, most of the names - and certainly the name of the tribe - were totally unknown Aboriginal words for me, although later on it was confirmed that the tribe was in the location which I had stated. Traditional Aboriginal personal names were also unknown to me - all the people I had ever met had Western names.

But the initiation was not yet finished: I was told to go to another time in my life, and go through the same process - and I did. By now I was speaking without hesitation, and I described another scene, another tribe and different people. Looking back now, I can see what a massive step I took that day: previously, I had never 'seen' anything, apart from that one experience in Carcassonne, but by the end of the initiation, I was 'seeing' - and *knowing* - things that were totally absent from my conscious mind. I don't know what the composition of the ochre was: did it have hallucinogenic qualities? Possibly - but I wouldn't have thought so. Although I don't know much about hallucinogenic drugs, I believe that the effects eventually wear off, whereas that has certainly never happened in my case.

The second - and higher - initiation took place several months later. I don't know who or what decided that it *was* the correct time, although part of my personal philosophy of life is that *everything* happens at the right time. (It is interesting that the Aboriginal saying is that 'Everything happens when it *wants* to happen', as though events have a life of their own, totally separate from the life of the people who experience them*). However, one day I was visiting the senior Aboriginal lady, and there were several visitors there from different countries, (none of whom I had met,) when she suddenly said, 'It is time for you to have your next initiation!', and it started there and then.

*N.B. *This is very similar to the 'seriality' of Paul Kammerer, which I mention in the earlier chapter on Synchronicity!*

This time I knew what was going to happen, so the process seemed to pass more quickly, although it still lasted almost two hours, to the fascination of many of the visitors. I was taken to several different lives, and asked even more searching questions, which I answered without hesitation. I described the places I visited, and all of these were verified by several of the Aborigines present, who knew the locations. However, the big thing which happened (what was going to be the first of many such events) was that I identified one of the people present (a Norwegian whom I had never met) as my son in a previous life, and I described his own tribal initiation as an adult. In fact, I was so totally overwhelmed with pride at the memory that I dissolved into tears - the first time that this had ever happened in my life. (As an aside, this is the aspect of increased sensitivity that I now find very uncomfortable. I can pick up emotions so easily that I am often reduced to tears, which clashes completely with the detachment of my basic Aquarian nature).

So this was the start of my own spiritual transformation. I cannot explain logically what happened in those two initiations, but I know that from that time my previous mental attachment to spiritual philosophy was enhanced by dramatically increased psychic sensitivity. But before I leave that period in Australia, I will tell of one incident which happened which confirmed in my mind the validity of what I had experienced in my first initiation.

I was visiting the senior Aboriginal lady, and when I walked into her house, she was in conversation with a visitor, so she told me to go through onto the verandah, where there was someone she wanted me to meet. I went through the house, and there, in front of me, was the Seeress of the local tribe. (The Seeress is the wise woman of the tribe, completely clairvoyant, who is consulted routinely on all important matters in the life of tribal members. In other indigenous cultures she would be known as a 'medicine woman'. In Australia, it is a position handed down from mother to daughter, and while I was there, I met all three generations of the Seeress family).

As soon as I saw her, I said, 'I know you'. She knew that we had never met, so she said, 'I don't think so'. Then I remembered, and said 'You were the grandmother of the tribe' - and she was. She was the first person I had seen behind the campfire in my first initiation, and was identical in every respect. She immediately realised that I was talking about a past life, went back herself to that life, gave me that same beaming smile, and said, 'Yes I was'. Once more, it was something that was scientifically impossible, and yet it happened.

A17: Tribal Initiation

On another occasion, I met the Seeress' daughter, a Seeress-in-waiting. Her first words to me were, 'You are a wizard'. I hadn't the slightest idea what she was talking about, but she said, 'You have the sign of the wizard on your forehead'! She explained that in Aboriginal tradition, a certain bone formation in the forehead (what appears under certain conditions to be a big V) is the sign of someone with special spiritual powers - and I have that very bone formation. I have no knowledge whatsoever whether that is true or not, and I have never felt that I have any special powers, but I find the idea of being called 'A Wizard of Oz' very amusing.

I have been back to Australia several times since then, and now five of my six children live there with their families. I have a great love of the country, and of the people, and I still remember vividly the flashbacks I had during those two initiations. It has been suggested that I will end my days in that wonderful country: I obviously don't know whether or not this is true, but if it is, then it would be a sort of returning to my roots, and a fitting end to this stage of my spiritual journey.

Chapter 18: Unhelpful Energies

I mentioned earlier that there is a reason why the first few hundred lives of our journey are spent experiencing lives as the worst kind of human beings, and I have written in detail about it in my earlier book on Metaphysics, in which I go fairly deeply into the scientific side of the subject, and explain the different dimensions and their inhabitants. For those who wish to study the topic more deeply, I refer them to my website www.wolfeagle.co.uk, which gives a link to it.

However, to give a short summary, there are a range of dimensions of ascending spiritual vibrations, and also a range of entities who are capable of an existence in those vibrations. Our universe is the only dimension in which the vibrations are compatible with physical existence, but there are many spiritual (positive) ones above us, and two negative ones below. Our dimension, the 3rd dimension, is in the middle, and one that can be influenced by either positive or negative entities.

The negative entities below us consist of elemental forces, principles of evil - usually called the seven deadly sins, although there are more than seven - and a hierarchy of entities of evil which are known by different names in different religions, but which are called in Christianity 'fallen angels'.

When human beings first come into incarnation, they are without any form of moral or ethical background; so they explore their new existence and do everything to extract the maximum pleasure from the experience, and in doing so inevitably hurt others. Now spiritual law states that no entity can interfere with the life of a human being unless it is asked to - but by initial self-indulgence, causing harm to others and bringing in negative energy, lower-level entities are contacted, and effectively *invited in*. Then, once in, they will feed on the negative energies which the human being is generating - and so begins a vicious spiral.

A18: Unhelpful Energies

However, after a few hundred lives or so, so much negative potential energy has built up between the individual human being and the ideal state of harmony - the white line in the middle of the road that we mentioned earlier - that it *has* to be neutralised.

A very simple analogy in everyone's life is the feeling in the air on the approach of a thunderstorm. As a storm gets nearer, the air gets very oppressive because the potential charge between the clouds and the earth increases, until eventually, it reaches the critical point at which it *has* to be discharged, by a lightning strike - after which the air once more feels pleasant and fresh.

The same sort of thing happens in human lives, with one big difference. In a thunderstorm, the potential builds up over a very short time, usually a matter of hours, whereas the potential energy in the lives has been building up over hundreds of lives - and so can't be all discharged in one go. If you think that each individual negative action, which has caused damage to another person, has to be neutralised, and this can be done only by the human being experiencing the same thing in reverse, you will see that it is going to take hundreds more lives to undo the damage that has already been done.

Eventually, of course, after very many painful lessons, all human beings start to realise that there might be a connection between what they do to others and what they themselves experience - the start of an understanding of the law of Cause and Effect - and when they want to learn more they are told about guides, helpers and other spiritual beings, and how to invite them in - and so starts the last stage of their spiritual journey.

Conclusion

We now come to the end of this Appendix, and of the book itself. The object of the whole exercise in producing the book was to provide basic information about the principles of spirituality. This is why the title is 'A Practical Spiritual Primer', rather than 'A Practical Spiritualist primer' - its scope is wider than a narrow consideration of Spiritualism. Every religion is - ultimately - about spirituality, although that fact is often hidden in the mass of dogma associated with the religion. And if you strip every religion to basics, devoid of dogma, you will find a remarkable amount of *agreement* between them.

Since I first came into contact with Spiritualism, the world has changed dramatically, and also Spiritualism has changed. There have always been two different sides to it - the phenomena (such as clairvoyance, clairaudience and clairsentience, proving the survival of the soul after the death of the physical body) and the philosophy (showing how and why things happen, and what the meaning of it all is). The former has come more and more to the fore over the past few years, so much so that demonstrations by celebrity mediums on TV have become part of the Entertainment industry, but the latter is becoming increasingly sidelined.

I am not against phenomena - they are very important, particularly in bringing in and helping those who are newly bereaved - or still grieving for the loss of a loved one. But the decline of philosophy means that there are now fewer speakers who are able to teach and, regrettably, fewer rank-and-file spiritualists who really *understand* what it is all about. So this is why I publish this book at this time, to state a few basic facts, devoid of dogma, of which all Spiritualists should be aware.

But the book is not just for established Spiritualists, it is also for total beginners, who have no background at all in the subject, and it provides an easy - and hopefully enjoyable - introduction to it. In general, the main book will be of more value for those who want such an introduction, whereas the Appendix will provide a study course for those who are already involved, or who are seeking to assimilate knowledge more quickly. However, for those who are keen to learn more thoroughly, there is no reason why the whole book shouldn't be read through from start to finish.

Just as the world and Spiritualism have changed over the last 50 years, I myself have changed as well. I no longer think of Spiritualism in the same way that I used to: in fact, I no longer consider it as a religion at all - I think of it as a way of life. The reasons why I no longer call it a religion are as follows:

Although Spiritualists believe in 'God', that God is not a personality, It (not He) is an energy, a force, a power - in fact, Spirit. The first principle is 'The Fatherhood of God', and prayers are often started with the words 'Father God' (sometimes these days 'Father/ Mother God)', but what 'God' is, is never fully defined.

There is no Holy Book of Spiritualism that has to be read, studied, learned or recited. Spiritualists use quotations from several spiritual sources.

There is no main historical or mythical figure, saint, prophet, guru who has to be revered, followed or obeyed. There are many spiritual Masters, most of whom are historical figures (Jesus, Buddha, St Germain) but none is more important than the others.

There is no rigid code of dietary or morality rules that have to be slavishly followed. 'Freedom of Interpretation' is allowed.

In the absence of all of the above facets of other religions, it is difficult to call Spiritualism a religion at all. So what is its purpose?

It exists for one reason only - to teach about, and prove, the continuation of existence of something after the death of the physical body.

It is that very fact which is its great strength, particularly at this crucial time in the history of the world, because the energies by which the Earth is being bombarded are now changing, and are impelling Mankind to more awareness that Reality is far greater than anything which has been imagined to date. This is creating a world of polarities, of opposites: those who are already religious are becoming more extreme, evangelical, committed. Many of those who are not are going in the opposite direction, becoming more violently atheist. More and more people are dropping out of the rat race, and seeking alternative lifestyles - going back to Nature - while others are abandoning any traditional forms of morality or behaviour, and living for the moment only.

Somewhere in the middle are the vast numbers of people who want to know what life is all about, but without all the dogma and trappings of religion - and Spiritualism is ideally placed to provide the answers. I believe that something dramatic is about to happen, which will really make Mankind wake up, and I have had a vision of queues forming at the doors of churches and spiritual centres, wanting information about what is happening. At that time, as predicted in the Bible, 'the harvest will certainly be plentiful, but the reapers will be few'.

Finally, where am I now being led in my own spiritual quest? Before writing my major channelled book a few years ago, I was introduced to Metaphysics, which is the area beyond Science and also beyond Religion - but strangely enough it is where Science and Religion meet and mutually support each other. I asked how this was possible a while ago, and I was given this fascinating little analogy:

Two men stood back to back on the Equator, and went off into opposite directions, one to the East and one to the West. As they travelled they grew further apart, until when halfway through their journey they were at their most distant from each other. But then something strange started to happen, as from this point the further they travelled the closer they came together, until eventually, on the other side of the Earth from where they started, they met face-to-face.

And this is what has been happening between Science and Religion: at one time, all scientists were religious, and many of the religious houses had their own monk/scientists. But then, in the late Middle Ages, Science and Religion parted company, when the Christian Church refused to accept that the Earth was not the centre of Universe - and even burnt Giordano Bruno at the stake for daring to maintain the scientific truth that the planets rotated round the sun. But with the invention of the telescope, the matter was proved, and an uneasy truce was called, in which

A19: Conclusion

everything that concerned practical matters was the province of Science, while all matters of philosophy came under the scope of Religion.

But in the modern scientific revolution, and the latest discoveries of Quantum Physics, scientists are coming dangerously near to what some enlightened theologians have been talking about for centuries. In fact, they are almost at the level where they will find the last link in the scientific chain, the building blocks of the Universe, and at that time - paradoxically - they will prove the existence of 'God'. Unfortunately, most religions will still be far from the meeting point - many are still arguing about the correct *name* of the Creative Force.

So that is the area I am currently exploring, and on which I am giving talks. Perhaps there is another book in me which will go into this in greater detail - we shall see.

I will close the book by quoting once more the last sentence of my autobiography. I believe that everything always works out exactly as it is meant to - although we usually can't see the pattern, and so now - as always:

ALL IS WELL!

Index

Index

exorcism 128
Expenses 111

F
Faith 70
Fear 72, 106, 112
final interface 201
first subtle body 200
flashback 273
Flower People 158
Follow the Rabbit-Proof Fence 276
Fontainebleau 11
Frank 11
Free Will 161

G
Gatekeeper 143
Gautama 182
ghost-busting 128
God 24, 53, 69, 188
Golden Age 222
Gorbachev, Mikhael 106
Great Teacher of the Zodiac 115
Group Therapy 70
guide, healing 143
guide, mediumship 143
Guide, Personal 142
guide, speaking 143

H
Haggard, H. Rider 42
Handicaps 271
Harry 11
Hate 98
Hay, Louise 67, 91, 188, 234
Hay, Louise L. 51, 56, 226

Healing 21
Helen 114
Hell 127
helpers 143
Higher Dimension 135
Higher Self 34, 135, 160, 162
Hilarion 182
Hinduism 243
Husein, Imam 171

I
Infatuation 151
Infinity Clairvoyance 1, 193
inspirers 143
instruments 21
Interfaces 200
into the Light 205
Invictus Games 272
Isaiah 88
Iscariot, Judas 88

J
James 62, 66, 67, 81, 166, 168
Jean 159
Jehovah 24, 53
Jerry 239
Jesus 166
Jill 119
Joan 74, 237
John Laing Construction Company 17
Jonah 119
Jung, Carl 64

K
Kammerer, Paul 64, 279
Karma 24, 36, 177, 250, 264, 271

Index

www.ingramcontent.com/pod-product-compliance
Lightning Source LLC
Chambersburg PA
CBHW070528090426
42735CB00013B/2904